Soviet-Type
Economic Systems

ECONOMICS INFORMATION GUIDE SERIES

Series Editor: Robert W. Haseltine, Associate Professor of Economics, State University College of Arts and Science at Geneseo, Geneseo, New York

---

The above series is part of the

GALE INFORMATION GUIDE LIBRARY

The Library consists of a number of separate series of guides covering major areas in the social sciences, humanities, and current affairs.

General Editor: Paul Wasserman, Professor and former Dean, School of Library and Information Services, University of Maryland

Managing Editor: Denise Allard Adzigian, Gale Research Company

Soviet-Type Economic Systems

A GUIDE TO INFORMATION SOURCES

Volume 12 in the Economics Information Guide Series

WITHDRAWN

Z. Edward O'Relley

Associate Professor of Economics
North Dakota State University, Fargo

Gale Research Company
Book Tower, Detroit, Michigan 48226

Library of Congress Cataloging in Publication Data

O'Relley, Z   Edward.
    Soviet-type economic systems.

    (Economic information guide series; v.12)
    Includes index.
    1. Europe, Eastern--Economic conditions--Bibliography. 2. Europe,
Eastern--Economic policy--Bibliography.
I. Title.
Z7154.E2066   [HC244]   016.3309'47   73-17583
ISBN 0-8103-1306-5

VITA

O'Relley is associate professor of economics at North Dakota State University in Fargo. He received his B.S. degree in business administration (finance) from Virginia Polytechnic Institute and State University, and his Ph.D. in economics from the University of Tennessee. In addition to teaching both graduate and undergraduate students, his interests include research in comparative economic systems, economic development, and contemporary economic policy. He has published articles in several journals and compendia; his latest contribution, dealing with Hungarian agricultural performance and policy, appeared in the 1977 Joint Economic Committee compendium on Eastern Europe. O'Relley maintains active membership in numerous honorary, civic, and professional organizations and societies.

CONTENTS

Contents

PREFACE

The purpose of this compilation is to direct the reader, as expeditiously as possible, to particular references in his subarea of interest within the broader framework of Soviet-type economic systems or Soviet-type economies. The rationale is to provide a bibliographic aid which permits the user to bypass the laborious process of searching through the many books and journals which may have some relevance to his topic. The main criteria used in the selection of the bibliography were the following: originality of contribution, quality of exposition of a topic or particular point of view, and timeliness.

In a volume dealing with both economics and the economies of several countries--in this case Bulgaria, Czechoslovakia, East Germany, Hungary, Poland, Rumania, and the Soviet Union--the number of possible sources that could be cited becomes immense. Especially in the past two decades the number of articles and books published concerning the various aspects of Soviet-type economies has expanded enormously. Consequently, to make the volume a practical one, a great deal of selectivity was necessary. The number of citations has been streamlined so as to emphasize the _economic_ (as opposed to accounting or business) aspects of the respective economies. However, whenever some insight into, say, accounting methods was deemed useful for a more thorough understanding of the functioning and performance of the economies, such topics were not excluded. The same principle was applied to studies of particular industries, as well as to Soviet and East European contributions to mathematical economics and econometrics.

There are many foreign language sources that could be included in a bibliography of Soviet-type economic systems. As an editorial policy, no foreign language sources have been cited in the volume; however, many articles written originally by Soviet and East European authors have been included in translation. Those interested in further references and those who possess the necessary language competence are referred to the appropriate Soviet and East European journals and economic newspapers, such as VOPROSI EKONOMIKI, PLANOVOE KHOZIAISTVO, EKONOMISTA, GOSPODARKA PLANOWA, PROBLEME ECONOMICE, KOZGAZDASAGI SZEMLE, FIGYELO, and others. Additionally, to gain insight into current economic problems, plans, policies, and accomplishments, the reader should consult the appropriate party's daily such as PRAVDA, NEUES DEUTSCHLAND, RUDE PRAVO, or NEPSZABADSAG.

Preface

Because of the similarity of economic processes in Soviet-type economies, the material is organized primarily according to functional categories instead of particular countries. Semantically, no attempt is made to emphasize the distinctions among "Socialist," "Communist," or "Soviet-type" economies. Rather, and often following the author's terminology without necessarily endorsing it, the adjectives "Socialist" and "Communist" are used synonymously with "Soviet-type," "centrally-planned," or "command economies." As the Chinese and Yugoslav models and economies are excluded from the present bibliography, references to actual, functioning economies will be to the economies of Bulgaria, Czechoslovakia, East Germany, Hungary, Poland, Rumania, or the Soviet Union. When referring to theoretical concepts or models, the adjectives are used to denote those models most similar to the "Soviet model."

The compilation is presented with full cognizance of the fact that many more contributions perhaps need to be recorded. Users are, therefore, invited to communicate any suggestions for improvement to the volume editor, who alone bears full responsibility for the contents. It is through such suggestions that the editor's errors and omissions can be corrected and the volume can become an even more useful reference guide.

Z.E.O.

ABBREVIATIONS

CMEA   Council for Mutual Economic Assistance

COMECON   See CMEA

DDR   See GDR

EEC   European Economic Community

EFTA   European Free Trade Association

GATT   General Agreement on Tariffs and Trade

GDP   Gross Domestic Product

GDR   German Democratic Republic

GNP   Gross National Product

IBEC   International Bank for Economic Cooperation

IIB   International Investment Bank

MTS   Machine Tractor Station

NEM   New Economic Mechanism or Model

NEP   New Economic Policy

NMP   Net Material Product

OECD   Organization for Economic Cooperation and Development

R&D   Research and Development

VVB   Association of Nationally Owned Factories

Chapter 1

OVERVIEW

Baykov, Alexander. THE DEVELOPMENT OF THE SOVIET ECONOMIC SYS-
TEM; AN ESSAY ON THE EXPERIENCE OF PLANNING IN THE U.S.S.R.
New York: Macmillan Co., 1948. xv, 514 p.

> A careful, exhaustive study of Soviet economic institutions and
> practices from the revolution through 1940. Topics covered in-
> clude industry, agriculture, labor, foreign trade and payments,
> and planning during the periods of war communism, NEP, and the
> plan era.

Bergson, Abram. THE ECONOMICS OF SOVIET PLANNING. New Haven,
Conn.: Yale University Press, 1964. xvii, 394 p. Tables, appendixes, and
index.

> Excellent overview of the organization, functioning, problems, and
> accomplishments of the Soviet economy.

Brown, J. F. BULGARIA UNDER COMMUNIST RULE. New York: Frederick
A. Praeger, 1970. ix, 339 p. Tables, appendixes, and index.

> A summary of events up to 1953, followed by a detailed account,
> both political and economic, of the 1954-68 period.

Brzeski, Andrzej. "Two Decades of East European Industrialization in Retrospect." EAST EUROPEAN QUARTERLY 3 (March 1969): 1-14.

> An essay on the postwar industrialization of Eastern Europe.

Brzezinski, Zbigniew K. THE SOVIET BLOC: UNITY AND CONFLICT.
Rev. ed. New York: Frederick A. Praeger, 1961. xv, 543 p. Tables,
appendixes, and index.

> An excellent, scholarly work, providing the political background
> and perspective necessary to the understanding of postwar economic
> developments in Eastern Europe.

Campbell, Robert W. SOVIET ECONOMIC POWER: ITS ORGANIZATION,
GROWTH, AND CHALLENGE. Cambridge, Mass.: Riverside Press, 1960.

xii, 209 p. Tables, figures, and index. Paperback.

A well written, introductory discussion of the major issues relevant to the organization and functioning of the Soviet economy.

_____. THE SOVIET-TYPE ECONOMIES: PERFORMANCE AND EVOLU-TION. 3d ed. Boston: Houghton Mifflin Co., 1974. xi, 259 p. Figures, tables, and index. Paperback.

An updated and expanded version of the first edition, published in 1960 under the title SOVIET ECONOMIC POWER: ITS OR-GANIZATION, GROWTH, AND CHALLENGE. The expanded version includes discussions concerning basic economic institutions and organization, the Soviet growth model and its application in Eastern Europe, planning principles and practices, the record of Soviet growth, and economic reforms in the Soviet Union and Eastern Europe.

Carson, Richard L. COMPARATIVE ECONOMIC SYSTEMS. New York: Macmillan Co., 1973. xiii, 717 p. Tables, figures, and index.

An organizational approach to the study of economic systems, in-cluding discussions on efficiency, optimality, and the functioning of command economies.

Crawford, J.T., and Haberstroh, John. "Survey of Economic Policy Issues in Eastern Europe: Technology, Trade, and the Consumer." In REORIENTA-TION AND COMMERCIAL RELATIONS OF THE ECONOMIES OF EASTERN EUROPE, Joint Economic Committee, 93d Cong., 2d sess., pp. 32-50. Washington, D.C.: Government Printing Office, 1974. Tables.

A discussion and assessment of the policy issues which are likely to become more critical for Eastern European decision makers during the 1970s.

Dobrin, Bogoslav. BULGARIAN ECONOMIC DEVELOPMENT SINCE WORLD WAR II. New York: Praeger, 1973. xv, 185 p. Tables.

An examination of the salient aspects of the postwar Bulgarian economic experience: economic planning, development strategy, the foreign trade experience, growth, and the economic reform.

Eckstein, Alexander. "Economic Development and Political Change in Com-munist Systems." WORLD POLITICS 22 (July 1970): 475-95.

An investigation of the imperatives imposed by the stage of eco-nomic development upon Communist political and social systems.

Elliott, John E. COMPARATIVE ECONOMIC SYSTEMS. Englewood Cliffs, N.J.: Prentice-Hall, 1973. xv, 540 p. Tables, figures, appendixes, and index.

A recent, excellent, analytical contribution to the literature of economic systems.

Gilberg, Trond. MODERNIZATION IN ROMANIA SINCE WORLD WAR II. New York: Praeger, 1975. xiii, 261 p. Tables.

A discussion of postwar Rumanian political, social, and economic developments.

Grossman, Gregory. ECONOMIC SYSTEMS. 2d ed. Englewood Cliffs, N.J.: Prentice-Hall, 1974. xii, 195 p. Index. Paperback.

An introductory, concise survey and summary of the field usually identified as comparative economic systems.

_____. "The Structure and Organization of the Soviet Economy." SLAVIC REVIEW 21 (June 1962): 203-22.

A lucid explanation of the organization and functioning of the Soviet economy.

Guins, George C. "Claims and Realities of Soviet Socialism." RUSSIAN REVIEW 11 (July 1952): 138-47.

Background views on Soviet aims, problems, and accomplishments.

Halm, George N. ECONOMIC SYSTEMS: A COMPARATIVE ANALYSIS. 3d ed. New York: Holt, Rinehart & Winston, 1968. xi, 420 p. Tables, figures, and index.

A well written overview of economic systems, including that of authoritarian socialism.

Hanson, Philip. "East-West Comparisons and Comparative Economic Systems." SOVIET STUDIES 22 (January 1971): 327-43. Tables.

Arguments to the effect that East-West comparisons cannot provide evidence for the relative merits of socialism vs. capitalism, nor any conclusive evidence for the comparative efficiency of U.S. and Soviet economic institutions.

Karcz, Jerzy F. "Reflections on the Economics of Nationalism and Communism in Eastern Europe." EAST EUROPEAN QUARTERLY 5 (June 1971): 232-59.

A commentary on the interplay between the forces of nationalism and communism as that interplay affected postwar economic developments in Eastern Europe.

Kaser, Michael [C.]. SOVIET ECONOMICS. New York: McGraw-Hill Book Co., World University Library, 1970. 256 p. Tables, figures, and index. Paperback.

An introduction to the functioning of the Soviet economy and a description of the historical and political forces which helped shape it.

Kohler, Heinz. WELFARE AND PLANNING: AN ANALYSIS OF CAPITALISM VERSUS SOCIALISM. New York: John Wiley and Sons, 1966. xv, 175 p. Tables, figures, and index.

A brief, clear introduction to the questions of planning and efficiency.

Koopmans, Tjalling C., and Montias, John Michael. "On the Description and Comparison of Economic Systems." In COMPARISON OF ECONOMIC SYSTEMS: THEORETICAL AND METHODOLOGICAL APPROACHES, edited by Alexander Eckstein, pp. 27-78. Berkeley and Los Angeles: University of California Press, 1971.

A suggestion for the description and comparison of economic systems.

Kulski, W.W. "Soviet Colonialism and Anti-Colonialism." RUSSIAN REVIEW 18 (April 1959): 113-25.

An essay concerning Soviet policies in Eastern Europe and in the less developed countries.

Loucks, William N., and Whitney, William G. COMPARATIVE ECONOMIC SYSTEMS. 9th ed. New York: Harper & Row, Publishers, 1973. viii, 411 p. Index.

A well known work in its ninth edition (with Whitney), providing a good overview of the theoretical principles and actual operations of the various economic systems.

Matusek, Ivan. "Eastern Europe: The Political Context." In REORIENTATION AND COMMERCIAL RELATIONS OF THE ECONOMIES OF EASTERN EUROPE, Joint Economic Committee, 93d Cong., 2d sess., pp. 17-31. Washington, D.C.: Government Printing Office, 1974. Tables and figures.

An examination of the political context which provides the framework for Eastern European economic policy.

Michal, Jan M. CENTRAL PLANNING IN CZECHOSLOVAKIA: ORGANIZATION FOR GROWTH IN A MATURE ECONOMY. Stanford, Calif.: Stanford University Press, 1960. xii, 274 p. Tables, appendix, and index.

A thorough and skillful examination of the Czechoslovak economy in terms of its national income and product, population and manpower, industry, agriculture, trade, transport, foreign trade, money and prices, investment, budgetary matters, and standard of living.

Millar, James R. "On the Merits of the Convergence Hypothesis." JOURNAL OF ECONOMIC ISSUES 2 (March 1968): 60-68.

An analysis of the issues and arguments involved in the convergence hypothesis.

Nagy, Imre. ON COMMUNISM: IN DEFENSE OF THE NEW COURSE. New York: Frederick A. Praeger, 1957. xliv, 306 p.

An examination of Hungary's economic experiences during 1945-55, including agricultural, industrial, and foreign trade policies.

Nove, Alec. THE SOVIET ECONOMY; AN INTRODUCTION. 2d rev. ed. New York: Frederick A. Praeger, 1968. xiv, 373 p. Index.

A well written introduction to the issues related to the functioning of the Soviet economy.

Osborne, R.H. EAST-CENTRAL EUROPE: A GEOGRAPHICAL INTRODUCTION TO SEVEN SOCIALIST STATES. London: Chatto & Windus, 1967. 384 p. Tables, figures, appendixes, and index.

A historical, economic, demographic, and geographic background to Eastern Europe.

Pickersgill, Gary M., and Pickersgill, Joyce E. CONTEMPORARY ECONOMIC SYSTEMS: A COMPARATIVE VIEW. Englewood Cliffs, N.J.: Prentice-Hall, 1974. x, 356 p. Tables, figures, and index.

An overview of economic systems, including that of the Soviet-type command economy.

Schnitzer, Martin. EAST AND WEST GERMANY: A COMPARATIVE ECONOMIC ANALYSIS. New York: Praeger, 1972. xxii, 446 p. Tables and figures.

A description of the general characteristics of the East German economic and political system, followed by a discussion of the salient features of industry, agriculture, trade, money and banking, fiscal policy, and income distribution. Relevant comparisons with West Germany.

Schwartz, Harry. THE SOVIET ECONOMY SINCE STALIN. New York: J.B. Lippincott Co., 1965. 256 p. Figures, tables, appendix, and index.

A readable, introductory volume dealing with Soviet agriculture, industry, and foreign economic relations.

Spulber, Nicolas. THE ECONOMICS OF COMMUNIST EASTERN EUROPE. New York: Technology Press of M.I.T. and John Wiley and Sons, 1957. xxviii, 525 p. Tables, figures, and index.

A careful and thorough examination and analysis of the economic experiences (primarily structural changes and growth performance) of the Eastern European countries from the end of World War II until the mid 1950s.

_____. THE SOVIET ECONOMY; STRUCTURE, PRINCIPLES, PROBLEMS. Rev. ed. New York: W. W. Norton & Co., 1969. xiv, 329 p. Tables, figures, and index.

A well written introduction to the Soviet economy, including a discussion of plan construction and coordination, the role of prices and market mechanisms, industry and agriculture, labor, fiscal and monetary institutions and mechanisms, national income and product accounts, and foreign trade and payments.

_____. THE STATE AND ECONOMIC DEVELOPMENT IN EASTERN EUROPE. New York: Random House, 1966. xii, 177 p. Tables and index.

An examination of the relationship between state activities and the pace and nature of industrialization, the role of nonindigenous entrepreneurs, and changes in the economic structure of the Balkan countries during 1860–1960.

Stackelberg, Georg A. von. "The Problem of Soviet Colonialism." STUDIES ON THE SOVIET UNION, no. 5 (1960): 15–30.

A discussion of the role of ethnic minorities within the USSR and the relations between the USSR and its satellites.

Stahl, Z. "The Soviet Union and the East European Bloc." STUDIES ON THE SOVIET UNION, no. 1 (1957): 58–73.

A description of Soviet expansion in Eastern Europe after 1939.

Turgeon, Lynn. THE CONTRASTING ECONOMIES: A STUDY OF MODERN ECONOMIC SYSTEMS. Boston: Allyn and Bacon, 1969. xi, 445 p. Tables and index.

An overview of the major differences between centrally planned and market economies. Examined are consumption and investment decision making, public finance and taxation, price and labor policies, and international trade practices under the two systems.

Wellisz, Stanislaw. THE ECONOMIES OF THE SOVIET BLOC: A STUDY OF DECISION MAKING AND RESOURCE ALLOCATION. New York: McGraw-Hill Book Co., 1964. vi, 245 p. Tables and index.

A brief introduction to the economics of Soviet-type economies, designed for the general reader.

Wilczynski, J. THE ECONOMICS OF SOCIALISM. Chicago: Aldine Publishing Co., 1970. 233 p. Tables, figures, and index.

A general survey of the economics of Soviet-type economies, including a discussion of growth strategy, planning principles, pricing, monetary and fiscal policy, and domestic and foreign trade.

Wolfe, Bertram D. "The Durability of Despotism in the Soviet System: I." RUSSIAN REVIEW 17 (January 1958): 83-93.

An examination of the totalitarian heritage of Soviet communism.

_____. "The Durability of Despotism in the Soviet Union: II." RUSSIAN REVIEW 17 (July 1958): 163-75.

A brief survey of post-Stalin political developments in the Soviet Union.

Zinam, Oleg. "Impact of Modernization on the USSR: Convergence or Divergence." RUSSIAN REVIEW 32 (July 1963): 254-63.

Thoughtful comments on the forces of modernization and their impact.

Chapter 2

ECONOMIC ORGANIZATION AND STRUCTURE

Ames, Edward. SOVIET ECONOMIC PROCESSES. Homewood, Ill.: Richard D. Irwin, 1965. 257 p. Tables, figures, and index. Paperback.

> An excellent overview of the Soviet economy, with particular attention to economic organization, planning on the macro and micro levels, fiscal and monetary policy, international trade, and economic performance.

Bandera, V.N. "The New Economic Policy (NEP) as an Economic System." JOURNAL OF POLITICAL ECONOMY 71 (June 1963): 265-79.

> An outline of the salient features of the Soviet economy between 1922 and 1927, a system based upon the coexistence of private and public sectors.

Baykov, Alexander. THE DEVELOPMENT OF THE SOVIET ECONOMIC SYSTEM; AN ESSAY ON THE EXPERIENCE OF PLANNING IN THE U.S.S.R. New York: Macmillan Co., 1948. xv, 514 p.

> A careful, exhaustive study of Soviet economic institutions and practices from the revolution through 1940. Topics covered include industry, agriculture, labor, foreign trade and payments, and planning during the periods of war communism, NEP, and the plan era.

Campbell, Robert W. SOVIET ECONOMIC POWER; ITS ORGANIZATION, GROWTH, AND CHALLENGE. Cambridge, Mass.: Riverside Press, 1960. xii, 209 p. Tables, figures, and index.

> A well written, introductory discussion of the major issues relevant to the organization and functioning of the Soviet economy.

_____. THE SOVIET-TYPE ECONOMIES: PERFORMANCE AND EVOLUTION. 3d ed. Boston: Houghton Mifflin Co., 1974. xi, 259 p. Figures, tables, and index. Paperback.

> An updated and expanded version of the first edition, published in 1960 under the title SOVIET ECONOMIC POWER: ITS ORGANIZATION, GROWTH, AND CHALLENGE. The expanded version

includes discussions concerning basic economic institutions and organization, the Soviet growth model and its application in Eastern Europe, planning principles and practices, the record of Soviet growth, and economic reforms in the Soviet Union and Eastern Europe.

Csikos-Nagy, Bela. "Macrostructural and Microstructural Performance of the Economy." SOVIET STUDIES 23 (January 1972): 474-83.

A discussion of the guided market concept and the role of prices, as envisioned initially by the architects of the Hungarian reform of 1968.

Dobb, Maurice. SOVIET ECONOMIC DEVELOPMENT SINCE 1917. New York: International Publishers, 1948. vii, 475 p. Tables and index.

A detailed, sympathetic account of the unfolding Soviet economic organization and development strategy. Topics discussed include the periods of war communism and NEP, the growth of industry and agriculture, the financial system, and the five-year plans.

Dolan, Edwin G. "Structural Interdependence of the Soviet Economy before the Industrialization Drive." SOVIET STUDIES 19 (July 1967): 66-73.

An examination of the foundations of balance and patterns of interdependence during the NEP.

Dorovskikh, A. "Some Problems in the Theory and Practice of the Interbranch Balance." PROBLEMS OF ECONOMICS 11 (August 1968): 12-20.

A discussion of the difficulties in the use of existing planning methodologies and basic requirements for the formulation of an Interbranch Balance.

Friedrich, Gerd. "Problems of Economic Direction in the VVB's and Factories as Posed by Differentiated Conditions of Reproduction." EASTERN EUROPEAN ECONOMICS 6 (Winter 1967-68): 39-54.

An evaluation of the role and effectiveness of VVB's (Associations of Nationally Owned Factories) in the East German economy.

Gilberg, Trond. "Ceausescu's Romania." PROBLEMS OF COMMUNISM 23 (July-August 1974): 29-43.

A discussion of the political factors and of Ceausescu's role in providing a framework for economic policy in Rumania.

Granick, David. "An Organizational Model of Soviet Industrial Planning." JOURNAL OF POLITICAL ECONOMY 67 (April 1959): 109-30.

An assessment of the influence on Soviet industrial organization of

changes in capital resources, in technology, and in the characteristics of the labor force.

Grossman, Gregory. "The Structure and Organization of the Soviet Economy."
SLAVIC REVIEW 21 (June 1962): 203-22.

A lucid explanation of the organization and functioning of the
Soviet economy.

Hoeffding, Oleg. "The Soviet Industrial Reorganization of 1957." AMERI-
CAN ECONOMIC REVIEW 49 (May 1959): 65-77.

A discussion of selected aspects of the Soviet industrial reorganization of 1957.

Jasny, Naum. THE SOCIALIZED AGRICULTURE OF THE USSR: PLANS AND
PERFORMANCE. Stanford, Calif.: Stanford University Press, 1949. xv,
837 p. Tables, figures, appendixes, and index.

A careful and thorough analysis of the development of Soviet agriculture. Topics discussed include prerevolutionary land tenure,
precollectivization peasant farming, the collectivization drive,
agricultural output, and methods of agricultural planning.

Michal, Jan M. CENTRAL PLANNING IN CZECHOSLOVAKIA: ORGANI-
ZATION FOR GROWTH IN A MATURE ECONOMY. Stanford, Calif.:
Stanford University Press, 1960. xii, 274 p. Tables, appendix, and index.

A thorough and skillful examination of the Czechoslovak economy
in terms of its national income and product, population and manpower, industry, agriculture, trade, transport, foreign trade, money
and prices, investment, budgetary matters, and standard of living.

Pryor, Frederic L. PROPERTY AND INDUSTRIAL ORGANIZATION IN COM-
MUNIST AND CAPITALIST NATIONS. Bloomington: Indiana University
Press, 1973. xviii, 513 p. Tables, appendixes, and index.

An analysis of the pattern of public ownership, property and labor
incomes, property rights, and the size of production units.

Stolper, Wolfgang F. THE STRUCTURE OF THE EAST GERMAN ECONOMY.
Cambridge, Mass.: Harvard University Press, 1960. xxv, 478 p. Tables and
index.

A thorough examination of the functioning and performance of the
East German economy, including a discussion of national income
methodology, population and labor force, industrial and agricultural output, and transportation, communication, and distribution
problems and accomplishments.

Swearer, Howard R. "Decentralization in Recent Soviet Administrative Practice." SLAVIC REVIEW 21 (September 1962): 456-70.

A description of the problems of Soviet administrative decentralization, consolidation, and territorialization.

Treml, Vladimir G. "The 1959 Soviet Input-Output Table (As Reconstructed)." In NEW DIRECTIONS IN THE SOVIET ECONOMY, Joint Economic Committee, 89th Cong., 2d sess., pp. 257-70. Washington, D.C.: Government Printing Office, 1966. Tables.

An expanded and corrected version of the reconstructed 1959 Input-Output Table, originally published by the same author in 1964.

Treml, Vladimir G., et al. "Interindustry Structure of the Soviet Economy: 1959 and 1966." In SOVIET ECONOMIC PROSPECTS FOR THE SEVENTIES, Joint Economic Committee, 93d Cong., 1st sess., pp. 246-69. Washington, D.C.: Government Printing Office, 1973. Tables and appendixes.

Presentation of Soviet input-output tables for 1959 and 1966 in a format which allows comparisons.

_____. THE STRUCTURE OF THE SOVIET ECONOMY: ANALYSIS AND RECONSTRUCTION OF THE 1966 INPUT-OUTPUT TABLE. New York: Praeger Publishers, 1972. xxiv, 660 p. Tables, appendixes, and index.

One of a series of studies involving the reconstruction and analysis of Soviet input-output tables.

Vergner, Zdenek. "Problems of the Economic Level Already Attained in Czechoslovakia and of Its Future Development." EASTERN EUROPEAN ECONOMICS 1 (Spring 1963): 29-33.

A discussion of problems of economic structure, efficiency, and labor utilization.

Voznesensky, Nikolai A. THE ECONOMY OF THE USSR DURING WORLD WAR II. Washington, D.C.: Public Affairs Press, 1948. 115 p.

A discussion of the organization and functioning of the war economy of the Soviet Union during World War II by the chief of the State Planning Commission. Included in the discussion are aspects of economic planning, agricultural, industrial, financial, and credit policy, as well as transport and distribution policies.

Vutov, Vasil. "Analysis of the Branch Structure of the Bulgarian National Economy." EASTERN EUROPEAN ECONOMICS 3 (Fall 1964): 16-25. Tables.

An examination of Bulgarian economic organization, the sectoral distribution of employment, and the sources and magnitude of Bulgarian national income in selected years.

Ward, Benjamin N. THE SOCIALIST ECONOMY--A STUDY OF ORGANI-

ZATIONAL ALTERNATIVES. New York: Random House, 1967. ix, 272 p. Figures and index.

Alternative abstract models of socialism are contrasted and evaluated. A discussion of the prewar Socialist controversy is followed by a theoretical analysis of centralized and then decentralized socialism.

Wiles, Peter J.D. THE POLITICAL ECONOMY OF COMMUNISM. Oxford: Basil Blackwell, 1962. xv, 404 p. Tables, figures, and index.

A critical, analytical examination of the major issues relevant to the study of Soviet-type economies: economic organization; planning and resource allocation, including pricing, planners' preferences, and decentralization; and growth strategy and performance.

Chapter 3

WESTERN THEORIES OF SOCIALISM

Barone, E. "The Ministry of Production in the Collectivist State." In COL-
LECTIVIST ECONOMIC PLANNING: CRITICAL STUDIES ON THE POSSI-
BILITIES OF SOCIALISM, edited by F.A. von Hayek, pp. 245-90. London:
Routledge & Kegan Paul, 1935. Figures.

> A pathbreaking contribution to economic analysis, dealing with
> the problem of directing production in a Socialist state.

Bergson, Abram. "Market Socialism Revisited." JOURNAL OF POLITICAL
ECONOMY 75 (October 1967): 655-73. Figures.

> An analysis of the economic efficiency of market socialism.

_____. "Socialist Economics." In A SURVEY OF CONTEMPORARY ECO-
NOMICS, VOL. I, edited by Howard S. Ellis, pp. 412-48. Homewood,
Ill.: Richard D. Irwin, 1948.

> An analytical discussion and evaluation of the major theoretical
> issues in Socialist economics.

Dickinson, H.D. "Price Formation in a Socialist Community." ECONOMIC
JOURNAL 43 (June 1933): 237-50.

> An early attempt to show that a rational pricing system is at least
> a theoretical possibility in a Socialist economy.

Drewnowski, Jan. "The Economic Theory of Socialism: A Suggestion for Re-
consideration." JOURNAL OF POLITICAL ECONOMY 69 (August 1961):
341-54.

> A critique of Pareto, Barone, Lange, and Lerner, followed by an
> effort to lay a basis for a "realistic" theory of a Socialist economy.

Hayek, F.A. von. "The Nature and History of the Problem." In his COL-
LECTIVIST ECONOMIC PLANNING, pp. 1-40. London: George Routledge
& Sons, 1935.

> Thoughts on socialism, capitalism, and planning.

_____. "Socialist Calculation: The Competitive 'Solution.'" ECONOMICA 7 (May 1940): 125-49.

Comments on Lange's and Dickinson's proposals for competitive socialism.

Lange, Oskar. "On the Economic Theory of Socialism: Part One." REVIEW OF ECONOMIC STUDIES 4 (1936-37): 53-71.

A clear statement by Lange concerning his economic theory of socialism.

_____. "On the Economic Theory of Socialism: Part Two." REVIEW OF ECONOMIC STUDIES 4 (1936-37): 123-42.

A statement of the economist's case for socialism by one of socialism's proponents.

Lerner, A.P. "Economic Theory and Socialist Economy." REVIEW OF ECONOMIC STUDIES 2 (1934-35): 51-61.

Thoughtful comments on the Socialist controversy.

Roberts, Paul Craig. "Oskar Lange's Theory of Socialist Planning." JOURNAL OF POLITICAL ECONOMY 79 (May/June 1971): 562-77.

An analysis of Lange's theory of Socialist planning in which Roberts attempts to show that the belief of the existence of an alternative to the market for a modern economy is erroneous.

Spulber, Nicolas. "On Some Issues in the Theory of the 'Socialist Economy.'" KYKLOS 25 (1972): 715-35.

An examination of the salient points of Western debates about the theory of the "socialist" economy (including resource allocation under "socialism," objectives and controls under alternative modes of organization, etc.) and Eastern and Western interpretations of the concept of a "socialist economy."

Taylor, Fred M. "The Guidance of Production in a Socialist State." In ON THE ECONOMIC THEORY OF SOCIALISM, by Oskar Lange and Fred M. Taylor, edited by Benjamin E. Lippincott, pp. 39-54, 1938. Reprint. New York: McGraw-Hill Book Co., 1964. Paperback.

Taylor's presidential address, dealing with the methods that could be used by a Socialist state to derive an output assortment, delivered at the forty-first annual meeting of the American Economic Association in Chicago in 1928. Reprinted in AMERICAN ECONOMIC REVIEW 19 (March 1929): 1-8.

Von Mises, Ludwig. "Economic Calculation in the Socialist Commonwealth." In COLLECTIVIST ECONOMIC PLANNING: CRITICAL STUDIES ON THE

POSSIBILITIES OF SOCIALISM, edited by F.A. von Hayek, pp. 87-130. London: Routledge & Kegan Paul, 1935.

An examination of the concept of economic calculation and the possibilities of rational calculation in a Socialist economy.

_____. SOCIALISM: AN ECONOMIC AND SOCIOLOGICAL ANALYSIS. Translated by J. Kahane. New Haven, Conn.: Yale University Press, 1951. 599 p. Index.

Mises' thoughts on the nature of economic activity, the organization of production and distribution of income under socialism, socialism under dynamic and static conditions, foreign trade under socialism, and certain sociological aspects of socialism.

Ward, Benjamin N. THE SOCIALIST ECONOMY--A STUDY OF ORGANIZATIONAL ALTERNATIVES. New York: Random House, 1967. ix, 272 p. Figures and index.

An evaluation of alternative abstract models of socialism. A discussion of the prewar Socialist controversy is followed by a theoretical analysis of centralized and then decentralized socialism.

Chapter 4
GROWTH AND DEVELOPMENT

NATIONAL INCOME ESTIMATES AND METHODOLOGY

Alton, Thad P[aul]. "Economic Growth and Resource Allocation in Eastern Europe." In REORIENTATION AND COMMERCIAL RELATIONS OF THE ECONOMIES OF EASTERN EUROPE, Joint Economic Committee, 93d Cong., 2d sess., pp. 251-98. Washington, D.C.: Government Printing Office, 1974. Tables and appendix.

> Analysis of rates of economic growth, changes in the structure of economic activity, and labor and capital productivity in Bulgaria, Czechoslovakia, East Germany, Hungary, Poland, and Rumania.

_____. "Economic Structure and Growth in Eastern Europe." In ECONOMIC DEVELOPMENTS IN COUNTRIES OF EASTERN EUROPE, Joint Economic Committee, 91st Cong., 2d sess., pp. 41-67. Washington, D.C.: Government Printing Office, 1970. Tables and appendix.

> A statistical approach, using both official data and independent estimates to describe the composition of economic activity, measure its growth, and show trends in labor and capital productivity in Eastern Europe.

Alton, Thad Paul, et al. CZECHOSLOVAK NATIONAL INCOME AND PRODUCT: 1947-1948 AND 1955-1956. New York: Columbia University Press, 1962. xiv, 255 p. Tables, appendixes, and index.

> Presentation of sectoral and consolidated national accounts in market prices, followed by an analysis of GNP by sectors of origin and final use at factor cost.

_____. HUNGARIAN NATIONAL INCOME AND PRODUCT IN 1955. New York: Columbia University Press, 1963. xv, 254 p. Tables, appendixes, and index.

> An analysis of the contribution of the various sectors of production to national product and the allocation of this product to end uses. A part of a larger study of the structure and growth of Soviet-type

economies carried on by the Research Project on National Income in East Central Europe.

_____. POLISH NATIONAL INCOME AND PRODUCT IN 1954, 1955, AND 1956. New York: Columbia University Press, 1965. viii, 252 p. Appendixes and index.

A calculation of GNP by analyzing the contribution of the various sectors of production at factor cost.

Baran, Paul A. "National Income and Product of the U.S.S.R. in 1940." REVIEW OF ECONOMICS AND STATISTICS 29 (November 1947): 226-34. Tables and appendix.

Explanation of sources of upward bias in Soviet national income statistics, followed by comparisons between U.S. and Soviet national income concepts. Soviet national income for 1940 is given at both factor cost and at market prices.

Becker, Abraham S. "National Income Accounting in the USSR." In SOVIET ECONOMIC STATISTICS, edited by Vladimir G. Treml and John P. Hardt, pp. 69-119. Durham, N.C.: Duke University Press, 1972. Tables.

Analysis of Soviet national income concepts and procedures and testing of the reliability of official data.

_____. SOVIET NATIONAL INCOME 1958-1964. Berkeley and Los Angeles: University of California Press, 1969. xvii, 608 p. Tables, figures, appendixes, and index.

A comprehensive analysis of Soviet national income and product accounts, including an analysis of incomes and outlays at current prevailing prices, national product at current factor cost and at constant prices, and military outlays.

Bergson, Abram. "National Income." In ECONOMIC TRENDS IN THE SOVIET UNION, edited by Abram Bergson and Simon Kuznets, pp. 1-37. Cambridge, Mass.: Harvard University Press, 1963. Tables and appendix.

An analysis of Soviet national income growth and growth in factor productivity in the USSR, accompanied by U.S.-USSR comparisons.

_____. THE REAL NATIONAL INCOME OF SOVIET RUSSIA SINCE 1928. Cambridge, Mass.: Harvard University Press, 1961. xix, 472 p. Tables, appendixes, and index.

An explanation of the Soviet national income concept and calculation of Soviet national income in prevailing and adjusted rubles; comparisons between U.S. and USSR national incomes.

_____. SOVIET NATIONAL INCOME AND PRODUCT IN 1937. New York: Columbia University Press, 1953. viii, 156 p. Tables and appendixes.

Presentation of Soviet national income estimates in current rubles and at adjusted factor cost.

_____. "Soviet National Income and Product in 1937, Part I: National Income Accounts in Current Rubles." QUARTERLY JOURNAL OF ECONOMICS 64 (May 1950): 208-41. Tables.

Explanation of the various account categories and the role of the budget.

_____. "Soviet National Income and Product in 1937, Part II: Ruble Prices and the Valuation Problem." QUARTERLY JOURNAL OF ECONOMICS 64 (August 1950): 408-41. Tables.

An examination of retail prices, wages, collective farm prices, and national product in terms of adjusted rubles and national income according to ruble and dollar valuations.

_____. "Toward a New Growth Model." PROBLEMS OF COMMUNISM 22 (March-April 1973): 1-9. Tables.

A review of past trends in the Soviet economy, followed by alternative projections for future GNP on the basis of different rates of growth in the capital stock and in factor productivity.

Bergson, Abram, and Heymann, Hans, Jr. SOVIET NATIONAL INCOME AND PRODUCT, 1940-1948. New York: Columbia University Press, 1954. xii, 235 p. Tables, figures, and appendixes.

Estimates for Soviet national income in current rubles and at adjusted factor cost.

Berri, L. "Questions in the Methodology of National Economic Planning." PROBLEMS OF ECONOMICS 11 (December 1968): 3-11.

A reaffirmation of the role of balances and model building in national economic planning.

Bornstein, Morris. "Soviet National Income Accounts for 1955." REVIEW OF ECONOMICS AND STATISTICS 44 (November 1962): 446-57. Tables.

Estimates of national income and product of the USSR for 1955.

Campbell, Robert W., et al. "Methodological Problems Comparing the U.S. and U.S.S.R. Economies." In SOVIET ECONOMIC PROSPECTS FOR THE SEVENTIES, Joint Economic Committee, 93d Cong., 1st sess., pp. 122-46. Washington, D.C.: Government Printing Office, 1973. Tables.

Illustration of methodological problems by supplying estimates of U.S. and USSR economic aggregates and by interpreting these aggregates. Discussion of the use of economic comparisons in defense policy issues.

Cohn, Stanley H. "National Income Growth Statistics." In SOVIET ECO-NOMIC STATISTICS, edited by Vladimir G. Treml and John P. Hardt, pp. 120-47. Durham, N.C.: Duke University Press, 1972. Tables.

A careful examination of Soviet national income growth statistics, with attention to questions of reliability and divergences between Western-computed and official indexes.

Falkus, M.E. "Russia's National Income, 1913: A Revaluation." ECONOM-ICA 35 (February 1963): 52-73. Tables and appendix.

Revised estimates for Russia's national income for 1913.

Hagen, Everett E., and Hawrylyshyn, Oli. "Analysis of World Income and Growth, 1955-1965." ECONOMIC DEVELOPMENT AND CULTURAL CHANGE 18, pt. 2 (October 1969): 1-96. Tables, figures, and appendix.

Analysis of estimates for gross domestic product in selected years, rates of growth of GDP, and availability of goods and services.

Hoeffding, Oleg. SOVIET NATIONAL INCOME AND PRODUCT IN 1928. New York: Columbia University Press, 1954. 156 p. Tables and appendixes.

Estimates are presented for the national income of the USSR in 1928, in a form comparable to estimates by Bergson and Heymann in their SOVIET NATIONAL INCOME AND PRODUCT, 1940-1948 (New York: Columbia University Press, 1954).

Holesovsky, Vaclav. "Karl Marx and Soviet National Income Theory." AMERICAN ECONOMIC REVIEW 51 (June 1961): 325-44.

An analysis of the connections between contemporary Soviet na-tional income theory and Marxist ideas on the subject.

Jackson, E.F. "Social Accounting in Eastern Europe." In INCOME AND WEALTH, Series IV, edited by Milton Gilbert and Richard Stone, pp. 242-61. London: Bowes and Bowes, 1955. Tables.

A discussion of Eastern European national income accounting meth-odology and practices.

Jasny, N[aum]. "A Short Cut to Growth Rates in Soviet National Income." SOVIET STUDIES 15 (July 1963): 38-42.

A brief discussion of Soviet national income indexes.

_____. THE SOVIET ECONOMY DURING THE PLAN ERA. Stanford, Calif.: Stanford University Press, 1951. xi, 116 p. Tables, appendix, and index.

An analysis of the sources and uses of national income in the Soviet Union during 1928-48.

_____. "The Soviet Statistical Yearbooks for 1955 through 1960." SLAVIC REVIEW 21 (March 1962): 121-56.

An explanation of the breakdown and concepts used in Soviet statistical handbooks.

_____. "Soviet Statistics." REVIEW OF ECONOMICS AND STATISTICS 32 (February 1950): 92-99.

A critical view at Soviet statistics.

Kaser, M[ichael].C. "Estimating the Soviet National Income." ECONOMIC JOURNAL 67 (March 1957): 83-104. Appendix.

A survey of the inadequacies of official Soviet data and Western estimates of Soviet national income.

_____. "A Survey of the National Accounts of Eastern Europe." In INCOME AND WEALTH, SERIES IX, edited by Phyllis Deane, pp. 131-77. London: Bowes and Bowes, 1961.

Examination of Eastern European and Soviet national income accounting concepts, methodology, and data availability and comparability.

Krejci, Jaroslav. "Gross National Product in the United Kingdom and Czechoslovakia--A Comparative Analysis." SOVIET STUDIES 22 (January 1971): 370-75.

A recalculation of GNP figures for Czechoslovakia according to methods used by the UN Statistical Department.

Lazarcik, Gregor. "Growth of Output, Expenses, and Gross and Net Product in East European Agriculture." In ECONOMIC DEVELOPMENTS IN COUNTRIES OF EASTERN EUROPE, Joint Economic Committee, 91st Cong., 2d sess., pp. 463-527. Washington, D.C.: Government Printing Office, 1970. Tables and appendixes.

A statistical study, dealing with production and input measures, production per capita, changes in land and labor productivity, and investment as they pertain to East European agriculture.

Notkin, A.I. "Aggregate and End Social Product." PROBLEMS OF ECONOMICS 6 (February 1964): 14-26. Tables.

A methodological discussion concerning the concepts of aggregate and end social product.

Nove, A[lec]. "Some Notes on Soviet National Income Statistics." SOVIET STUDIES 6 (January 1955): 247-80.

A discussion and illustration of the methods and problems involved in Soviet national income accounting.

_____. "Some Problems in Soviet Agricultural Statistics." SOVIET STUDIES 7 (January 1956): 248-68.

A discussion of problems of Soviet agricultural gross and net output, productivity, and cost of production statistics.

Pryor, Frederic L., and Staller, George J. "The Dollar Values of the Gross National Products in Eastern Europe in 1955." ECONOMICS OF PLANNING 6 (1966): 1-26. Tables and appendixes.

Estimates of dollar values of GNP for Bulgaria, Czechoslovakia, East Germany, Hungary, Poland, Rumania, Yugoslavia, and the USSR.

Seers, Dudley. "A Note on the Current Marxist Definitions of the National Income." OXFORD ECONOMIC PAPERS 1 (June 1949): 260-68.

An explanation of the Marxist concept of national income.

Seton, Francis. "The Social Accounts of the Soviet Union in 1934." REVIEW OF ECONOMICS AND STATISTICS 36 (August 1954): 290-308. Tables.

Recomputation of Soviet social accounts for 1934.

Starovskii, V. "On the Methodology of Comparing Economic Indices of the USSR and the USA." PROBLEMS OF ECONOMICS 3 (July 1960): 14-24. Tables.

A discussion of methodological questions concerning the comparisons of national income, living standards, labor productivity, and the volume of industrial and agricultural output in the United States and the Soviet Union.

Stolper, Wolfgang [F.]. "The National Product of East Germany." KYKLOS 12 (1959): 131-66. Tables and appendix.

Estimates for the sectoral origin and uses of East German GNP for the period 1936-57.

_____. THE STRUCTURE OF THE EAST GERMAN ECONOMY. Cambridge, Mass.: Harvard University Press, 1960. xxv, 478 p. Tables and index.

A thorough examination of the functioning and performance of the East German economy, including a discussion of national income methodology, population and labor force, industrial and agricultural output, and transportation, communication, and distribution problems and accomplishments.

Tarn, Alexander. "A Comparison of Dollar and Ruble Values of the Industrial Output of the USA and the USSR." SOVIET STUDIES 19 (April 1968): 482-500. Tables.

A serious attempt, on a comprehensive basis, to evaluate the magnitude of Soviet industrial output and to compare it to the value of U.S. industrial output.

Tarn, Alexander, and Campbell, Robert [W.]. "A Comparison of U.S. and Soviet Industrial Output." AMERICAN ECONOMIC REVIEW 52 (September 1962): 703-27. Tables and appendix.

A comparison of Soviet and U.S. industrial output, including a careful explanation of the method used in obtaining the result.

Treml, Vladimir G., et al. THE STRUCTURE OF THE SOVIET ECONOMY: ANALYSIS AND RECONSTRUCTION OF THE 1966 INPUT-OUTPUT TABLE. New York: Praeger Publishers, 1972. xxiv, 660 p. Tables, appendixes, and index.

One of a series of studies involving the reconstruction and analysis of Soviet input-output tables.

United Nations. Economic Commission for Europe. "An Estimate of the National Accounts of the Soviet Union for 1955." ECONOMIC BULLETIN FOR EUROPE 9 (May 1957): 89-107. Tables and appendix.

Soviet national income accounts estimates for 1955.

_____. "A Note on Some Aspects of National Accounting Methodology in Eastern Europe and the Soviet Union." ECONOMIC BULLETIN FOR EUROPE 11 (November 1959): 52-68. Tables.

Explanation of Soviet and East European national income accounting concepts and methods.

Vikhliaev, A. [V.]. "The Method of Valuation of Gross Agricultural Production." PROBLEMS OF ECONOMICS 3 (September 1960): 55-60. Tables.

A methodological discussion concerning the valuation of agricultural output.

GROWTH AND DEVELOPMENT THEORY, STRATEGY, AND POLICY

Alton, Thad Paul. POLISH POSTWAR ECONOMY. New York: Columbia University Press, 1955. 330 p. Tables, appendixes, and index.

Survey of early postwar Polish economic planning and developments. Topics covered include planning in industry, agriculture, finance, and foreign trade.

Baykov, Alexander. THE DEVELOPMENT OF THE SOVIET ECONOMIC SYSTEM; AN ESSAY ON THE EXPERIENCE OF PLANNING IN THE U.S.S.R. New York: Macmillan Co., 1948. xv, 514 p.

A careful, exhaustive study of Soviet economic institutions and practices from the revolution through 1940. Topics covered include industry, agriculture, labor, foreign trade and payments, and planning during the periods of war communism, NEP, and the plan era.

Berend, Ivan T. "The Historical Background of the Recent Economic Reforms in East Europe." EAST EUROPEAN QUARTERLY 2 (March 1968): 75-90.

An essay on the postwar economic experiences of Hungary.

Berend, I[van]. T., and Ranki, G. HUNGARY: A CENTURY OF ECONOMIC DEVELOPMENT. New York: Harper & Row Publishers, 1974. 263 p. Tables, figures, and index.

A discussion of Hungarian economic development strategy and a brief survey of the attained results.

Bergson, Abram. "Toward a New Growth Model." PROBLEMS OF COMMUNISM 22 (March-April 1973): 1-9. Tables.

A review of past trends in the Soviet economy, followed by alternative projections for future GNP on the basis of different rates of growth in the capital stock and in factor productivity. Some thoughts concerning the reasons for the apparent erosion of the traditional Soviet growth model.

Bernasek, Miloslav. "The Czechoslovak Economic Recession, 1962-65." SOVIET STUDIES 20 (April 1969): 444-61. Appendix.

An examination of the causes of the 1962-65 stagnation in Czechoslovakia--the growth strategy and the Soviet system of centralized planning.

Bhalla, A.S. "From Fel'dman to Mahalanobis in Economic Planning." KYKLOS 18 (1965): 9-26. Tables.

A comparison of the Feldman, Harrod-Domar, and Mahalanobis growth models. Stress on the superiority of the Soviet model.

Brus, W[lodzimierz]., and Laski, K. "Problems in the Theory of Growth under Socialism." In PROBLEMS IN ECONOMIC DEVELOPMENT: PROCEEDINGS OF A CONFERENCE HELD BY THE INTERNATIONAL ECONOMIC ASSOCIATION, edited by E.A.G. Robinson, pp. 21-54. New York: St. Martin's Press, 1965. Figures.

An analysis of growth promoting and limiting factors under conditions of central planning. Integration of Kalecki's growth theory with the authors' extensions.

Brzeski, Andrzej. "Forced-Draft Industrialization with Unlimited Supply of

Money: Poland, 1945-1964." In MONEY AND PLAN--FINANCIAL ASPECTS OF EAST EUROPEAN ECONOMIC REFORMS, edited by Gregory Grossman, pp. 17-37. Berkeley and Los Angeles: University of California Press, 1968. Appendix.

> A discussion of supply and demand for money, inflation, and economic growth in postwar Poland.

_____. "Two Decades of East European Industrialization in Retrospect." EAST EUROPEAN QUARTERLY 3 (March 1969): 1-14.

> Essay on the postwar industrialization of Eastern Europe.

Campbell, Robert W. THE SOVIET-TYPE ECONOMIES: PERFORMANCE AND EVOLUTION. 3d ed. Boston: Houghton Mifflin Co., 1974. xi, 259 p. Figures, tables, and index. Paperback.

> An updated and expanded version of the first edition, published in 1960 under the title SOVIET ECONOMIC POWER: ITS ORGANIZATION, GROWTH, AND CHALLENGE. The expanded version includes discussions on basic economic institutions and organization, the Soviet growth model and its application in Eastern Europe, planning principles and practices, the record of Soviet growth, and economic reforms in the Soviet Union and Eastern Europe.

Chilosi, Alberto. "The Theory of Growth of a Socialist Economy of M. Kalecki." ECONOMICS OF PLANNING 11 (1971): 161-88.

> An examination and appraisal of Kalecki's contribution to the theory of growth of a Socialist economy.

Cohn, Stanley H. ECONOMIC DEVELOPMENT IN THE SOVIET UNION. Lexington, Mass.: D.C. Heath, 1970. 135 p. Tables, appendixes, and index.

> A lucid explanation of the salient features of the Soviet economic experience since 1917, with emphasis on development strategy and performance.

Conolly, Violet. BEYOND THE URALS: ECONOMIC DEVELOPMENTS IN SOVIET ASIA. London: Oxford University Press, 1967. xx, 420 p. Tables, figures, appendixes, and index.

> A description of economic developments in Soviet Central Asia, Kazakhstan, Siberia, and in the Soviet Far East.

Coulter, Harris L. "The Hungarian Peasantry: 1948-1956." AMERICAN SLAVIC AND EAST EUROPEAN REVIEW 18 (December 1959): 539-54.

> A discussion of Hungarian agricultural policy between 1945-56.

Dalrymple, Dana G. "The Soviet Famine of 1932–1934." SOVIET STUDIES 15 (January 1964): 250–84.

A documented account of the manmade Soviet famine of 1932–34.

Davies, R.W. "Planning for Rapid Growth in the USSR." ECONOMICS OF PLANNING 5 (1965): 74–86. Tables.

A general survey of the background of Soviet industrialization, the alternative patterns available to the planners, and the actual alternative which was chosen.

Dobb, Maurice. PAPERS ON CAPITALISM, DEVELOPMENT AND PLANNING. New York: International Publishers, 1967. 274 p. Index.

A series of essays, concentrating on certain aspects of the Soviet mode of economic development and explaining the rationale behind the "investment priority for heavy industry" argument.

_____. SOVIET ECONOMIC DEVELOPMENT SINCE 1917. New York: International Publishers, 1948. vii, 475 p. Tables and index.

A detailed, sympathetic account of the unfolding Soviet economic organization and development strategy. Topics discussed include the periods of war communism and NEP, the growth of industry and agriculture, the financial system, and the five-year plans.

Dobrin, Bogoslav. BULGARIAN ECONOMIC DEVELOPMENT SINCE WORLD WAR II. New York: Praeger, 1973. xv, 185 p. Tables.

An examination of important aspects of the postwar Bulgarian economic experience: economic planning, development strategy, the foreign trade experience, growth, and the economic reform.

Dodge, Norton T., and Wilber, Charles K. "The Relevance of Soviet Industrial Experience for Less Developed Economies." SOVIET STUDIES 21 (January 1970): 330–49. Table.

A discussion of the main features of Soviet industrialization strategy (unbalanced growth, capital intensive technology, etc.) as they pertain to the less developed economies.

Erlich, Alexander. "Development Strategy and Planning: The Soviet Experience." In NATIONAL ECONOMIC PLANNING: A CONFERENCE OF THE UNIVERSITIES-NATIONAL BUREAU COMMITTEE FOR ECONOMIC RESEARCH, edited by Max F. Millikan, pp. 233–78. New York: National Bureau of Economic Research, 1967.

An examination of the Soviet development strategy and the role of the planning system in implementing that strategy.

_____. "Preobrazhenski and the Economics of Soviet Industrialization."

QUARTERLY JOURNAL OF ECONOMICS 64 (February 1950): 57-88.

Discussion of the "goods famine," the law of "primitive socialist accumulation," the arguments concerning the tempo of industrialization, and the solution of the "Preobrazhenski Dilemma."

_____. THE SOVIET INDUSTRIALIZATION DEBATE, 1924-1928. Cambridge, Mass.: Harvard University Press, 1960. xxiii, 214 p. Figures and index.

Careful analysis of the theories and strategies advanced by the major participants in the Soviet industrialization debate of the 1920s.

Fallenbuchl, Z[bigniew].M. "Collectivization and Economic Development." CANADIAN JOURNAL OF ECONOMICS AND POLITICAL SCIENCE 33 (February 1967): 1-15.

An examination, in light of the Soviet-bloc experience, of the possible connection between collectivization and economic development.

_____. "Investment Policy for Economic Development: Some Lessons of the Communist Experience." CANADIAN JOURNAL OF ECONOMICS AND POLITICAL SCIENCE 29 (February 1963): 26-39.

A review of Communist investment theories within the framework of Communist investment experience.

_____. "The Relevance of the Communist Experience for the Development of Underdeveloped Countries." CANADIAN SLAVONIC PAPERS 6 (1964): 44-58.

An analysis of the reasons for Soviet economic performance and a discussion of the applicability of the Soviet model to the problems facing developing nations.

_____. "Some Structural Aspects of Soviet-Type Investment Policy." SOVIET STUDIES 16 (April 1965): 432-47.

An exposition of the relationships between Soviet investment policy and (1) the structure of aggregate demand and aggregate supply; (2) the relative rates of growth of the producer and consumer goods sectors; and (3) the possible adverse effects on growth due to the stress on the expansion of heavy industry.

_____. "The Strategy of Development and Gierek's Economic Manoeuvre." CANADIAN SLAVONIC PAPERS 15 (Spring and Summer 1973): 52-70.

An assessment of the probable impact of Gierek's economic policies on the further development of the Polish economy.

Feiwel, George R. THE ECONOMICS OF A SOCIALIST ENTERPRISE: A

CASE STUDY OF THE POLISH FIRM. New York: Frederick A. Praeger, 1965. xvi, 398 p.

A detailed review of the Polish economy after World War II, of the different planning philosophies, and of the actual plans as they affect Polish industrial enterprises. The views of leading Polish planners and economists as they relate to greater decentralization in planning are presented with great thoroughness.

_____. "The Inverse Economic Miracle: Sources of Growth and Retrogression in Postwar Czechoslovakia." ECONOMIC DEVELOPMENT AND CULTURAL CHANGE 19 (April 1971): 347-77. Tables.

A comprehensive examination of Czechoslovakia's postwar economic achievements and problems.

_____. NEW ECONOMIC PATTERNS IN CZECHOSLOVAKIA: IMPACT OF GROWTH, PLANNING AND THE MARKET. New York: Frederick A. Praeger, 1968. xxiv, 589 p. Tables and figures.

A thorough discussion of the major currents of Czechoslovak economic development, planning, and reforms.

_____. POLAND'S INDUSTRIALIZATION POLICY: A CURRENT ANALYSIS; SOURCES OF ECONOMIC GROWTH AND RETROGRESSION. Vol. 1. New York: Frederick A. Praeger, 1971. xxv, 748 p. Tables and appendix.

An exposition of the Soviet growth strategy and the case for planning, followed by a detailed description of the various Polish economic plans from 1947 to 1970.

_____. THE SOVIET QUEST FOR ECONOMIC EFFICIENCY--ISSUES, CONTROVERSIES, AND REFORMS. New York: Praeger, 1972. xxiv, 790 p.

An expanded and updated version of the first edition (1967). A very comprehensive and exhaustive treatment of the issues related to Soviet economic development, planning, efficiency, reform proposals, and implementation.

Fel'd, S. "Planning the Most Important Branch and Territorial Proportions of Soviet Reproduction." PROBLEMS OF ECONOMICS 9 (June 1966): 3-16. Tables.

An explanation of the reasons for planning production proportions and the appropriate proportions among the major sectors and branches of the economy.

Gerschenkron, Alexander. ECONOMIC BACKWARDNESS IN HISTORICAL PERSPECTIVE: A BOOK OF ESSAYS. Cambridge, Mass.: Harvard University Press, 1966. 456 p. Tables, appendixes, and index.

A collection of stimulating essays, concerned with patterns and problems of Soviet economic development, the rate of industrial growth in Soviet Russia, and the dollar index of output of Soviet heavy industry.

Gisser, Micha, and Jonas, Paul. "Soviet Growth in Absence of Centralized Planning: A Hypothetical Alternative." JOURNAL OF POLITICAL ECONOMY 82 (March/April 1974): 333-51. Tables and appendixes.

An investigation of whether the Soviet Union would be richer or poorer today had it adopted a decentralized, agriculture-propelled economic policy.

Goldmann, Josef. "Fluctuations and Trend in the Rate of Economic Growth in Some Socialist Countries." ECONOMICS OF PLANNING 4 (1964): 88-98. Tables and figures.

An analysis of the reasons for fluctuations in growth rates in Czechoslovakia, Poland, Hungary, and East Germany.

Goldmann, J[osef]., and Flek, J. "Economic Growth in Czechoslovakia: Experimental Application of Kalecki's Model to Czechoslovak Statistical Data." ECONOMICS OF PLANNING 6 (1966): 125-37. Figures.

Kalecki's model is utilized in analyzing Czechoslovakia's growth experience during 1950-65.

Goldmann, Josef, and Kouba, Karel. ECONOMIC GROWTH IN CZECHO-SLOVAKIA. White Plains, N.Y.: International Arts and Sciences Press, 1969. 150 p. Tables, figures, and index.

An experimental application of Kalecki's growth model to Czecho-slovak empirical data in an effort to discover the growth-promoting and growth-retarding factors in the Czechoslovak economy.

Granick, David. "The Pattern of Foreign Trade in Eastern Europe and Its Relation to Economic Development Policy." QUARTERLY JOURNAL OF ECONOMICS 68 (August 1954): 377-400. Tables.

A discussion of economic development and trade patterns in Eastern Europe, including some hypotheses regarding internal development and foreign trade patterns in the Soviet bloc.

Gregory, Paul R., and Stuart, Robert C. SOVIET ECONOMIC STRUCTURE AND PERFORMANCE. New York: Harper & Row Publishers, 1974. . x, 478 p. Tables, figures, and index. Paperback.

A comprehensive discussion and analysis of the salient issues relevant to the Soviet economy. Included are discussions concerning the economic experiences of the periods of war communism and New Economic Policy, pricing, planning methods and principles, agriculture, growth strategy and performance, foreign trade, monetary and financial controls and policy, and economic reforms.

Grossman, Gregory. "Thirty Years of Soviet Industrialization." SOVIET SURVEY 26 (October-December 1958): 15-21.

Perceptive views on Soviet industrialization.

Hardt, John P. "East European Economic Development: Two Decades of Interrelationships and Interactions with the Soviet Union." In ECONOMIC DEVELOPMENTS IN COUNTRIES OF EASTERN EUROPE, Joint Economic Committee, 91st Cong., 2d sess., pp. 5-40. Washington, D.C.: Government Printing Office, 1970. Tables.

An excellent description of the similarities and differences of East European and Soviet economic development patterns as well as a discussion of the dilemmas of reform in light of the changing Soviet party and government sovereignty in East Europe.

_____. "Industrial Investment in the U.S.S.R." In COMPARISONS OF THE UNITED STATES AND SOVIET ECONOMIES, Joint Economic Committee, 86th Cong., 1st sess., pp. 121-41. Washington, D.C.: Government Printing Office, 1959. Appendix.

An examination of Soviet industrial investment policy under Stalin and Krushchev.

_____. "Soviet Economic Development and Policy Alternatives." In THE DEVELOPMENT OF THE SOVIET ECONOMY: PLAN AND PERFORMANCE, edited by Vladimir G. Treml, pp. 1-23. New York: Frederick A. Praeger, 1968.

A concise summary of the major phases of Soviet economic development: war communism, New Economic Policy, developments under Stalin, and post-Stalin economic development.

Hardt, John P., et al. "Institutional Stagnation and Changing Economic Strategy in the Soviet Union." In NEW DIRECTIONS IN THE SOVIET ECONOMY, Joint Economic Committee, 89th Cong., 2d sess., pp. 19-62. Washington, D.C.: Government Printing Office, 1966.

An examination of the economic slowdown experienced during the Soviet Seven-Year Plan (1959-65), followed by a discussion of the changing conceptions of economic management in the USSR.

Hoeffding, Oleg. "State Planning and Forced Industrialization." PROBLEMS OF COMMUNISM 8 (November-December 1959): 38-46.

An inquiry into the applicability of the Soviet methods of planning and development to the problems of the underdeveloped countries of Asia.

Hunter, Holland. "The Overambitious First Soviet Five-Year Plan." SLAVIC REVIEW 32 (June 1973): 237-57. Tables and figures.

A test for the plan's feasibility is described and alternative feasible growth paths are indicated.

_____. "Transport in Soviet and Chinese Development." ECONOMIC DEVELOPMENT AND CULTURAL CHANGE 14 (October 1965): 71-84. Tables.

An inquiry into the role of the transport sector in Soviet and Chinese economic development.

Hutchings, Raymond. SOVIET ECONOMIC DEVELOPMENT. New York: Barnes & Noble, 1971. xiii, 314 p. Tables, figures, appendix, and index.

An examination of the extent and causes of economic development during World War I, war communism, the New Economic Policy, and the plan era.

Iiudina, E., and Oleinik, I. "Structural Changes in the Economies of Socialist Countries." PROBLEMS OF ECONOMICS 15 (March 1973): 21-43. Tables.

Changes in the sectoral contribution to national income, and differences in the growth rates of producer and consumer goods industries and in different industrial branches between 1950 and 1970 are noted for Bulgaria, Hungary, East Germany, Poland, Rumania, Czechoslovakia, and the USSR.

Janossy, Ferenc. "The Origins of Contradictions in Our Economy and the Path to Their Solution." EASTERN EUROPEAN ECONOMICS 8 (Summer 1970): 357-90.

Familiarization with postwar Hungarian economic development policy.

Jasny, Naum. THE SOVIET ECONOMY DURING THE PLAN ERA. Stanford, Calif.: Stanford University Press, 1951. xi, 116 p. Tables, appendix, and index.

An analysis of the sources and uses of national income in the Soviet Union during 1928-48.

Kahan, Arcadius. "The Collective Farm System in Russia: Some Aspects of Its Contribution to Soviet Economic Development." In AGRICULTURE IN ECONOMIC DEVELOPMENT, edited by Carl Eicher and Lawrence Witt, pp. 251-71. New York: McGraw-Hill Book Co., 1964. Tables.

A discussion of the role of collective farms in the implementation of Soviet growth strategy.

Kalecki, Michal. INTRODUCTION TO THE THEORY OF GROWTH IN A SOCIALIST ECONOMY. Translated by Zdzislaw Sadowski. Oxford: Basil Blackwell, 1969. vi, 125 p. Figures and appendix.

One of Kalecki's major contributions to economic analysis. Topics covered include growth under unlimited and limited labor supply, foreign trade as a limiting factor to growth, the problem of choice of capital-output ratios, and the structure of investment.

_____. SELECTED ESSAYS ON THE ECONOMIC GROWTH OF THE SO-CIALIST AND THE MIXED ECONOMY. Cambridge, Mass.: Cambridge University Press, 1972. vii, 176 p. Figures and index.

A theory of growth for Soviet-type economies.

Kalo, John. "The Bulgarian Economy." SURVEY 39 (December 1961): 86-95.

A discussion of Bulgarian development strategy and results during the late 1950s and early 1960s.

Kaser, Michael [C.]. "The Soviet Ideology of Industrialization: A Review Article." JOURNAL OF DEVELOPMENT STUDIES 3 (October 1966): 63-75.

A brief review of the Soviet industrialization strategy.

Kemeny, George. ECONOMIC PLANNING IN HUNGARY: 1947-9. London: Royal Institute of International Affairs, 1952. x, 146 p. Tables, appendix, and index.

A description of Hungarian economic planning and development policy during Hungary's first Three-Year Plan (1947-49).

Khachaturov, T. "Questions Concerning the Theory of Socialist Reproduction." PROBLEMS OF ECONOMICS 12 (September 1969): 3-28. Tables.

An exposition concerning the concept, component parts, and growth of the social product.

Koropeckyj, I[wan].S. "Equalization of Regional Development in Socialist Countries: An Empirical Study." ECONOMIC DEVELOPMENT AND CULTURAL CHANGE 21 (October 1972): 68-86. Tables and appendix.

A glance at the record of the Soviet-type economies in regard to the equalization of regional development.

_____. "Industrial Location Policy in the U.S.S.R. During the Postwar Period." In ECONOMIC PERFORMANCE AND THE MILITARY BURDEN IN THE SOVIET UNION, Joint Economic Committee, 91st Cong., 2d sess., pp. 235-95. Washington, D.C.: Government Printing Office, 1970. Tables, figures, and appendix.

An analysis of the major causes for regionalization, as well as an attempt to determine empirically whether the official objectives were decisive in investment allocation.

Kouba, Karel. "Investment and Economic Growth in Czechoslovakia." In PLANNING AND MARKETS: MODERN TRENDS IN VARIOUS ECONOMIC SYSTEMS, edited by John T. Dunlap and Nikolay P. Fedorenko, pp. 229-40. New York: McGraw-Hill Book Co., 1969. Tables.

An investigation of short and long-term trends in investment and economic growth in Czechoslovakia.

Laptev, I. "Rates and Proportions in the Development of Industry and Agriculture." PROBLEMS OF ECONOMICS 9 (May 1966): 23-33. Tables.

A discussion concerning the appropriate nature of the relationship between the two major sectors of the economy (industry and agriculture) and their rates of growth.

Laski, K. THE RATE OF GROWTH AND THE RATE OF INTEREST IN THE SOCIALIST ECONOMY. New York: Springer-Verlag, 1972. 238 p. Figures.

Based on Kalecki's growth theory, this is a further exposition of theories of growth, accumulation, profit, and technological progress.

Lee, Pong S. "Structural Changes in Rumanian Industry, 1938-63." SOVIET STUDIES 20 (October 1968): 219-28. Tables.

An examination of the changes in Rumanian industrial structure and of the divergence of this change from what might be expected from a non-Communist country in a similar stage of development.

Maddison, Angus. ECONOMIC GROWTH IN JAPAN AND THE USSR. New York: W.W. Norton & Co., 1969. xxviii, 174 p. Tables, appendixes, and index. Paperback.

An excellent brief survey of Japanese and Soviet economic history and a comparison with the economic history of the West. Favorable and unfavorable factors for growth and the significance of the Japanese and Soviet growth experience are discussed.

Mazour, Anatole G. SOVIET ECONOMIC DEVELOPMENT: OPERATION OUTSTRIP, 1921-1965. Princeton, N.J.: D. Van Nostrand, 1967. 191 p. Tables, figures, and index.

Brief survey of Soviet economic development from the period of war communism to 1965.

Montias, John Michael. ECONOMIC DEVELOPMENT IN COMMUNIST RUMANIA. Cambridge, Mass.: MIT Press, 1967. xiv, 327 p. Tables, appendixes, and index.

A thorough examination of Rumania's postwar industrialization, agricultural development, and foreign trade policies.

Moravcik, Ivo. "The Marxian Model of Growth and the 'General Plan' of Soviet Economic Development." KYKLOS 14 (1961): 548-74.

An exposition of early Soviet discussions concerning planning methodology and attempts to adapt the Marxist growth model to the needs of the Soviet economy in the form of a long-term plan.

Nagy, Imre. ON COMMUNISM: IN DEFENSE OF THE NEW COURSE. New York: Frederick A. Praeger, 1957. xliv, 306 p.

An examination of Hungary's economic experiences during 1945-55, including agricultural, industrial, and foreign trade policies.

Notkin, A. [I.]. "Development Rates and the Optimum of Production Accumulation and Consumption in Socialist Countries." PROBLEMS OF ECONOMICS 7 (April 1965): 21-34. Tables.

A restatement of the orthodox Soviet position concerning rates and optimal combinations of consumption and investment, the importance of increasing production efficiency, and the relationship between the rate of increase in the production of means of production and means of consumption.

_____. "Higher Economic Effectiveness and the Basic Proportions of Development of Social Production under the New Five-Year Plan." PROBLEMS OF ECONOMICS 7 (January 1965): 18-26.

A stress on the importance of production efficiency and of the maintenance of the relative growth rates of agriculture and industry and of groups A and B within industry.

_____. "Proportionality and Planning in Economic Development." PROBLEMS OF ECONOMICS 11 (September 1968): 3-9.

A discussion of past trends in the structural changes of the Soviet economy.

_____. "The Rate of Soviet Economic Development during the Construction of Communist Society." PROBLEMS OF ECONOMICS 5 (October 1962): 40-48. Tables.

An exposition concerning the determinants of the rate of growth and development of the Soviet economy.

_____. "Rates of Development of Socialist Production and the Rise in Public Consumption." PROBLEMS OF ECONOMICS 9 (January-March 1967): 22-65. Tables.

Traditional Soviet views on economic growth, production efficiency, the appropriate relations between the growth of consumer and producer good production, and optimum rates of accumulation and consumption.

Nove, Alec, and Newth, J.A. THE SOVIET MIDDLE EAST: A COMMU-
NIST MODEL FOR DEVELOPMENT. New York: Frederick A. Praeger, 1966.
160 p. Tables, appendix, and index.

An inquiry into the economic development of Soviet Central Asia
and Transcaucasia.

Nuti, Domenico Mario. "Capitalism, Socialism and Steady Growth." ECO-
NOMIC JOURNAL 80 (March 1970): 32-57. Figures and appendix.

A close look at the choice of production techniques from the
standpoint of both the Socialist planner maximizing per capita
consumption consistent with the maintenance of a given growth
rate and the capitalist entrepreneur maximizing his firm's assets
at a given rate of interest.

Powell, Raymond P. "Industrial Production." In ECONOMIC TRENDS IN
THE SOVIET UNION, edited by Abram Bergson and Simon Kuznets, pp. 150-
202. Cambridge, Mass.: Harvard University Press, 1963. Tables and appendix.

An inquiry into the strategy of Soviet industrialization and into
the sources of Soviet growth.

Preobrazhensky, Evgeny. THE NEW ECONOMICS. Translated by Brian
Pearce. Oxford: Clarendon Press, 1965. xx, 310 p. Appendix and index.

Magnum opus of the leading economic theorist of the Left Opposi-
tion. An inquiry into the law of primitive Socialist accumulation
and into the law of value in the Soviet economy.

Roberts, Paul Craig. "'War Communism': A Re-examination." SLAVIC RE-
VIEW 29 (June 1970): 238-61.

A critical analysis of the usual Anglo-American interpretation of
the period of war communism.

Rutgaizer, V. "Structural Changes in the Economies of the European Members
of Comecon." PROBLEMS OF ECONOMICS 8 (September 1965): 41-51.
Tables.

A report on the economic development of the Eastern European
Soviet-bloc countries.

Searing, Marjory E. "Education and Economic Growth: The Postwar Experience in Hungary and Poland." In REORIENTATION AND COMMERCIAL RE-
LATIONS OF THE ECONOMIES OF EASTERN EUROPE, Joint Economic Committee, 93d Cong., 2d sess., pp. 479-528. Washington, D.C.: Government
Printing Office, 1974. Tables and appendix.

An assessment of the role of education in the economic development
of Hungary and Poland.

Seton, Francis. "Planning and Economic Growth: Asia, Africa, and the Soviet Model." SOVIET SURVEY 31 (January-March 1960): 38-44.

Thoughts on the applicability of the Soviet model of growth to the problems of the less developed countries.

Sik, Ota. "The Economic Impact of Stalinism." PROBLEMS OF COMMUNISM 20 (May-June 1971): 1-10.

Interesting description of the impact of Stalinism on the growth and efficiency of the Czechoslovakian economy of one of the chief architects of Czechoslovakia's economic reform program of 1965-68.

Sirc, Ljubo. ECONOMIC DEVOLUTION IN EASTERN EUROPE. London: Longmans, Green and Co., 1969. xii, 165 p. Tables and appendix.

An analysis of Eastern European economic problems pertaining to pricing, foreign trade, economic growth, planning methods, and economic reforms.

Sorokin, G. "The Building of Communism and Long-Range Planning." PROBLEMS OF ECONOMICS 3 (September 1960): 23-32. Tables.

A retrospective glance at past achievements and an expectation of future successes for Soviet economic growth and development.

Spulber, Nicolas. "Contrasting Economic Patterns: Chinese and Soviet Development Strategies." SOVIET STUDIES 15 (July 1963): 1-16.

A careful examination of the main characteristics of the Soviet strategy of development, the Chinese resource problem, and Mao's basic development strategy and its influence on China's strategy of industrialization.

_____, ed. FOUNDATIONS OF SOVIET STRATEGY FOR ECONOMIC GROWTH; SELECTED SOVIET ESSAYS, 1924-1930. Bloomington: Indiana University Press, 1964. xii, 530 p. Tables, figures, and index.

A compendium of articles (translated from the Russian), written by such notables as Preobrazhenski, Feldman, Shanin, Bazarov, Groman, and Strumilin. Topics include macroeconomic models, growth strategy, and planning theories and methods.

Stolper, Wolfgang F. "The Labor Force and Industrial Development in Soviet Germany." QUARTERLY JOURNAL OF ECONOMICS 71 (November 1957): 518-45. Tables.

An appraisal of the industrial development of East Germany; some relevant comparisons with West Germany.

Strumilin, S. "Concerning the Problem of Optimum Proportions." PROBLEMS

OF ECONOMICS 5 (July 1962): 3-14. Tables.

> An examination of various proportions of consumption and accumu-
> lation funds and their impact on growth.

Sutton, Antony C. WESTERN TECHNOLOGY AND SOVIET ECONOMIC DE-
VELOPMENT, 1917 TO 1930. Stanford, Calif.: Hoover Institution on War,
Revolution, and Peace, 1968. xx, 381 p. Tables, figures, appendixes, and
index.

> An analysis of foreign concessions and technological transfers and
> of their significance for Soviet economic development.

Swianiewicz, S. FORCED LABOUR AND ECONOMIC DEVELOPMENT: AN
ENQUIRY INTO THE EXPERIENCE OF SOVIET INDUSTRIALIZATION. New
York: Oxford University Press, 1965. ix, 321 p. Tables, appendix, and
index.

> A discussion of the extent and role of forced labor in the economic
> development of the Soviet Union during 1928-41.

United Nations. Economic Commission for Europe. "Economic Development
in Rumania." ECONOMIC BULLETIN FOR EUROPE 8 (November 1961):
55-107. Tables, figures, and appendix.

> Examination of Rumania's postwar economic experience in terms of
> national income growth, industrial and agricultural development,
> allocation of investment, foreign trade, and personal consumption.

_____. "Economic Developments in the Soviet Union." ECONOMIC BUL-
LETIN FOR EUROPE 3, no. 3 (1952): 125-47. Tables and appendix.

> Survey of the results achieved in the growth of national income,
> industrial and agricultural production, and housing construction in
> the USSR.

Vajda, Imre. "Brakes and Bottlenecks in Hungary's Economic Growth." ECO-
NOMICS OF PLANNING 6 (1966): 228-40.

> Comments on Hungary's postwar growth experience and the role of
> the Comecon in that experience.

Vutov, Vasil. "Analysis of the Branch Structure of the Bulgarian National
Economy." EASTERN EUROPEAN ECONOMICS 3 (Fall 1964): 16-25.
Tables.

> Examination of Bulgarian economic organization, the sectoral dis-
> tribution of employment, and the sources and magnitude of Bul-
> garian national income in selected years.

Whalley, John. "Polish Postwar Economic Growth from the Viewpoint of
Soviet Experience." SOVIET STUDIES 24 (April 1973): 531-49. Appendix.

An attempt to assess the generality of the postwar Soviet growth experience by scrutinizing the postwar growth experience of Polish industry.

Wilber, Charles K. "The Role of Agriculture in Soviet Economic Development." LAND ECONOMICS (February 1969): 87-96. Tables.

An essay on the contribution of the agricultural sector to Soviet economic development.

_____. THE SOVIET MODEL AND UNDERDEVELOPED COUNTRIES. Chapel Hill: University of North Carolina Press, 1969. xiii, 241 p. Tables and index.

Thoughts on the relevance of the Soviet growth strategy to the problems of underdeveloped countries.

Wilczynski, J. SOCIALIST ECONOMIC DEVELOPMENT AND REFORMS. New York: Praeger, 1972. xvii, 350 p. Tables and index.

Discussion of growth strategy, orthodox planning practices, prices, financial and monetary policies, foreign trade criteria and practices, reforms, and growth performance in the Soviet-type economies.

Zaleski, Eugene. PLANNING FOR ECONOMIC GROWTH IN THE SOVIET UNION, 1918-1932. Chapel Hill: University of North Carolina Press, 1971. xxxviii, 425 p. Tables, figures, appendix, and index.

Discussion of plan construction and implementation in the USSR during 1918-32, as well as an evaluation of Soviet planning and development strategy.

Zauberman, Alfred. "A Few Remarks on Kalecki's Theory of Economic Growth under Socialism." KYKLOS 19 (1966): 411-24.

An elucidation of Kalecki's growth theory for normatively planned economic systems.

_____. "Soviet and Chinese Strategy for Economic Growth." INTERNATIONAL AFFAIRS 38 (July 1962): 339-52.

Comparison of Soviet and Chinese growth strategies.

Zyzniewski, Stanley J. "The Soviet Economic Impact on Poland." AMERICAN SLAVIC AND EAST EUROPEAN REVIEW 18 (April 1959): 205-25. Tables.

A description of the main features of postwar Polish-Soviet economic relations, with emphasis on the events of 1956.

PERFORMANCE

Berend, I[van]. T., and Ranki, G. HUNGARY: A CENTURY OF ECO-
NOMIC DEVELOPMENT. New York: Harper & Row Publishers, 1974. 263 p.
Tables, figures, and index.

> A discussion of Hungarian economic development strategy and a
> brief survey of the attained results.

Bornstein, Morris. "A Comparison of Soviet and United States National Product." In COMPARISONS OF THE UNITED STATES AND SOVIET ECONO-
MIES, Joint Economic Committee, 86th Cong., 1st sess., pp. 377-95. Washington, D.C.: Government Printing Office, 1959. Tables.

> Analysis of the comparative size, structure, and growth of U.S.
> and USSR national products.

Campbell, Robert W. THE SOVIET-TYPE ECONOMIES: PERFORMANCE AND
EVOLUTION. 3d ed. Boston: Houghton Mifflin Co., 1974. xi, 259 p.
Figures, tables, and index. Paperback.

> An updated and expanded version of the first edition, published in
> 1960 under the title SOVIET ECONOMIC POWER: ITS ORGANI-
> ZATION, GROWTH, AND CHALLENGE. The expanded version
> includes discussions concerning basic economic institutions and
> organization, the Soviet growth model and its application in East-
> ern Europe, planning principles and practices, the record of Soviet
> growth, and economic reforms in the Soviet Union and Eastern
> Europe.

Cohn, Stanley H. ECONOMIC DEVELOPMENT IN THE SOVIET UNION.
Lexington, Mass.: D.C. Heath, 1970. 135 p. Tables, appendixes, and
index.

> Clear explanation of the Soviet economic experience since 1917,
> with emphasis on development strategy and performance.

_____. "General Growth Performance of the Soviet Economy." In ECO-
NOMIC PERFORMANCE AND THE MILITARY BURDEN IN THE SOVIET UNION,
Joint Economic Committee, 91st Cong., 2d sess., pp. 9-17. Washington,
D.C.: Government Printing Office, 1970. Tables and appendix.

> A survey of growth trends in Soviet GNP and in its principal uses;
> output comparisons with selected market economies.

_____. "The Gross National Product in the Soviet Union: Comparative
Growth Rates." In DIMENSIONS OF SOVIET ECONOMIC POWER, Joint
Economic Committee, 87th Cong., 2d sess., pp. 67-89. Washington, D.C.:
Government Printing Office, 1962. Tables.

> Selective comparison of the economic growth of the USSR with
> that of the United States, France, Italy, West Germany, Britain,

and Japan during the decade 1950-60.

_____. "National Income Growth Statistics." In SOVIET ECONOMIC STATISTICS, edited by Vladimir G. Treml and John P. Hardt, pp. 120-47. Durham, N.C.: Duke University Press, 1972. Tables.

Careful examination of Soviet national income growth statistics, with attention to questions of reliability and divergences between Western-computed and official indexes.

_____. "The Soviet Economy: Performance and Growth." In THE DEVELOPMENT OF THE SOVIET ECONOMY: PLAN AND PERFORMANCE, edited by Vladimir G. Treml, pp. 24-54. New York: Frederick A. Praeger, 1968. Tables and appendixes.

Quantitative evaluation of Soviet growth performance during 1917-67.

_____. "Soviet Growth Retardation: Trends in Resource Availability and Efficiency." In NEW DIRECTIONS IN THE SOVIET ECONOMY, Joint Economic Committee, 89th Cong., 2d sess., pp. 99-132. Washington, D.C.: Government Printing Office, 1966. Tables and appendixes.

A careful look at Soviet economic structure, trends in GNP, factor availability and productivity, and the future growth prospects of the USSR. Certain comparisons are made with the United States, United Kingdom, West Germany, Japan, France, and Italy.

Czirjak, Laszlo. "Industrial Structure, Growth, and Productivity in Eastern Europe." In ECONOMIC DEVELOPMENTS IN COUNTRIES OF EASTERN EUROPE, Joint Economic Committee, 91st Cong., 2d sess., pp. 434-62. Washington, D.C.: Government Printing Office, 1970. Tables and appendixes.

An examination of rates of growth and the structure of industry on the basis of factor costs, and of trends in factor productivities.

Dobb, Maurice. SOVIET ECONOMIC DEVELOPMENT SINCE 1917. New York: International Publishers, 1948. vii, 475 p. Tables and index.

A detailed, sympathetic account of the unfolding Soviet economic organization and development strategy. Topics discussed include the periods of war communism and NEP, the growth of industry and agriculture, the financial system, and the five-year plans.

Ernst, Maurice. "Overstatement of Industrial Growth in Poland." QUARTERLY JOURNAL OF ECONOMICS 79 (November 1965): 632-41. Tables.

Evaluation of the official Polish index of industrial production.

_____. "Postwar Economic Growth in Eastern Europe; A Comparison with

Western Europe." In NEW DIRECTIONS IN THE SOVIET ECONOMY, Joint Economic Committee, 89th Cong., 2d sess., pp. 873-916. Washington, D.C.: Government Printing Office, 1966. Tables and appendixes.

> An evaluation of postwar economic growth in Eastern Europe by means of comparisons with Western Europe. Characteristics of the Eastern European economies (Bulgaria, Czechoslovakia, East Germany, Hungary, Poland, and Rumania) are provided, along with a discussion of output growth, trends in consumption and consumer welfare, the cost of economic growth, and external factors.

Fallenbuchl, Zbigniew [M.]. "The Strategy of Development and Gierek's Economic Manoeuvre." CANADIAN SLAVONIC PAPERS 15 (Spring and Summer 1973): 52-70.

> A discussion of the probable impact of Gierek's economic policies on the further development of the Polish economy.

Gerschenkron, Alexander. ECONOMIC BACKWARDNESS IN HISTORICAL PERSPECTIVE: A BOOK OF ESSAYS. Cambridge, Mass.: Harvard University Press, 1966. 456 p. Tables, appendixes, and index.

> A collection of stimulating essays, concerned with patterns and problems of Soviet economic development, the rate of industrial growth in Soviet Russia, and the dollar index of output of Soviet heavy industry.

_____. "Soviet Heavy Industry: A Dollar Index of Output, 1927/28-1937." REVIEW OF ECONOMICS AND STATISTICS 37 (May 1955): 120-30. Tables.

> Estimates of output growth indexes for the following branches of Soviet heavy industry: iron and steel, machine building, coal, petroleum, and electric power.

_____. "The Soviet Indices of Industrial Production." REVIEW OF ECO- NOMICS AND STATISTICS 29 (November 1947): 217-26. Tables.

> A description of Soviet industrial output indexes and an examina- tion of their validity.

Greenslade, Rush V. "Industrial Production Statistics in the USSR." In SO- VIET ECONOMIC STATISTICS, edited by Vladimir G. Treml and John P. Hardt, pp. 155-94. Durham, N.C.: Duke University Press, 1972. Tables and appendix.

> Careful analysis and evaluation of Soviet industrial production statistics.

Greenslade, Rush V., and Robertson, Wade E. "Industrial Production in the U.S.S.R." In SOVIET ECONOMIC PROSPECTS FOR THE SEVENTIES, Joint Economic Committee, 93d Cong., 1st sess., pp. 270-80. Washington, D.C.:

Government Printing Office, 1973. Tables and appendixes.

An updating of civilian industrial production indexes, a revision of weights to a 1968 price basis, and a discussion of recent trends in the various industrial branches.

Greenslade, Rush V., and Wallace, Phyllis. "Industrial Production in the U.S.S.R." In DIMENSIONS OF SOVIET ECONOMIC POWER, Joint Economic Committee, 87th Cong., 2d sess., pp. 115-36. Washington, D.C.: Government Printing Office, 1962. Tables, figures, and appendixes.

An examination of the growth of industrial production in the USSR for the period 1950-61 on the basis of an independently constructed index.

Gregory, Paul R., and Stuart, Robert C. SOVIET ECONOMIC STRUCTURE AND PERFORMANCE. New York: Harper & Row Publishers, 1974. x, 478 p. Tables, figures, and index. Paperback.

Comprehensive discussion and analysis of issues relevant to the Soviet economy. Included are discussions concerning the economic experiences of the periods of war communism and New Economic Policy, pricing, planning methods and principles, agriculture, growth strategy and performance, foreign trade, monetary and financial controls and policy, and economic reforms.

Grossman, Gregory. "Soviet Growth: Routine, Inertia, and Pressure." AMERICAN ECONOMIC REVIEW 50 (May 1960): 62-72.

A discussion of some of the institutional factors which affect Soviet growth performance.

_____. SOVIET STATISTICS OF PHYSICAL OUTPUT OF INDUSTRIAL COMMODITIES; THEIR COMPILATION AND QUALITY. A Study by the National Bureau of Economic Research. Princeton, N.J.: Princeton University Press, 1960. 151 p. Tables.

A reexamination of the usability and reliability of Soviet statistics of the physical output of industrial commodities, with special attention to the period beginning with the five-year plans.

Hodgman, Donald R. SOVIET INDUSTRIAL PRODUCTION, 1928-1951. Cambridge, Mass.: Harvard University Press, 1954. xix, 241 p. Tables, figures, appendixes, and index.

Construction of Soviet industrial production index for 1928-51 and assessment, on the basis of the revised index, of Soviet industrial growth.

Hutchings, Raymond. "Periodic Fluctuation in Soviet Industrial Growth Rates." SOVIET STUDIES 20 (January 1969): 331-52. Tables and figures.

A close look at the reasons for the fluctuations in Soviet industrial growth rates.

Johnson, D. Gale. "Agricultural Production." In ECONOMIC TRENDS IN THE SOVIET UNION, edited by Abram Bergson and Simon Kuznets, pp. 203-34. Cambridge, Mass.: Harvard University Press, 1963. Tables.

Measurement and analysis of the factors associated with changes in Soviet agricultural output.

Kaplan, Norman M. "The Growth of Output and Inputs in Soviet Transport and Communications." AMERICAN ECONOMIC REVIEW 57 (December 1967): 1154-67. Tables.

A summary of the results of an attempt to construct and use output indexes for Soviet transport and communication. The author explores also growth retardation by distinguishing between changes in the rates of increase in factor inputs and in combined factor productivity.

_____. "Retardation in Soviet Growth." REVIEW OF ECONOMICS AND STATISTICS 50 (August 1968): 293-303. Tables.

Explanation of the reasons for the deceleration of Soviet growth rates.

Kaplan, Norman M., and Moorsteen, Richard H. "An Index of Soviet Industrial Output." AMERICAN ECONOMIC REVIEW 50 (June 1960): 295-318. Tables.

A careful examination of Soviet industrial output indexes.

Lazarcik, Gregor. "Agricultural Output and Productivity in Eastern Europe and Some Comparisons with the U.S.S.R. and U.S.A." In REORIENTATION AND COMMERCIAL RELATIONS OF THE ECONOMIES OF EASTERN EUROPE, Joint Economic Committee, 93d Cong., 2d sess., pp. 328-93. Washington, D.C.: Government Printing Office, 1974. Tables and appendixes.

An exposition of the role of agriculture in East European economies, the growth and structure of agricultural output and inputs, per capita trends and levels of agricultural output, and land and labor productivity trends. Additionally, size comparisons of output are made among Eastern Europe, the Soviet Union, and the United States.

Maddison, Angus. ECONOMIC GROWTH IN JAPAN AND THE USSR. New York: W.W. Norton & Co., 1969. xxviii, 174 p. Tables, appendixes, and index. Paperback.

An excellent brief survey of Japanese and Soviet economic history and a comparison with the economic history of the West. Favorable and unfavorable factors for growth and the significance of the Japanese and Soviet growth experience are discussed.

Noren, James H. "Soviet Industry Trends in Output, Inputs, and Productivity." In NEW DIRECTIONS IN THE SOVIET ECONOMY, Joint Economic Committee, 89th Cong., 2d sess., pp. 271-325. Washington, D.C.: Government Printing Office, 1966. Tables, figures, and appendixes.

>   Authoritative analysis of the growth of Soviet industrial output, inputs, and factor productivity between 1951 and 1965, followed by an analysis of the causes of the decline in industrial growth during the 1950s and 1960s.

Nutter, G. Warren. GROWTH OF INDUSTRIAL PRODUCTION IN THE SO-VIET UNION. A Study by the National Bureau of Economic Research. Princeton, N.J.: Princeton University Press, 1962. xxvii, 706 p. Tables, figures, appendixes, and index.

>   A well known, exhaustive study of Soviet industrial growth.

_____. "The Structure and Growth of Soviet Industry: A Comparison with the United States." In COMPARISONS OF THE UNITED STATES AND SO-VIET ECONOMIES, Joint Economic Committee, 86th Cong., 1st sess., pp. 95-120. Washington, D.C.: Government Printing Office, 1959. Tables and figures.

>   Analysis of Soviet industrial growth and comparisons with the growth of U.S. industry.

Powell, Raymond P. "An Index of Soviet Construction, 1927/28 to 1955." REVIEW OF ECONOMICS AND STATISTICS 41 (May 1959): 170-77. Tables.

>   A discussion of Soviet construction activity indexes.

Siman, Miklos. "Sources of Economic Growth in Hungary, 1967-1972." EASTERN EUROPEAN ECONOMICS 13 (Fall 1974): 25-58. Tables.

>   Presentation of economic growth statistics by major sectors and branches and appraisal of the role of capital and labor inputs, incomplete investments, capital-output ratios, and productivity changes in the growth of the Hungarian economy.

Snell, Edwin M., and Harper, Marilyn. "Postwar Economic Growth in East Germany: A Comparison with West Germany." In ECONOMIC DEVELOP-MENTS IN COUNTRIES OF EASTERN EUROPE, Joint Economic Committee, 91st Cong., 2d sess., pp. 558-607. Washington, D.C.: Government Printing Office, 1970. Tables and appendixes.

>   Analysis of the effects of domestic institutions and policies, external factors retarding East German development, the East German economic reforms, and the postwar recovery and growth of East and West Germany.

Staller, George J. "Czechoslovak Industrial Growth: 1948-1959." AMERI-CAN ECONOMIC REVIEW 52 (June 1962): 385-407. Tables.

Measurement of the growth of Czechoslovak industrial output between 1948 and 1959.

Stolper, Wolfgang F. THE STRUCTURE OF THE EAST GERMAN ECONOMY. Cambridge, Mass.: Harvard University Press, 1960. xxv, 478 p. Tables and index.

Thorough examination of the functioning and performance of the East German economy, including a discussion of national income methodology, population and labor force, industrial and agricultural output, and transportation, communication, and distribution problems and accomplishments.

Sutton, Antony C. WESTERN TECHNOLOGY AND SOVIET ECONOMIC DEVELOPMENT, 1945 TO 1965. Stanford, Calif.: Hoover Institution Press, 1973. xxxi, 482 p. Tables, figures, and index.

An examination of the transfer mechanisms, the role of technical transfers in Soviet industry, and the implications of technical transfers for the fulfillment of economic objectives.

Tarn, Alexander. "A Comparison of Dollar and Ruble Values of the Industrial Output of the USA and the USSR." SOVIET STUDIES 19 (April 1968): 482-500. Tables.

A serious attempt, on a comprehensive basis, to evaluate the magnitude of Soviet industrial output and to compare it to the value of U.S. industrial output.

Tarn, Alexander, and Campbell, Robert [W.]. "A Comparison of U.S. and Soviet Industrial Output." AMERICAN ECONOMIC REVIEW 52 (September 1962): 703-27. Tables and appendix.

A comparison of Soviet and U.S. industrial output, including a careful explanation of the method used in obtaining the result.

Thornton, Judith. "Factors in the Recent Decline in Soviet Growth." SLAVIC REVIEW 25 (March 1966): 101-19. Tables.

Analysis of the growth retarding factors in the Soviet economy.

Tucek, Miroslav. "Monetary Equilibrium and Future Economic Growth in Czechoslovakia." EASTERN EUROPEAN ECONOMICS 6 (Summer 1968): 3-12.

Examination and evaluation of the basic concepts of the mechanism of monetary equilibrium in Czechoslovakia, followed by an appraisal of the relationship between monetary equilibrium and future economic growth.

United Nations. Economic Commission for Europe. "Economic Developments in the Soviet Union." ECONOMIC BULLETIN FOR EUROPE 3, no. 3 (1952): 125-47. Tables and appendix.

Survey of the results achieved in the growth of national income, industrial and agricultural production, and housing construction in the USSR.

_____. "A Fifteen-Year Review of Investment and Output in Eastern Europe and the Soviet Union." ECONOMIC BULLETIN FOR EUROPE 18 (November 1966): 31-64. Tables, figures, and appendix.

Survey of the changes in the volume of investment, its composition, and output effects between 1950 and 1965.

Veverka, Jindrich. "Long-term Measures of Soviet Industrial Output." SOVIET STUDIES 16 (January 1965): 285-301. Tables.

An examination of the problems involved in calculating measures of long-term changes in industrial output.

Weitzman, Martin L. "Soviet Postwar Growth and Capital-Labor Substitution." AMERICAN ECONOMIC REVIEW 60 (September 1970): 676-92. Tables.

A review of some basic facts concerning Soviet postwar growth, and an analysis of the role of the elasticity of substitution in explaining Soviet growth. Comparisons are made with the American economy.

Whitehouse, F. Douglas, and Havelka, Joseph F. "Comparisons of Farm Output in the US and USSR, 1950-1971." In SOVIET ECONOMIC PROSPECTS FOR THE SEVENTIES, Joint Economic Committee, 93d Cong., 1st sess., pp. 340-74. Washington, D.C.: Government Printing Office, 1973. Tables, figures, and appendixes.

A comparison of the volume growth of agricultural output and its major components in the USSR and in the United States for 1950-71.

Wilczynski, J. SOCIALIST ECONOMIC DEVELOPMENT AND REFORMS. New York: Praeger, 1972. xvii, 350 p. Tables and index.

Discussion of growth strategy, orthodox planning practices, prices, financial and monetary policies, foreign trade criteria and practices, reforms, and growth performance in the Soviet-type economies.

Wiles, Peter J.D. THE POLITICAL ECONOMY OF COMMUNISM. Oxford: Basil Blackwell, 1962. xv, 404 p. Tables, figures, and index.

A critical, analytical examination of the major issues relevant to the study of Soviet-type economies: economic organization; planning and resource allocation, including pricing, planners' preferences, and decentralization; and growth strategy and performance.

Zauberman, Alfred. INDUSTRIAL PROGRESS IN POLAND, CZECHOSLOVA-KIA, AND EAST GERMANY, 1937-1962. London: Oxford University Press, 1964. xiv, 338 p. Tables and index.

A detailed account of the growth of industrial output in Poland, East Germany, and Czechoslovakia, accompanied by a survey of central planning and its evolution, Communist growth strategy, and the international economic relations of the three countries.

Zeman, Karel. "Development in the Position of the COMECON Complex in the World Economy." SOVIET AND EASTERN EUROPEAN FOREIGN TRADE 10 (Summer 1974): 30-59. Tables.

A description of the volume and structure of output and foreign trade of Comecon countries.

Chapter 5

PLANNING THEORY, PRACTICES, AND METHODS

Alton, Thad Paul. POLISH POSTWAR ECONOMY. New York: Columbia University Press, 1955. 330 p. Tables, appendixes, and index.

>Survey of early postwar Polish economic planning and develop-
ments. Topics covered include planning in industry, agriculture,
finance, and foreign trade.

Ames, Edward. SOVIET ECONOMIC PROCESSES. Homewood, Ill.: Richard D. Irwin, 1965. 257 p. Tables, figures, and index. Paperback.

>An excellent overview of the Soviet economy, with particular at-
tention to economic organization, planning on the macro and micro
levels, fiscal and monetary policy, international trade, and economic performance.

Atlas, Z. "Profits and Profitability as Criteria of the Effectiveness of Production." PROBLEMS OF ECONOMICS 16 (December 1973): 56-80.

>A review of the role and shortcomings of the profitability index,
and an evaluation of profit as a local criterion of effectiveness.

Atlas, Z., and Vinokur, R. "The Economic Essence of Profit and Profitability
under Socialism." PROBLEMS OF ECONOMICS 12 (May 1969): 3-32.
Tables.

>An examination of the economic category and functions of profit,
differences between profit under socialism and capitalism, and the
increasing role of profit and profitability under the economic reform.

Azrael, Jeremy R. MANAGERIAL POWER AND SOVIET POLITICS. Cambridge, Mass.: Harvard University Press, 1966. ix, 258 p. Index.

>A chronological survey of the behavior and practices of Soviet
managers.

Bachurin, A. "Strengthening the Integrated Systems Approach in Planning."

PROBLEMS OF ECONOMICS 15 (December 1972): 3-25.

An emphasis on the importance of systems analysis and an integrated approach to planning problems.

Bachurin, A., and Pervukhin, A. "Concerning Profit under Socialism." PROBLEMS OF ECONOMICS 7 (August 1964): 16-26.

A critical reexamination of the role of profit under socialism.

Balassa, Bela A. THE HUNGARIAN EXPERIENCE IN ECONOMIC PLANNING. New Haven, Conn.: Yale University Press, 1959. xii, 285 p. Tables, appendixes, and index.

An outstanding theoretical and empirical study, concentrating on pre-1959 Hungarian planning methods, pricing principles and theory, and enterprise behavior.

Balinky, Alexander [S.], et al. PLANNING AND THE MARKET IN THE U.S.S.R.: THE 1960'S. New Brunswick, N.J.: Rutgers University Press, 1967. vi, 132 p.

A compendium of essays, dealing with the nature and implications of the Soviet economic reforms of the 1960s.

Baykov, Alexander. THE DEVELOPMENT OF THE SOVIET ECONOMIC SYSTEM; AN ESSAY ON THE EXPERIENCE OF PLANNING IN THE U.S.S.R. New York: Macmillan Co., 1948. xv, 514 p.

A careful, exhaustive study of Soviet economic institutions and practices from the revolution through 1940. Topics covered include industry, agriculture, labor, foreign trade and payments, and planning during the periods of war communism, NEP, and the plan era.

Belik, Iu. "Planning the Relationship between Consumption and Accumulation." PROBLEMS OF ECONOMICS 9 (May 1966): 3-12.

A brief glance at orthodox Soviet planning principles and methods.

Belkin, V., and Birman, A. "Independence of the Enterprise and Economic Stimuli." PROBLEMS OF ECONOMICS 8 (July 1965): 37-40.

A call for economic incentives for influencing enterprise behavior.

Berend, Ivan T. "The Historical Background of the Recent Economic Reforms in East Europe." EAST EUROPEAN QUARTERLY 2 (March 1968): 75-90.

Essay on the postwar economic experiences of Hungary.

Berghianu, Maxim. "Romanian Socialist Planning in the Context of the World-wide Planning Phenomenon." SOVIET AND EASTERN EUROPEAN FOREIGN TRADE 8 (Fall-Winter 1972-73): 263-300.

A description of the Rumanian planning system by the president of the State Planning Committee.

Berliner, Joseph S. FACTORY AND MANAGER IN THE USSR. Cambridge, Mass.: Harvard University Press, 1957. xv, 386 p. Appendix and index.

An investigation of Soviet managerial goals and methods as well as of controls over management.

_____. "The Informal Organization of the Soviet Firm." QUARTERLY JOURNAL OF ECONOMICS 66 (August 1952): 342-65.

An appraisal of Soviet managerial goals, expectations, and behavior, based on a series of interviews with former Soviet managers.

_____. "Managerial Incentives and Decisionmaking: A Comparison of the United States and the Soviet Union." In COMPARISONS OF THE UNITED STATES AND SOVIET ECONOMIES, Joint Economic Committee, 86th Cong., 1st sess., pp. 349-76. Washington, D.C.: Government Printing Office, 1959.

A discussion of Soviet managerial incentives, recruitment, and decision making, with appropriate U.S. comparisons.

Berri, L., and Efimov, A. "Methods of Preparing an Inter-Branch Balance." PROBLEMS OF ECONOMICS 3 (December 1960): 17-28. Tables.

A discussion of the essence of interbranch balances and their role in the solution of planning problems.

Berri, L., et al. "The Inter-Branch Balance and Its Use in Planning." PROBLEMS OF ECONOMICS 5 (August 1962): 13-24. Tables.

A description of the function of the interbranch balance in the planning process.

Birman, A. "Profit Today." PROBLEMS OF ECONOMICS 10 (January 1968): 3-13.

A discussion concerning the essence of profit and the relationships between profit and prices and bonuses.

Boiarskii, A. "Mathematical Methods and Optimal Planning." PROBLEMS OF ECONOMICS 17 (August 1974): 3-20.

An explanation of the meaning of optimality and the uses of mathematical methods in optimal planning.

Bor, Mikhail. AIMS AND METHODS OF SOVIET PLANNING. London: Lawrence and Wishart, 1967. 255 p. Tables and index.

An attempt by Bor, a Soviet economist, to describe and analyze

Soviet planning theory and practices prevalent during the mid-1960s.

Bozyk, Pawel. "Functions of Planning and Forecasting in International Trade." SOVIET AND EASTERN EUROPEAN FOREIGN TRADE 9 (Winter 1973-74): 3-18.

A description of foreign trade planning, particularly as it is related to the Polish economy.

Campbell, Robert W. ACCOUNTING IN SOVIET PLANNING AND MANAGEMENT. Cambridge, Mass.: Harvard University Press, 1963. 315 p. Tables and index.

A thoughtful exposition of the role of Soviet accounting in plan fulfillment.

_____. "Soviet Accounting and Economic Decisions." In VALUE AND PLAN--ECONOMIC CALCULATION AND ORGANIZATION IN EASTERN EUROPE, edited by Gregory Grossman, pp. 76-94. Berkeley and Los Angeles: University of California Press, 1960.

An inquiry into whether Soviet accounting practices facilitate or hinder rational economic decision making.

_____. THE SOVIET-TYPE ECONOMIES: PERFORMANCE AND EVOLUTION. 3d ed. Boston: Houghton Mifflin Co., 1974. xi, 259 p. Figures, tables, and index. Paperback.

An updated and expanded version of the first edition, published in 1960 under the title SOVIET ECONOMIC POWER: ITS ORGANIZATION, GROWTH, AND CHALLENGE. The expanded version includes discussions concerning basic economic institutions and organization, the Soviet growth model and its application in Eastern Europe, planning principles and practices, the record of Soviet growth, and economic reforms in the Soviet Union and Eastern Europe.

Csikos-Nagy, Bela. SOCIALIST ECONOMIC POLICY. New York: St. Martin's Press, 1973. 238 p. Index.

An explanation, by a well known Hungarian economist, of Soviet-type economic organization, planning, financial policies, price and incomes policies, and distribution and foreign trade policies.

Dadaian, V. [S.]. "The Principles and Criteria of Optimum Planning." PROBLEMS OF ECONOMICS 9 (November 1966): 16-29. Tables.

A discussion of the necessary conditions for optimal planning, characteristics of optimal plans, and criteria for optimality.

Davies, R.W. "Planning a Mature Economy in the USSR." ECONOMICS OF PLANNING 6 (1966): 138-53.

A survey of Soviet planning experience and a brief consideration of the prospects for reform.

_____. "The Soviet Planning Process for Rapid Industrialization." ECONOMICS OF PLANNING 6 (1966): 53-67. Figures.

Schematic illustrations of the traditional Soviet planning process.

Dobrin, Bogoslav. BULGARIAN ECONOMIC DEVELOPMENT SINCE WORLD WAR II. New York: Praeger, 1973. xv, 185 p. Tables.

Examination of the postwar Bulgarian economic experience: economic planning, development strategy, the foreign trade experience, growth, and the economic reform.

Dolan, Edwin G. "The Teleological Period in Soviet Economic Planning." YALE ECONOMIC ESSAYS 10 (Spring 1970): 3-41. Figures.

Analysis of the intellectual origins of teleological planning, followed by the construction of a model to be used for the evaluation of the effectiveness of teleological planning.

Dorovskikh, A. "Some Problems in the Theory and Practice of the Interbranch Balance." PROBLEMS OF ECONOMICS 11 (August 1968): 12-20.

A look at the use of existing planning methodologies and basic requirements for the formulation of an interbranch balance.

Efimov, A. "The Interbranch Balance and Questions of Planning." PROBLEMS OF ECONOMICS 12 (January 1970): 3-21.

Explanation of the interbranch balance and its use in planning.

Eidel'man, M. "The Experience of Preparing an Intersectoral Balance Account of Production and Distribution of Output in the Soviet National Economy." PROBLEMS OF ECONOMICS 5 (May 1962): 3-20. Tables.

An examination of certain methodological problems of intersectoral balances and of their use in the analysis of economic growth and planning.

_____. "The New Ex Post Interbranch Balance of Production and Distribution of Output in the National Economy of the USSR." PROBLEMS OF ECONOMICS 16 (May 1973): 3-34. Tables.

A description of the special features of the ex-post interbranch balance for 1972.

_____. "The Structure of an Inter-Branch Balance of Production and Distribution in the Soviet National Economy." PROBLEMS OF ECONOMICS 3 (June 1960): 3-10. Tables.

A discussion of general questions and principles of compiling an interbranch balance in the Soviet Union.

Ellman, Michael [J.]. "Optimal Planning." SOVIET STUDIES 20 (July 1968): 112-36.

A review article, discussing primarily Soviet views concerning the nature of optimal planning, uses of linear programming, and the relationship between optimal planning and economic policy.

_____. SOVIET PLANNING TODAY--PROPOSALS FOR AN OPTIMALLY FUNCTIONING ECONOMIC SYSTEM. Cambridge: At the University Press, 1971. xv, 219 p. Tables, figures, and appendixes.

Familiarization with Soviet planning theory and practices in light of the reforms.

_____. "The Use of Input-Output in Regional Economic Planning: The Soviet Experience." ECONOMIC JOURNAL 78 (December 1968): 855-67.

An explanation of the problems encountered in the construction of ex-post and ex-ante input-output tables and the use of such tables in Soviet regional planning.

Erlich, Alexander. "Development Strategy and Planning: The Soviet Experience." In NATIONAL ECONOMIC PLANNING; A CONFERENCE OF THE UNIVERSITIES-NATIONAL BUREAU COMMITTEE FOR ECONOMIC RESEARCH, edited by Max F. Millikan, pp. 233-78. New York: National Bureau of Economic Research, 1967.

A discussion of the Soviet development strategy and the role of the planning system in implementing that strategy.

Fedorenko, N[ikolay P.]. "Prices and Optimal Planning." PROBLEMS OF ECONOMICS 10 (November 1967): 11-21.

Statement on the principles governing the elaboration of optimal plans and the relationships between price and the optimal plan.

Feiwel, George R. THE ECONOMICS OF A SOCIALIST ENTERPRISE: A CASE STUDY OF THE POLISH FIRM. New York: Frederick A. Praeger, 1965. xvi, 398 p.

A detailed review of the Polish economy after World War II, of the different planning philosophies, and of the actual plans as they affect Polish industrial enterprises. The views of leading Polish planners and economists, as they pertain to greater decentralization in planning, are presented with great thoroughness.

_____. NEW ECONOMIC PATTERNS IN CZECHOSLOVAKIA: IMPACT OF GROWTH, PLANNING AND THE MARKET. New York: Frederick A. Praeger, 1968. xxiv, 589 p. Tables and figures.

A thorough discussion of the major currents of Czechoslovak economic development, planning, and reforms.

_____. POLAND'S INDUSTRIALIZATION POLICY: A CURRENT ANALYSIS; SOURCES OF ECONOMIC GROWTH AND RETROGRESSION. Vol. 1. New York: Frederick A. Praeger, 1971. xxv, 748 p. Tables and appendix.

An explanation of the Soviet growth strategy and the case for planning, followed by a detailed description of the various Polish economic plans from 1947 to 1970.

_____. PROBLEMS IN POLISH ECONOMIC PLANNING: CONTINUITY, CHANGE AND PROSPECTS. Vol. 2. New York: Frederick A. Praeger, 1971. xvii, 454 p. Tables and figures.

A discussion of the economic reforms in perspective, the financing of investments, the existing planning system, and the revamping of the system for the 1970s.

_____. THE SOVIET QUEST FOR ECONOMIC EFFICIENCY--ISSUES, CONTROVERSIES, AND REFORMS. 1967. Exp. and rev. New York: Praeger, 1972. xxiv, 790 p.

A very comprehensive and exhaustive treatment of the issues related to Soviet economic development, planning, efficiency, reform proposals, and implementation.

Fel'd, S. "Planning the Most Important Branch and Territorial Proportions of Soviet Reproduction." PROBLEMS OF ECONOMICS 9 (June 1966): 3-16. Tables.

An explanation of the reasons for planning production proportions and the appropriate proportions among the major sectors and branches of the economy.

FitzLyon, K. "Plan and Prediction." SOVIET STUDIES 21 (October 1969): 164-92. Tables and appendixes.

An attempt to determine whether a long-term prediction of Soviet economic performance is possible on the basis of published plan targets and results of implementation.

Garetovskii, N. "New Developments in the Formation and Utilization of the Enterprise Fund." PROBLEMS OF ECONOMICS 6 (April 1964): 54-61.

Familiarization with the rules pertaining to the formation and use of enterprise funds in the USSR following the 1963 changes.

Gatanova, A.A. "The Use of the Balance Method in Economic Planning." PROBLEMS OF ECONOMICS 6 (June 1963): 11-17.

A description of the classification and use of material balances in the Soviet Union.

Gatovskii, L. "The Role of Profit in a Socialist Economy." PROBLEMS OF ECONOMICS 5 (February 1963): 10-18.

A delineation of the distinctions between the role of profit from the standpoint of the national economy and that of the individual enterprise, and the relations between profits and prices and profits and turnover taxes.

Gavrilov, V. "Improving the Economic Collaboration of Socialist Countries." PROBLEMS OF ECONOMICS 16 (October 1973): 93-103.

A call for the coordination of long-range plans, a system of joint (as opposed to supranational) planning, and the creation of independent production associations.

Gindin, Sam. "A Model of the Soviet Firm." ECONOMICS OF PLANNING 10 (1970): 145-57. Figures.

Analytical model of the Soviet firm, including extensions of Ames's model.

Goldmann, Josef. "Fluctuations and Trend in the Rate of Economic Growth in Some Socialist Countries." ECONOMICS OF PLANNING 4 (1964): 88-98. Tables and figures.

An explanation of the reasons for fluctuations in growth rates for Czechoslovakia, Poland, Hungary, and East Germany.

Granick, David. "Initiative and Independence of Soviet Plant Management." AMERICAN SLAVIC AND EAST EUROPEAN REVIEW 10 (1951): 191-201.

Inquiry into the nature of decision making by plant managers in Soviet heavy industry during 1934-41.

_____. "A Management Model of East European, Centrally-Planned Economies." EUROPEAN ECONOMIC REVIEW 4 (June 1973): 135-61.

An examination of a model of managerial effectiveness of a representative, East European industrial system.

_____. MANAGEMENT OF THE INDUSTRIAL FIRM IN THE USSR: A STUDY IN SOVIET ECONOMIC PLANNING. New York: Columbia University Press, 1954. xiii, 346 p. Appendixes and index.

Study of Soviet economic planning and management as manifested in the behavior of enterprise managers in heavy industry during 1934-41. Discussion of plan construction, success criteria, implementation, and the role of the party.

_____. "The Orthodox Model of the Socialist Enterprise in the Light of Romanian Experience." SOVIET STUDIES 26 (April 1974): 205-23. Tables.

Statements concerning the inapplicability of the orthodox model of the Socialist enterprise to Rumanian enterprises of 1969-70, on the basis of a series of interviews by the author.

_____. "Technological Policy and Economic Calculation in Soviet Industry." In VALUE AND PLAN--ECONOMIC CALCULATION AND ORGANIZATION IN EASTERN EUROPE, edited by Gregory Grossman, pp. 271-94. Berkeley and Los Angeles: University of California Press, 1960. Tables.

An examination of the rationality of economic decisions in the Soviet metalworking industries.

Grebtsov, G. "Concerning the Elaboration of a Composite Material Balance." PROBLEMS OF ECONOMICS 2 (November 1959): 9-17. Tables.

Outline of the general characteristics of material balances, followed by a description of the methods used in the calculation of branch norms of labor and capital inputs.

Gregory, Paul R., and Stuart, Robert C. SOVIET ECONOMIC STRUCTURE AND PERFORMANCE. New York: Harper & Row Publishers, 1974. x, 478 p. Tables, figures, and index. Paperback.

Comprehensive analysis of issues relevant to the Soviet economy. Included are discussions of the economic experiences of the periods of war communism and New Economic Policy, pricing, planning methods and principles, agriculture, growth strategy and performance, foreign trade, monetary and financial controls and policy, and economic reforms.

Grossman, Gregory. "Notes for a Theory of the Command Economy." SOVIET STUDIES 15 (October 1963): 101-23.

An analysis of the relationships between individual production units and the command economy at large.

Hallaraker, Harald. "Soviet Discussion on Enterprise Incentives and Methods of Planning." ECONOMICS OF PLANNING 3 (April 1963): 53-68.

Compilation of contemporary Soviet views on plans, profits, bonuses, intensification of planning, and rationalization of production.

Hardt, John P., et al., eds. MATHEMATICS AND COMPUTERS IN SOVIET PLANNING. New Haven, Conn.: Yale University Press, 1967. xxii, 298 p. Tables, figures, appendix, and index.

An evaluation of the Soviet planning and information system, Soviet efforts in input-output and in linear programming, and applications of operations research at the industry and enterprise levels.

Hunter, Holland. "Optimum Tautness in Developmental Planning." ECONOMIC DEVELOPMENT AND CULTURAL CHANGE 9 (July 1961): 561-72.

A well known contribution to the theory of planning in Soviet-type economies.

_____. "The Overambitious First Soviet Five-Year Plan." SLAVIC REVIEW 32 (June 1973): 237-57. Tables and figures.

A test for the plan's feasibility, followed by a projection of alternative feasible growth paths.

Hutchings, Raymond. SOVIET ECONOMIC DEVELOPMENT. New York: Barnes & Noble, 1971. xiii, 314 p. Tables, figures, appendix, and index.

An examination of the extent and causes of economic development during World War I, war communism, the New Economic Policy, and the plan era.

Jasny, Naum. "Plan and Superplan." SURVEY 38 (October 1961): 29-43. Tables.

An analysis of the twenty-year perspective program for the Soviet economy, published in 1961.

_____. "A Soviet Planner--V.G. Groman." RUSSIAN REVIEW 13 (January 1954): 52-58.

An interesting insight into the early history of Soviet planning.

Kantorovich, L. "Optimal Mathematical Models in Planning the Development of a Branch and in Technical Policy." PROBLEMS OF ECONOMICS 11 (July 1968): 3-16.

A discussion of models of branch development and branch technical and economic policy.

Karagedov, R.G. "The Question of the Relationship between the Categories of Economic Effectiveness and Profitability." PROBLEMS OF ECONOMICS 13 (November 1970): 24-44.

A critique of Western and of some Soviet theories of profit, followed by a call for optimizing the process of economic development on the basis of centralized planning.

Kaser, M[ichael]. C. "Changes in Planning Methods During the Preparation of the Soviet Seven-Year Plan." SOVIET STUDIES 10 (April 1959): 321-38.

An analysis of the changes which occured during 1957-58 in the central planning mechanism, including a summary of the main features of Soviet economic administration at the start of the Seven-Year Plan.

_____. "The Nature of Soviet Planning; A Critique of Jasny's Appraisal." SOVIET STUDIES 14 (October 1962): 109-31.

A critique of Naum Jasny's "cyclic theory" of planning in the USSR.

Kemeny, George. ECONOMIC PLANNING IN HUNGARY: 1947-9. London: Royal Institute of International Affairs, 1952. x, 146 p. Tables, appendix, and index.

A discussion of Hungarian economic planning and development policy during Hungary's first Three-Year Plan (1947-49).

Keren, Michael. "On the Tautness of Plans." REVIEW OF ECONOMIC STUDIES 39 (October 1972): 469-86. Figures.

Theoretical analysis of the role which production targets may play in augmenting production.

_____. "Planning and Uncertainty in a Soviet-Type Economy." YALE ECONOMIC ESSAYS 11 (Spring-Fall 1971): 219-61. Tables and figures.

An evaluation of the process of resource allocation in Soviet-type economies, based on East German institutions and planning practices.

Kheinman, S. "The Scientific and Technical Revolution and Structural Changes in the USSR Economy." PROBLEMS OF ECONOMICS 12 (April 1970): 3-25.

Discourse on the role of scientific and technical advances in changing the branch structure of industry and of material production as a whole.

Koldomasov, Iu. "Development of Direct Economic Ties and Improvement of the Distribution of Means of Production." PROBLEMS OF ECONOMICS 8 (April 1966): 23-33.

Comments concerning material allocation under the post-1965 system of industrial management.

Konnik, I. "Plan and Market in the Socialist Economy." PROBLEMS OF ECONOMICS 9 (December 1966): 24-35.

Views on supply and demand under socialism, the role of the market, and the planned regulation of economic proportions.

Kornai, Janos. "Mathematical Programming as a Tool in Drawing Up the

Five-Year Economic Plan." ECONOMICS OF PLANNING 5 (1966): 3-18.

A close look at the role of mathematical programming in the construction of Hungarian medium-term plans.

_____. OVERCENTRALIZATION IN ECONOMIC ADMINISTRATION. Translated by John Knapp. London: Oxford University Press, 1959. xviii, 236 p. Tables.

Examination of the Hungarian experience with traditional planning, as shown by the problems encountered in Hungarian light industry.

Kornai, J[anos]., and Liptak, T. "A Mathematical Investigation of Some Economic Effects of Profit Sharing in Socialist Firms." ECONOMETRICA 30 (January 1967): 140-61. Figures.

By means of linear and nonlinear programming methods, an examination of the problems associated with profit sharing and price regulation in Hungary.

Kotov, F. "New Methodological Principles of Preparing the State Plan." PROBLEMS OF ECONOMICS 4 (June 1961): 28-35.

A discussion of the principles of plan construction in the USSR.

Krylov, P. "The Balance Method of Planning." PROBLEMS OF ECONOMICS 11 (May 1968): 11-17.

A description of the function and construction of material balances, value balances, and of the methods used in balance calculations.

Krylov, P., and Chistiakov, M. "Problems in Improving the Methods of National Economic Planning." PROBLEMS OF ECONOMICS 15 (August 1972): 21-40.

Views concerning methods of planning and substantiating plan indexes.

Leeman, Wayne A. "Bonus Formulae and Soviet Managerial Performance." SOUTHERN ECONOMIC JOURNAL 36 (April 1970): 434-45. Figures.

A rigorous examination of the principles of Soviet physical planning.

Lemeshev, M. "Concerning Integrated Programs of Economic Development." PROBLEMS OF ECONOMICS 15 (August 1972): 3-20.

A call for an interbranch approach to the planning and management of production.

Levine, Herbert S. "The Centralized Planning of Supply in Soviet Industry."

In COMPARISONS OF THE UNITED STATES AND SOVIET ECONOMIES, Joint Economic Committee, 86th Cong., 1st sess., pp. 151-76. Washington, D.C.: Government Printing Office, 1959. Figures.

> An analysis of plan construction in Soviet industry, including a discussion of the chronology of plan construction, the role of material balances, and weaknesses of supply planning.

_____. "The Effects of Foreign Trade on Soviet Planning Practices." In INTERNATIONAL TRADE AND CENTRAL PLANNING--AN ANALYSIS OF ECONOMIC INTERACTIONS, edited by Alan A. Brown and Egon Neuberger, pp. 255-76. Berkeley and Los Angeles: University of California Press, 1968.

> An assessment of the effects of foreign trade on Soviet planning methodology.

_____. "Input-Output Analysis and Soviet Planning." AMERICAN ECONOMIC REVIEW 52 (May 1962): 127-37. Appendix.

> A discussion of input-output analysis and its application in the construction of Soviet annual plans.

_____. "Recent Developments in Soviet Planning." In DIMENSIONS OF SOVIET ECONOMIC POWER, Joint Economic Committee, 87th Cong., 2d sess., pp. 47-65. Washington, D.C.: Government Printing Office, 1962.

> An examination of Soviet planning problems and procedures prevalent between the 1957 reorganization and 1962.

Liberman, E.G. "Planning Production and Standards of Long-Term Operation." PROBLEMS OF ECONOMICS 5 (December 1962): 16-22.

> An inquiry into the incentive system contained in the existing methods of industrial management.

_____. "Plan, Profits, Bonuses." PROBLEMS OF ECONOMICS 8 (July 1965): 3-8.

> Proposals concerning the appropriate role of financial incentives.

Long, Neal B., Jr. "An Input-Output Comparison of the Economic Structure of the U.S. and the U.S.S.R." REVIEW OF ECONOMICS AND STATISTICS 52 (November 1970): 434-41. Tables.

> Procedures for using input-output tables for making intercountry comparisons for comparing the economic structure of the United States with that of the USSR.

Lovell, C.A. Knox. "Profits and Cybernetics as Sources of Increased Efficiency in Soviet Planning." SOUTHERN ECONOMIC JOURNAL 34 (January 1968): 392-405. Tables.

A discussion of the cybernetic approach to planning and Liberman's proposals.

McAuley, Alastair N.D. "Rationality and Central Planning." SOVIET STUDIES 18 (January 1967): 340-55.

A discussion concerning the applicability and implications of formal welfare economics to economies with different institutions from those assumed in traditional theory.

Manove, Michael. "A Model of Soviet-Type Economic Planning." AMERICAN ECONOMIC REVIEW 61 (June 1971): 390-406.

A theoretical analysis of the traditional Soviet-type planning procedure, with special attention to the concept of consistency in plan construction.

Marczewski, Jan. CRISIS IN SOCIALIST PLANNING: EASTERN EUROPE AND THE USSR. Translated by Noel Lindsay. New York: Praeger, 1974. xvii, 245 p. Tables and index.

A discussion of the orthodox Soviet-type planning system and planning reforms, primarily in Soviet and Eastern European industry. Foreign trade and monetary and financial planning and policies are also discussed.

Michal, Jan M. CENTRAL PLANNING IN CZECHOSLOVAKIA: ORGANIZATION FOR GROWTH IN A MATURE ECONOMY. Stanford, Calif.: Stanford University Press, 1960. xii, 274 p. Tables, appendix, and index.

Thorough and skillful examination of the Czechoslovak economy in terms of its national income and product, population and manpower, industry, agriculture, trade, transport, foreign trade, money and prices, investment, budgetary matters, and standard of living.

Mieczkowski, Z. "The Economic Regionalization of the Soviet Union in the Lenin and Stalin Period." CANADIAN SLAVONIC PAPERS 8 (1966): 89-124. Figures.

A survey of Goelro and Gosplan regionalization efforts.

Minc, Bronislaw. "The Problem of Optimization in Planning." In PLANNING AND MARKETS: MODERN TRENDS IN VARIOUS ECONOMIC SYSTEMS, edited by John T. Dunlop and Nikolay P. Fedorenko, pp. 241-53. New York: McGraw-Hill Book Co., 1969.

A description of the concept and use of constrained optimization in Socialist planning.

Montias, John Michael. CENTRAL PLANNING IN POLAND. New Haven,

Conn.: Yale University Press, 1962. xv, 410 p. Tables, figures, appendixes, and index.

A well known, systematic, analytical exposition of orthodox, command-type planning theory and practice.

_____. "Planning with Material Balances in Soviet-Type Economies." AMERICAN ECONOMIC REVIEW 49 (December 1959): 963-85.

A well known article concerning the role of material balances in Soviet planning by reference to the theoretical models of administrative planning and by comparison of those models with actual planning methods.

_____. "The Polish 'Economic Model.'" PROBLEMS OF COMMUNISM 9 (March-April 1960): 16-24.

Instructive comments on the Polish reform efforts during the late 1950s.

Morton, George, and Zauberman, Alfred. "Von Neumann's Model and Soviet Long-Term (Perspective) Planning." KYKLOS 22 (1969): 45-61.

A discussion of the use made of the Von Neumann model by Kantorovich and Makarov.

Nagy, Imre. ON COMMUNISM: IN DEFENSE OF THE NEW COURSE. New York: Frederick A. Praeger, 1957. xliv, 306 p.

An examination of Hungary's economic experiences during 1945-55, including agricultural, industrial, and foreign trade policies.

Nemchinov, V. "Mathematics and Electronics in the Service of Planning." PROBLEMS OF ECONOMICS 4 (November 1961): 3-9.

A familiarization with the use of mathematics and mathematical model building in economic planning.

_____. "The Plan Target and Material Incentive." PROBLEMS OF ECONOMICS 8 (July 1965): 9-13.

Comments on Liberman's proposals.

Neuberger, Egon. "Central Planning and Its Legacies: Implications for Foreign Trade." In INTERNATIONAL TRADE AND CENTRAL PLANNING--AN ANALYSIS OF ECONOMIC INTERACTIONS, edited by Alan A. Brown and Egon Neuberger, pp. 349-77. Berkeley and Los Angeles: University of California Press, 1968. Tables.

An attempt to analyze the positive and negative legacies of Soviet-type central planning, with special attention to the Yugoslav experience.

Nove, Alec. "The Industrial Planning System: Reforms in Prospect." SO-
VIET STUDIES 14 (July 1962): 1-15.

A discussion of the changes in the industrial planning system between 1957 and 1962, followed by an analysis of the reasons why
further changes could be expected.

_____. "Planners' Preferences, Priorities, and Reforms." ECONOMIC
JOURNAL 86 (June 1966): 267-77.

An analysis of the meaning of "planners' preferences" and of
"priorities."

_____. "The Problem of 'Success Indicators' in Soviet Industry." ECONOM-
ICA 25 (February 1958): 1-13.

Discussion of the problems associated with the system of quantitative success indicators in the USSR during the 1960s.

Novozhilov, V.V. "On the Problem of Developing the Theory of Optimal
Planning in the Present Stage." PROBLEMS OF ECONOMICS 14 (July 1971):
3-22.

A delineation of approaches to the elaboration of planning methods
and problems of optimization.

Nuti, D[omenico]. M[ario]. "Discounting Methods in Polish Planning." SO-
VIET STUDIES 23 (October 1971): 309-17.

An assessment of the efficiency index, adopted for Polish investment planning in 1970.

Pantilie, N. "The Enterprise-Central Ministry Relationship." EASTERN EU-
ROPEAN ECONOMICS 11 (Winter 1972-73): 80-91.

A description of the relationship between enterprises and associations in Rumanian industrial planning and management.

Portes, R[ichard]. D. "The Enterprise under Central Planning." REVIEW OF
ECONOMIC STUDIES 36 (April 1969): 197-212.

A formal model of enterprise behavior in a centrally planned economy.

Porwit, Krzysztof. CENTRAL PLANNING; EVALUATION OF VARIANTS.
Translated by Jozef Stadler, translation edited by Helen Infeld. New York:
Pergamon Press, 1967. vi, 200 p. Tables, figures, appendixes, and index.

A call for a new methodology for the construction of long-term
plans, one which explicitly recognizes the necessity of studying
several variants.

Postyshev, A. "The Labor Theory of Value and Optimal Planning." PROB-LEMS OF ECONOMICS 10 (December 1967): 3-15.

An analysis of mathematical programming and the theory of value, as well as the prospects for the use of mathematics in planned price formation.

Richman, Barry M. "Formulation of Enterprise Operating Plans in Soviet Industry." SOVIET STUDIES 15 (July 1963): 58-71. Appendix.

A description of the process of plan formulation in Soviet industrial enterprises.

_____. MANAGEMENT: DEVELOPMENT AND EDUCATION IN THE SO-VIET UNION. East Lansing: Institute for International Business and Economic Development Studies, Michigan State University, 1967. xviii, 308 p. Tables, figures, appendixes, and index.

An examination of the Soviet manager, his job, and his education.

_____. SOVIET MANAGEMENT; WITH SIGNIFICANT AMERICAN COM-PARISONS. Englewood Cliffs, N.J.: Prentice-Hall, 1965. vii, 279 p. Figures, tables, and appendixes.

A careful account of the organizational structure of Soviet industry and its enterprises, the industrial planning process, and some fundamental problems of the Soviet administrative-economic system to 1962. Comparisons between Soviet and American managers.

Rybakov, O. "Improvements in Planning Methods of Collaboration among Comecon Countries." PROBLEMS OF ECONOMICS 15 (March 1973): 3-20.

Comments on the perspectives of long-term intrabloc plan coordination.

_____. "Some Organizational and Methodological Problems Relating to the Elaboration of Long-Range Plans for Collaboration between the USSR and Socialist Countries." PROBLEMS OF ECONOMICS 16 (October 1973): 3-19.

Discussion of problems related to long-range plan coordination within the CMEA.

Rybakov, O., and Khmelevskii, N. "Certain Methodological Aspects in the Planning of Integration Measures." PROBLEMS OF ECONOMICS 17 (September 1974): 3-19.

A discussion of bilateral and multilateral plan coordination within the Comecon for 1971-75 and 1976-80.

Schlesinger, Rudolf. "A Note on the Context of Early Soviet Planning." SOVIET STUDIES 16 (July 1964): 22-44.

A note on the impact on contemporary planning theories of Soviet economists of the 1920s, the timing of the party decision in favor of full-scale industrialization, and the initial variants of the First Five-Year Plan.

_____. "Some Observations on the Historical and Social Conditions of Planning." ECONOMICS OF PLANNING 5 (1965): 53-73.

General remarks concerning planning, the Russian Socialist tradition, and the competition between social systems.

Schroeder, Gertrude E. "Recent Developments in Soviet Planning and Incentives." In SOVIET ECONOMIC PROSPECTS FOR THE SEVENTIES, Joint Economic Committee, 93d Cong., 1st sess., pp. 11-38. Washington, D.C.: Government Printing Office, 1973.

An examination of modifications in planning approaches and techniques, as well as new developments in enterprise incentives.

Sherman, Howard J. "Marxist Economics and Soviet Planning." SOVIET STUDIES 18 (October 1966): 169-88.

An essay on the relationship between Marxist economics and Soviet planning.

Sik, Ota. "The Economic Impact of Stalinism." PROBLEMS OF COMMUNISM 20 (May-June 1971): 1-10.

Interesting description of the impact of Stalinism on the growth and efficiency of the Czechoslovakian economy by one of the chief architects of Czechoslovakia's economic reform program of 1965-68.

Sirc, Ljubo. ECONOMIC DEVOLUTION IN EASTERN EUROPE. London: Longmans, Green and Co., 1969. xii, 165 p. Tables and appendix.

An analysis of Eastern European economic problems as they pertain to pricing, foreign trade, economic growth, planning methods, and economic reforms.

Skriabin, A. "Problems of Optimal Planning of the National Economy." PROBLEMS OF ECONOMICS 11 (June 1968): 3-11.

Comparison of Soviet and Western theories and processes.

Smolinski, Leon. "Grinevetskii and Soviet Industrialisation." SURVEY 67 (April 1968): 100-115.

An essay on the concept and content of Grinevetskii's plan, a little known forerunner of the GOELRO plan.

_____. "Lenin and Economic Planning." STUDIES IN COMPARATIVE COMMUNISM 2 (January 1969): 96-114.

A survey of Lenin's writing on economic planning.

_____. "Planning without Theory, 1917-1967." SURVEY 64 (July 1967): 108-28.

A chronological survey of Soviet planning methodology and practices.

Smolinski, Leon, and Wiles, Peter [J.D.]. "The Soviet Planning Pendulum." PROBLEMS OF COMMUNISM 12 (November-December 1963): 21-34.

Analysis of those contradictions in the Soviet planning system which are responsible for the successive swings between centralizing and decentralizing measures in economic policy.

Spulber, Nicolas, ed. FOUNDATIONS OF SOVIET STRATEGY FOR ECONOMIC GROWTH; SELECTED SOVIET ESSAYS, 1924-1930. Bloomington: Indiana University Press, 1964. xii, 530 p. Tables, figures, and index.

A compendium of articles (translated from the Russian), written by such notables as Preobrazhenski, Feldman, Shanin, Bazarov, Groman, and Strumilin. Topics include macroeconomic models, growth strategy, and planning theories and methods.

Strumilin, S. "Material Incentive and Planning in the USSR." PROBLEMS OF ECONOMICS 6 (January 1964): 3-10.

Remarks concerning the functions of enterprise incentive funds and the "proper" relationship between profit and such funds.

Sukharevskii, B. "The Enterprise and Material Stimulation." PROBLEMS OF ECONOMICS 9 (August 1966): 42-49.

Views on production relations and incentives, profit under socialism, relations among enterprises, and the appropriate distribution of enterprise incomes.

_____. "On Improving the Forms and Methods of Material Incentives." PROBLEMS OF ECONOMICS 5 (April 1963): 3-12.

Comments concerning the Soviet system of material incentives and the Liberman proposals.

Treml, Vladimir G. "The 1959 Soviet Input-Output Table (As Reconstructed)." In NEW DIRECTIONS IN THE SOVIET ECONOMY, Joint Economic Committee, 89th Cong., 2d sess., pp. 257-70. Washington, D.C.: Government Printing Office, 1966. Tables.

An expanded and corrected version of the reconstructed 1959

Input-Output Table, originally published by the same author in 1964.

_____. "A Note on Soviet Input-Output Tables." SOVIET STUDIES 31 (July 1969): 21-34. Tables.

An introduction to Soviet input-output statistics in general and to the 1966 table in particular.

United Nations. Economic Commission for Europe. "A Note on the Introduction of Mathematical Techniques into Soviet Planning." ECONOMIC BULLETIN FOR EUROPE 12 (June 1960): 57-67.

Review of the mathematical techniques in use in Soviet planning.

Vainshtein, A.L. "The Criterion of Optimal Development in a Socialist National Economy." PROBLEMS OF ECONOMICS 13 (October 1970): 3-21.

An analysis of previously proposed national economic optimality criteria, followed by a review with the author's own criterion: maximum net output (including some services).

Ward, Benjamin [N.]. "Kantorovich on Economic Calculation." JOURNAL OF POLITICAL ECONOMY 68 (December 1960): 545-56.

An instructive, analytical review of Kantorovich's THE BEST USE OF ECONOMIC RESOURCES.

_____. "The Planners' Choice Variables." In VALUE AND PLAN--ECONOMIC CALCULATION AND ORGANIZATION IN EASTERN EUROPE, edited by Gregory Grossman, pp. 132-51. Berkeley and Los Angeles: University of California Press, 1960.

An investigation of the role of prices and the role of other economic levers in short-term Soviet-type planning.

Weitzman, Martin L. "Material Balances under Uncertainty." QUARTERLY JOURNAL OF ECONOMICS 85 (May 1971): 262-82. Appendix.

A study of optimal plan formulation and execution under uncertainty.

Wilczynski, J. "Dumping and Central Planning." JOURNAL OF POLITICAL ECONOMY 74 (June 1966): 250-64. Tables.

An examination of the problem of dumping within the context of command-type central planning.

_____. PROFIT, RISK AND INCENTIVES UNDER SOCIALIST ECONOMIC PLANNING. London: Macmillan and Co., 1973. viii, 231 p. Tables and index.

A survey of successive Eastern European views on profit, followed by a discussion of the ways in which profit is being used in Socialist economic planning.

_____. SOCIALIST ECONOMIC DEVELOPMENT AND REFORMS. New York: Praeger, 1972. xvii, 350 p. Tables and index.

A discussion of growth strategy, orthodox planning practices, prices, financial and monetary policies, foreign trade criteria and practices, reforms, and growth performance in the Soviet-type economies.

Wiles, P[eter]. J.D. THE POLITICAL ECONOMY OF COMMUNISM. Oxford: Basil Blackwell, 1962. xv, 404 p. Tables, figures, and index.

A critical, analytical examination of the major issues relevant to the study of Soviet-type economies: economic organization; planning and resource allocation, including pricing, planners' preferences, and decentralization; and growth strategy and performance.

_____. "Scarcity, Marxism, and Gosplan." OXFORD ECONOMIC PAPERS 5 (October 1953): 288-316.

Thoughts on the incompatibility of Marxism with the rational allocation of resources.

Wolf, Herbert. "Problems of the Lines of Development of Scientific Planning in the Comprehensive Building of Socialism in the German Democratic Republic." EASTERN EUROPEAN ECONOMICS 5 (Summer 1967): 3-22. Table.

A survey of East German planning criteria and perspectives and of development problems by the chairman of the State Planning Commission.

Zaleski, Eugene. PLANNING FOR ECONOMIC GROWTH IN THE SOVIET UNION, 1918-1932. Chapel Hill: University of North Carolina Press, 1971. xxxviii, 425 p. Tables, figures, appendix, and index.

A discussion of plan construction and implementation in the USSR during 1918-32, as well as an evaluation of Soviet planning and development strategy.

_____. "Planning for Industrial Growth." STUDIES ON THE SOVIET UNION 6, no. 4 (1967): 55-77. Tables.

Chronological discussion of Soviet planning theories and methods as well as of the results attained.

Zauberman, Alfred. ASPECTS OF PLANOMETRICS. New Haven, Conn.: Yale University Press, 1967. xiii, 318 p. Appendixes and index.

A broad range of studies in mathematical economics, most of them appearing in print for the first time. The topics covered include investment criteria, profit guidance, the objective function and optimal growth, foreign trade planning, and techniques in normative and indicative planning.

_____. "Recent Developments in Soviet Planning Techniques." ECONOMIA INTERNAZIONALE 20 (May 1967): 255-77.

An explanation of Soviet planning assumptions, models, and instruments.

Zielinski, Janusz G. "Economic Tools of Plan Fulfillment." ECONOMICS OF PLANNING 4 (1964): 129-42.

A discussion concerning the nature of management formulas in Soviet-type economies.

_____. "Notes on Incentive Systems of Socialist Enterprises." ECONOMICS OF PLANNING 7 (1967): 258-69. Figures.

A description of incentive systems and of incentives for optimal planning.

_____. "On the Theory of Success Indicators." ECONOMICS OF PLANNING 7 (1967): 1-29. Figures.

A theoretical examination of certain basic problems of success indicators in the state industrial enterprises of the centrally planned economies.

Chapter 6

PRICES AND INFLATION

Arnold, Arthur Z. BANKS, CREDIT AND MONEY IN SOVIET RUSSIA.
New York: Columbia University Press, 1937. xxiii, 559 p. Tables and index.

   A thorough, exhaustive discussion and explanation of Soviet financial and banking operations and inflationary pressures during 1917-
   37.

Ausch, Sandor, and Bartha, Ferenc. "Theoretical Problems Relating to Prices
in Trade between the Comecon Countries." SOVIET AND EASTERN EURO-
PEAN FOREIGN TRADE 4 (Summer 1968): 35-71. Tables.

   An examination of price formation, relative prices, and bilateral
   clearing within the Comecon.

Bazlova, A. "Improving Purchase Prices on Agricultural Output." PROBLEMS
OF ECONOMICS 16 (July 1973): 37-58. Tables.

   A discussion of the level, regional differentiation, and shortcomings
   of agricultural purchase prices.

Bergson, Abram. "Soviet National Income and Product in 1937, Part II:
Ruble Prices and the Valuation Problem." QUARTERLY JOURNAL OF ECO-
NOMICS 64 (August 1950): 408-41. Tables.

   A study of retail prices, wages, and collective farm prices; measurement of national product in terms of adjusted rubles and national
   income according to ruble and dollar valuations.

Bergson, Abram, et al. "Prices of Basic Industrial Products in the U.S.S.R.,
1928-1950." JOURNAL OF POLITICAL ECONOMY 64 (August 1956): 303-
28. Tables and figures.

   A careful examination and explanation of Soviet industrial price
   trends for the period 1928-50.

Boehme, Hans. "East German Price Formation Under the New Economic

System." SOVIET STUDIES 19 (January 1968): 340–58.

>A discussion and evaluation of the East German price reforms of 1964 and of the economic thought which underlies them.

Bornstein, Morris. "The Soviet Debate on Agricultural Price and Procurement Reforms." SOVIET STUDIES 21 (July 1969): 1–20. Tables.

>An analysis of the debates which took place in the Soviet Union during the late 1950s and during the 1960s concerning agricultural price formation and procurement policies.

_____. "The Soviet Price Reform Discussion." QUARTERLY JOURNAL OF ECONOMICS 78 (February 1964): 15–48.

>An appraisal of the background and content of the 1956–63 Soviet price debate.

_____. "Soviet Price Statistics." In SOVIET ECONOMIC STATISTICS, edited by Vladimir G. Treml and John P. Hardt, pp. 355–96. Durham, N.C.: Duke University Press, 1972.

>A description and evaluation of the major official Soviet price statistics, including coverage, collection procedures, methodology, and publication practices.

_____. "The Soviet Price System." AMERICAN ECONOMIC REVIEW 52 (March 1962): 64–103.

>An excellent analysis of the role of prices in the Soviet economy.

_____. "Soviet Price Theory and Policy." In NEW DIRECTIONS IN THE SOVIET ECONOMY, Joint Economic Committee, 89th Cong., 2d sess., pp. 63–98. Washington, D.C.: Government Printing Office, 1966. Tables.

>A discussion of the functions of prices in the Soviet economy precedes an examination of industrial wholesale prices, agricultural procurement prices, and retail prices. The Soviet price reform discussions of the fifties and sixties are also examined.

Bozyk, Pawel. "Domestic and Foreign Trade Prices in the Process of Integration in Comecon Countries." SOVIET AND EASTERN EUROPEAN FOREIGN TRADE 6 (Summer 1970): 125–39.

>A report on domestic price formation, the relationships between domestic and foreign prices, the influence of domestic price structures on intra-Comecon specialization, and the role of foreign exchange rates in linking intra-Comecon domestic prices.

Branik, Julius. "Internal and World Prices in the New System of Management." EASTERN EUROPEAN ECONOMICS 5 (Spring 1967): 39–48. Tables.

A discussion of the expected impact of world prices on Czechoslovak internal prices as a result of economic reform.

Brody, Andras. "Three Types of Price Systems." ECONOMICS OF PLAN-
NING 5 (1965): 58-66.

A mathematical presentation of the three types of price systems
proposed in Hungary through 1965.

Brus, Wlodzimierz. "On the Role of the Law of Value in Socialist Economy."
OXFORD ECONOMIC PAPERS 9 (June 1957): 209-21.

An exposition on prices and their role in planning under socialism.

Brzeski, Andrzej. "Forced-Draft Industrialization with Unlimited Supply of
Money: Poland, 1945-1964." In MONEY AND PLAN--FINANCIAL ASPECTS
OF EAST EUROPEAN ECONOMIC REFORMS, edited by Gregory Grossman,
pp. 17-37. Berkeley and Los Angeles: University of California Press, 1968.
Appendix.

An analysis of the supply and demand for money, inflation, and
economic growth in postwar Poland.

Campbell, Robert W. "Marx, Kantorovich, and Novozhilov: Stoimost' Versus
Reality." SLAVIC REVIEW 20 (October 1961): 402-18.

An assessment of the deficiencies in the labor theory of value and
value theories of Kantorovich and Novozhilov.

Chernysheva, V. "Summary of Discussion on Problems of Price Formation."
PROBLEMS OF ECONOMICS 7 (August 1964): 36-50.

A summary of discussions concerning geographic factors, product
quality, and demand and supply in price formation.

Csikos-Nagy, Bela. "Macrostructural and Microstructural Performance of the
Economy." SOVIET STUDIES 23 (January 1972): 474-83.

Comments on the guided market concept and the role of prices,
as envisioned initially by the architects of the Hungarian reform
of 1968.

_____. SOCIALIST ECONOMIC POLICY. New York: St. Martin's Press,
1973. 238 p. Index.

A discussion of Soviet-type economic organization, planning, financial policies, price and income policies, and distribution and
foreign trade policies.

Dadaian, V.S. "Developing a System of Incentive Prices." PROBLEMS OF
ECONOMICS 10 (July 1967): 3-8. Tables.

An examination of incentive prices and shadow prices and the relation between them.

Davies, R.W. THE DEVELOPMENT OF THE SOVIET BUDGETARY SYSTEM. Cambridge: At the University Press, 1958. xxi, 373 p. Tables, figures, and index.

A detailed study of the development of the Soviet budgetary and financial system from the period of war communism until the end of World War II.

D'iachenko, V. "Improvement of the Price System and of Price Formation in the USSR." PROBLEMS OF ECONOMICS 9 (August 1966): 15-26.

Comments concerning the appropriate functions of prices and ways of achieving them.

_____. "Main Trends in Improving Prices in Trade among Comecon Members." PROBLEMS OF ECONOMICS 11 (June 1968): 40-49.

An examination of the role and establishment of foreign trade prices within the Comecon, and a call for the establishment of Comecon's "own price basis."

_____. "The System of Price-Forming Factors and the Principles of Their Classification." PROBLEMS OF ECONOMICS 6 (November 1963): 30-42.

An essay on the theoretical aspects of price formation under socialism.

Fearn, Robert M. "Controls over Wage Funds and Inflationary Pressures in the USSR." INDUSTRIAL AND LABOR RELATIONS REVIEW 18 (January 1965): 186-95.

An investigation of repressed inflation in the USSR, as caused by wage fund overexpenditures and evasion of financial controls by enterprise managers.

Fedorenko, N[ikolay P.]. "Prices and Optimal Planning." PROBLEMS OF ECONOMICS 10 (November 1967): 11-21.

A statement of the principles governing the elaboration of optimal plans and the relationships between price and the optimal plan.

Frisch, Ragnar. "Rational Price Fixing in a Socialistic Society." ECONOMICS OF PLANNING 6 (1966): 97-124.

A theoretical analysis of price formation for a centrally planned economy.

Ganczer, Sandor. "Price Calculations in Hungary on the Basis of Mathematical

Methods." ECONOMICS OF PLANNING 5 (1965): 67-79.

> A brief survey of the five price systems considered and discussed in Hungary through 1965.

Grossman, Gregory. "Industrial Prices in the USSR." AMERICAN ECONOMIC REVIEW 49 (May 1959): 50-64.

> An inquiry into the role of prices in the Soviet economy during 1929-57.

Hewett, Edward A. FOREIGN TRADE PRICES IN THE COUNCIL FOR MUTUAL ECONOMIC ASSISTANCE. New York: Cambridge University Press, 1974. 196 p. Tables, figures, and index.

> A survey of literature on CMEA foreign trade price determination, analysis of CMEA foreign trade prices and their influence on intra-CMEA trade flows, and discussion of the proposals for reforming the CMEA pricing system.

Holzman, Franklyn D. "Commodity and Income Taxation in the Soviet Union." JOURNAL OF POLITICAL ECONOMY 58 (October 1950): 425-33.

> An exploration of the approaches open to the decision makers in the USSR in solving the problem of inflation.

_____. "Soviet Inflationary Pressures, 1928-1957: Causes and Cures." QUARTERLY JOURNAL OF ECONOMICS 74 (May 1960): 167-88. Tables.

> An analysis of Soviet price and wage trends.

_____. SOVIET TAXATION: THE FISCAL AND MONETARY PROBLEMS OF A PLANNED ECONOMY. Cambridge, Mass.: Harvard University Press, 1955. xix, 375 p. Tables, appendix, and index.

> An examination of the theory, alternative methods, and actual burden and functions of Soviet taxation.

Jasny, Naum. SOVIET INDUSTRIALIZATION, 1928-1952. Chicago: University of Chicago Press, 1961. xviii, 467 p. Tables, figures, appendixes, and index.

> A careful and thorough examination of the Soviet experience with industrialization, agriculture, investment, prices, transportation, and retail trade.

_____. THE SOVIET PRICE SYSTEM. Stanford, Calif.: Stanford University Press, 1951. ix, 179 p. Tables, figures, appendix, and index.

> A study of Soviet wages, producer prices, consumer prices, farm prices, and price-forming factors.

_____. "The Soviet Price System." AMERICAN ECONOMIC REVIEW 40 (December 1950): 845-62. Tables.

    An analysis of Soviet wage-price relationships, taxes, inflation, and budgetary expenditures.

_____. SOVIET PRICES OF PRODUCERS' GOODS. Stanford, Calif.: Stanford University Press, 1952. vii, 180 p. Tables, appendix, and index.

    A careful examination of Soviet fuel and metals prices, construction costs, and railway costs and rates.

Kalinov, Stefan, and Yordanov, Ivan. "Some Problems of Price Formation under the New System of Management of the National Economy." EASTERN EUROPEAN ECONOMICS 5 (Spring 1967): 9-16.

    A discussion concerning methods of price formation and the role of prices under the Bulgarian reform.

Kaplan, Norman M., and Wainstein, Eleanor S. "A Comparison of Soviet and American Retail Prices in 1950." JOURNAL OF POLITICAL ECONOMY 64 (December 1956): 470-91. Tables.

    A comparison of U.S. and USSR prices and real wages for 1950.

Karmiloff, G. "Soviet Economic Models, Investment Criteria and Prices." KYKLOS 16 (1963): 83-110.

    An analytical review of Soviet economic models, investment criteria, and the effects of mathematical analysis on economic theory.

Komin, A. "Economic Reform and Tasks in Further Improving Price Formation." PROBLEMS OF ECONOMICS 11 (December 1968): 39-46.

    A discussion of the role of wholesale prices and new methodological approaches to price formation in the USSR.

_____. "Price Formation--A Major Aspect of Economic Management." PROBLEMS OF ECONOMICS 17 (December 1974): 28-45.

    An elaboration on the role of central price determination in economic management.

_____. "Price Formation under the Ninth Five-Year Plan." PROBLEMS OF ECONOMICS 15 (October 1972): 23-40.

    An outline of the methods to increase the incentive role of prices in the USSR.

_____. "Problems in the Methodology and Practice of Planned Price Formation." PROBLEMS OF ECONOMICS 16 (May 1973): 35-49.

An examination of the role of costs of production, profitability, technical progress, capital intensity, and rent as they affect planned price formation.

Kondrashev, D. "The Development of Price Formation in the USSR." PROB-LEMS OF ECONOMICS 10 (March 1968): 30-37.

A historical survey of price formation in the Soviet Union from 1917 to 1967.

_____. "Development of the Wholesale Price System in Industry." PROBLEMS OF ECONOMICS 5 (December 1962): 40-47.

An explanation of the reasons for the revision of industrial whole-sale prices in the Soviet Union.

Kotov, V. "Prices: The Instrument of National Economic Planning and the Basis of the Value Indices of the Plan." PROBLEMS OF ECONOMICS 16 (May 1973): 50-69.

An assessment of the role of prices in the Soviet planned economy.

Kuligin, P. "Improvement of Price Formation under the Economic Reform." PROBLEMS OF ECONOMICS 12 (October 1969): 27-41.

An orthodox view according to which improvement of price forma-tion under the economic reform amounts to the "further consolida-tion of centralized planning."

Lur'e, A. "Price Formation and Comparison of Different Variants of Economic Measures." PROBLEMS OF ECONOMICS 10 (August 1967): 3-12.

A discussion of the role of shadow prices in price formation.

Maizenberg, L. "Improvements in the Wholesale Price System." PROBLEMS OF ECONOMICS 13 (February 1971): 49-72.

An explanation of the 1967 wholesale price system and its impact on product quality and enterprise accountability.

Mitrofanova, N. "Concerning the Interrelationship between Internal and For-eign Trade Prices in European Socialist Countries." PROBLEMS OF ECONOM-ICS 17 (May 1974): 85-97.

A study of the factors determining foreign trade prices and of the relationship between foreign trade and internal prices.

Montias, John Michael. "Price-Setting Problems in the Polish Economy." JOURNAL OF POLITICAL ECONOMY 65 (December 1957): 486-505.

A close look at price setting under central planning, the Polish experience with prices during 1949-56, and suggestions by Polish economists for a workable price system.

Moskoff, William, and Benz, G. William. "The USSR and Developing Countries: Politics and Export Prices, 1955-69." SOVIET STUDIES 24 (January 1973): 348-63. Tables and appendix.

A report on Soviet price policy toward the LDC's as a group, and on pricing practices in relation to political policy concerning individual countries.

Nemchinov, V. "Value and Price under Socialism." PROBLEMS OF ECONOMICS 4 (July 1961): 3-17.

A theoretical analysis of value and price under socialism.

Nimitz, Nancy. "Soviet Agricultural Prices and Costs." In COMPARISONS OF THE UNITED STATES AND SOVIET ECONOMIES, Joint Economic Committee, 86th Cong., 1st sess., pp. 239-84. Washington, D.C.: Government Printing Office, 1959. Tables and appendix.

An examination of agricultural procurement prices and realized prices and collective farm costs of production.

Nove, Alec. "The Changing Role of Soviet Prices." ECONOMICS OF PLANNING 3 (December 1963): 185-95.

Thoughts on the role of prices in the Stalin period and on post-Stalin price discussions in the USSR.

Novozhilov, V.[V.]. "Calculation of Outlays in a Socialist Economy." PROBLEMS OF ECONOMICS 4 (December 1962): 18-28.

An analysis of the relations between scarcity and value.

Oxenfeldt, Alfred R., and Van den Haag, Ernest. "Unemployment in Planned and Capitalist Economies." QUARTERLY JOURNAL OF ECONOMICS 68 (February 1954): 43-60.

An investigation of the problems of unemployment and inflation in market and centrally planned economies.

Oyrzanowski, Bronislaw. "Problems of Inflation under Socialism." In INFLATION: PROCEEDINGS OF A CONFERENCE HELD BY THE INTERNATIONAL ECONOMIC ASSOCIATION, edited by D.C. Hague, pp. 332-41. New York: St. Martin's Press, 1962.

A theoretical discussion, based upon Polish experience, of possible inflationary problems of centrally planned economies.

Pickersgill, Joyce E. "Hyperinflation and Monetary Reform in the Soviet Union, 1921-26." JOURNAL OF POLITICAL ECONOMY 76 (September-October 1968): 1037-48. Tables.

A specification of the demand function for money in the USSR by observing alterations in individuals' portfolios during and immediately after the hyperinflation of the early 1920s.

Reiher, Klaus, and Schierz, Erich. "The Relation between Prices and Production-Financial Planning in the New Economic System." EASTERN EUROPEAN ECONOMICS 5 (Summer 1967): 40-51. Tables.

An examination of the influence of prices on planning methods and of planning on prices in the East German economic reforms of the 1960s.

Rubinshtein, M. "Scientific and Technical Progress and Planned Price Formation." PROBLEMS OF ECONOMICS 16 (July 1973): 22-36.

A description of price formation and the role of Soviet prices.

Rychetnik, Ludek. "The Growth of Inflationary Pressure: 1955-1966." EASTERN EUROPEAN ECONOMICS 7 (Spring 1969): 3-11.

An investigation of the extent and reasons for inflationary pressures in Czechoslovakia during 1955-66.

Schroeder, Gertrude E. "The 1966-67 Soviet Industrial Price Reform: A Study in Complications." SOVIET STUDIES 20 (April 1969): 462-77. Tables.

A discussion of the functioning of the Soviet price fixing apparatus, the objectives of price reform, and the effects of the price revision.

Shekerov, Yordan. "The Problem of Bringing Commodity Prices Closer to Value and of Changes in Price Relationships." EASTERN EUROPEAN ECONOMICS 3 (Fall 1964): 37-43. Tables.

Discussion by Bulgarian economists concerning producer and consumer price formation.

Simon, Gyorgy. "Ex Post Examination of Macro-Economic Shadow Prices." ECONOMICS OF PLANNING 5 (1965): 80-93. Tables.

An insight into the calculation of shadow prices in Hungarian programming models; estimates of the deviation of actual from shadow prices during 1959-63.

Sirc, Ljubo. ECONOMIC DEVOLUTION IN EASTERN EUROPE. London: Longmans, Green and Co., 1969. xii, 165 p. Tables and appendix.

An analysis of Eastern European economic problems as they pertain to pricing, foreign trade, economic growth, planning methods, and economic reforms.

Sitnin, V. "The Economic Reform and the Revision of Wholesale Prices for Industrial Goods." PROBLEMS OF ECONOMICS 9 (December 1966): 15-23.

A glance at the role of prices and profitability and a call for wholesale price revision.

Stoliarov, S. "The Price of Industrial Output." PROBLEMS OF ECONOM-ICS 6 (September 1966): 15-19.

An explanation of the manner of fixing prices, including the determination of industrial and enterprise wholesale prices and of retail prices.

Sztyber, Wladyslaw. "Theoretical Basis for the Reform of Sale Prices in Socialist Countries." EASTERN EUROPEAN ECONOMICS 9 (Winter 1970-71): 91-131.

A discussion of the nature, scope, and extent of price reforms which were carried out in the Soviet-type economies during the 1960s.

Tarnovskii, O. "Price Formation on the World Socialist Market." PROBLEMS OF ECONOMICS 12 (October 1969): 42-57.

An explanation of the prices used in CMEA trade (i.e., world market prices, corrected for cyclical and monopoly factors).

Turetskii, Sh. "Price and Its Role in the System of Economic Methods of Management." PROBLEMS OF ECONOMICS 10 (May 1967): 3-14.

General remarks on the role of price policy in economic management.

_____. "Price Formation and Balance Relationships." PROBLEMS OF ECO-NOMICS 13 (August 1970): 21-35.

An essay on the impact of price changes on various balance relationships (interbranch proportions, interdependence among consumption, accumulation).

Wakar, Aleksy, and Zielinski, Janusz G. "Socialist Operational Price Systems." AMERICAN ECONOMIC REVIEW 53 (March 1963): 109-27.

A statement on the connections between prices and gross output, profit, and value-added incentives.

Ward, Benjamin [N.]. "The Planners' Choice Variables." In VALUE AND PLAN--ECONOMIC CALCULATION AND ORGANIZATION IN EASTERN EUROPE, edited by Gregory Grossman, pp. 132-51. Berkeley and Los Angeles: University of California Press, 1960.

A contribution dealing with the role of prices and that of other economic levers in short-term Soviet-type planning.

Wilczynski, J. SOCIALIST ECONOMIC DEVELOPMENT AND REFORMS. New York: Praeger, 1972. xvii, 350 p. Tables and index.

A discussion of growth strategy, orthodox planning practices, prices, financial and monetary policies, foreign trade criteria and practices, reforms, and growth performance in the Soviet-type economies.

Wiles, P[eter]. J.D. THE POLITICAL ECONOMY OF COMMUNISM. Oxford: Basil Blackwell, 1962. xv, 404 p. Tables, figures, and index.

A critical, analytical examination of the major issues relevant to the study of Soviet-type economies: economic organization; planning and resource allocation, including pricing, planners' preferences, and decentralization; and growth strategy and performance.

_____. "Scarcity, Marxism, and Gosplan." OXFORD ECONOMIC PAPERS 5 (October 1953): 288-316.

An argument stressing that Marxism is incompatible with the rational allocation of resources.

Wyczalkowski, Marcin R. "The Soviet Price System and the Ruble Exchange Rate." INTERNATIONAL MONETARY FUND STAFF PAPERS 1 (September 1950): 203-23.

An examination of Soviet price formation in 1950, the meaning of the ruble exchange rate, and the significance of ruble revaluation.

Zauberman, Alfred. "The Soviet Debate on the Law of Value and Price Formation." In VALUE AND PLAN--ECONOMIC CALCULATION AND ORGANIZATION IN EASTERN EUROPE, edited by Gregory Grossman, pp. 17-35. Berkeley and Los Angeles: University of California Press, 1960.

A systematic survey of the principal Soviet debates on price formation during the late 1950s.

Chapter 7

CAPITAL AND INVESTMENT

Abouchar, Alan. "The New Soviet Standard Methodology for Investment Allocation." SOVIET STUDIES 24 (January 1973): 402-10.

A review of the changes between the 1959 and 1969 methods for investment allocation.

Bajt, Alexander. "Investment Cycles in European Socialist Economies: A Review Article." JOURNAL OF ECONOMIC LITERATURE 9 (March 1971): 53-63. Figures.

A survey of Soviet and East European literature dealing with the meaning and occurrence of investment cycles in Communist countries.

Bettelheim, Charles. "The Discussion on the Problem of Choice between Alternative Investment Projects." SOVIET STUDIES 2 (July 1950): 22-42. Tables.

A comparison and explanation of Western and Soviet views concerning the problem of resource allocation in a Soviet-type economy.

Brubaker, Earl R. "The Age of Capital and Growth in the Soviet Nonagricultural and Nonresidential Sector." SOVIET STUDIES 21 (January 1970): 350-59. Tables.

An attempt to explore the quantitative importance of the contribution to growth of technical change as it was embodied in fixed capital investments in the Soviet nonagricultural nonresidential sector.

_____. "Embodied Technology, the Asymptotic Behavior of Capital's Age, and Soviet Growth." REVIEW OF ECONOMICS AND STATISTICS 50 (August 1968): 304-11. Tables.

An analysis of the relationship between embodied technical change and Soviet growth.

Bunich, P. "The New Depreciation Allowance Rates and Control over Their Application by Financial Agencies." PROBLEMS OF ECONOMICS 6 (March 1964): 36–42. Tables.

> An explanation of depreciation rates effective 1 January 1963 and a comparison between these rates and those prevailing prior to 1963.

Campbell, Robert W. "Accounting for Depreciation in the Soviet Economy." QUARTERLY JOURNAL OF ECONOMICS 70 (November 1956): 481–506. Tables.

> A discussion of the Soviet method of fixed asset valuation and depreciation rate determination.

Eidel'man, M. "On the Question of the Structure of Fixed Capital in the USSR." PROBLEMS OF ECONOMICS 13 (October 1970): 22–46. Tables.

> Provision of basic indexes of the interbranch balance of fixed capital for 1966 in a consolidated grouping, showing the availability and composition of the fixed productive capital of the USSR.

Emel'ianov, A., and Krasovskii, V. "Methods of Determining the Economic Effectiveness of Mechanization and Automation." PROBLEMS OF ECONOMICS 3 (March 1961): 29–35.

> An illustration of investment efficiency calculations in industry, agriculture, and construction.

Fallenbuchl, Z[bigniew]. M. "Investment Policy for Economic Development: Some Lessons of the Communist Experience." CANADIAN JOURNAL OF ECONOMICS AND POLITICAL SCIENCE 29 (February 1963): 26–39.

> An examination of Communist investment theories within the framework of Communist investment experience.

_____. "Some Structural Aspects of Soviet-Type Investment Policy." SOVIET STUDIES 16 (April 1965): 432–47.

> An exposition of the relationships between Soviet investment policy and (1) the structure of aggregate demand and aggregate supply (2) the relative rates of growth of the producer and consumer goods sectors and (3) the possible adverse effects on growth resulting from the stress on the expansion of heavy industry.

Granick, David. "Economic Development and Productivity Analysis: The Case of Soviet Metalworking." QUARTERLY JOURNAL OF ECONOMICS 71 (May 1957): 205–33.

> An examination of the problem of factor proportions and the substitution of labor for capital in the Soviet economy.

Grossman, Gregory. "Scarce Capital and Soviet Doctrine." QUARTERLY JOURNAL OF ECONOMICS 67 (August 1953): 311-43.

An examination, in historical perspective, of the conflict between Marxist value theory and the problem of resource allocation in the Soviet economy.

Hardt, John P. "Industrial Investment in the U.S.S.R." In COMPARISONS OF THE UNITED STATES AND SOVIET ECONOMIES, Joint Economic Committee, 86th Cong., 1st sess., pp. 121-41. Washington, D.C.: Government Printing Office, 1959. Appendix.

An evaluation of Soviet industrial investment policy under Stalin and Krushchev.

Holzman, Franklyn D. "The Soviet Ural-Kuznetsk Combine: A Study in Investment Criteria and Industrialization Policies." QUARTERLY JOURNAL OF ECONOMICS 71 (August 1957): 368-405. Tables.

A review of the history of the Ural-Kuznetsk Combine; evaluation of the Combine in terms of the planners' objectives on the basis of a social marginal productivity criterion.

Hunter, Holland. "The Planning of Investments in the Soviet Union." REVIEW OF ECONOMICS AND STATISTICS 31 (February 1949): 54-62.

An assessment of Khachaturov's ideas concerning the rational allocation of investible resources; some comparisons with related Western concepts.

Huszar, J., and Mandel, M. "The Investment Decision-Making System in Hungary." EASTERN EUROPEAN ECONOMICS 11 (Spring 1973): 27-49. Tables.

A description of the system of investment allocation in Hungary during 1968-72.

Jackson, Marvin R. "Information and Incentives in Planning Soviet Investment Projects." SOVIET STUDIES 23 (July 1971): 3-25.

An illustration of the Soviet system of investment project decision making, including a discussion of investment problems and their sources.

Jarkovsky, Vladimir. "The Dynamic Determination of Economically Efficient Capital Investment and New Technology." EASTERN EUROPEAN ECONOMICS 11 (Summer 1973): 86-112. Figures.

An analysis of investment efficiency calculations in Czechoslovakia, including a discussion of the methods and basic considerations of determining economic efficiency, the question of capital asset retirement, and the determination of the optimum size and life of plants.

Jasny, Naum. SOVIET INDUSTRIALIZATION, 1928-1952. Chicago: University of Chicago Press, 1961. xviii, 467 p. Tables, figures, appendixes, and index.

A careful and thorough examination of the Soviet experience with industrialization, agriculture, investment, prices, transportation, and retail trade.

Kaplan, Norman. "Capital Stock." In ECONOMIC TRENDS IN THE SOVIET UNION, edited by Abram Bergson and Simon Kuznets, pp. 96-149. Cambridge, Mass.: Harvard University Press, 1963. Tables and appendix.

A description of and comments on the 1959 Soviet capital revaluation procedures and on the allocation of capital in the USSR.

Karmiloff, G. "Soviet Economic Models, Investment Criteria and Prices." KYKLOS 16 (1963): 83-110.

An analytical review of Soviet economic models, investment criteria, and the effects of mathematical analysis on economic theory.

Khachaturov, T. "The Economic Effectiveness of Capital Investments." PROBLEMS OF ECONOMICS 10 (September 1967): 3-12.

Remarks concerning past results and future perspectives for investment effectiveness.

_____. "The Economic Reform and Problems of the Effectiveness of Capital Investments." PROBLEMS OF ECONOMICS 10 (March 1968): 12-24.

An examination of the principles and techniques for calculating the effectiveness of capital investments prior to and under the 1965 reform.

_____. "Ways of Increasing the Economic Effectiveness of Capital Investments." PROBLEMS OF ECONOMICS 7 (September 1964): 29-39.

Some thoughts concerning the ways of reducing the capital-output ratio.

Klykov, V. "Joint Capital Construction in Comecon Countries and the Determination of Its Economic Effectiveness." PROBLEMS OF ECONOMICS 16 (January 1974): 91-104.

A consideration of the rationale for and the respective benefits of joint capital construction projects within the CMEA.

Kouba, Karel. "Investment and Economic Growth in Czechoslovakia." In PLANNING AND MARKETS: MODERN TRENDS IN VARIOUS ECONOMIC SYSTEMS, edited by John T. Dunlap and Nikolay P. Fedorenko, pp. 229-40. New York: McGraw-Hill Book Co., 1969. Tables.

An investigation of short and long-term trends in investment and economic growth in Czechoslovakia.

Kvasha, Ia. "Direct and Total Capital-Output Ratios in Consumer Goods." PROBLEMS OF ECONOMICS 15 (June 1972): 22-44. Tables.

A discussion of methods of calculation of capital-output ratios, accompanied by numerical ratios for various branches and groups of branches.

Kvasha, Ia., and Krasovskii, V. "Economic Effectiveness of Capital Investments." PROBLEMS OF ECONOMICS 4 (February 1962): 21-29. Tables.

An attempt to explore the relation between investment effectiveness and growth rates and the ways of increasing the economic efficiency of capital investments.

Malyshev, P.A. "The Capital-Output Ratio and the Rate of Socialist Accumulation." PROBLEMS OF ECONOMICS 8 (September 1965): 27-34. Tables.

An examination of the prospects of raising investment efficiency.

Moorsteen, Richard, and Powell, Raymond P. THE SOVIET CAPITAL STOCK, 1928-1962. A publication of the Economic Growth Center, Yale University. Homewood, Ill.: Richard D. Irwin, 1966. xxiii, 671 p. Tables and appendixes.

A provision of basic capital estimates, analysis of those estimates, and examination of the contribution of the Soviet capital stock (and the growth of that stock) to the growth of the Soviet economy.

Neuberger, Egon. "The Theory of Interest in Centrally Planned Economies." ECONOMIA INTERNAZIONALE 14 (1961): 616-32.

Analysis of theoretical aspects of the problem of using a rate of interest in planned economies.

Nuti, Domenico Mario. "Capitalism, Socialism and Steady Growth." ECONOMIC JOURNAL 80 (March 1970): 32-57. Figures and appendix.

An investigation of the choice of production techniques from the standpoint of both the Socialist planner, who is maximizing per capita consumption consistent with the maintenance of a given growth rate, and the capitalist entrepreneur, who is maximizing his firm's assets at a given rate of interest.

_____. "Investment Reforms in Czechoslovakia." SOVIET STUDIES 21 (January 1970): 360-70.

A summary of the investment rules prevailing in Czechoslovakia before and after 1967, in light of their implications for economic planning.

Poletaev, P. "Capital Investment in Agriculture." PROBLEMS OF ECO-
NOMICS 14 (February 1972): 19-34.

An explanation of the further need for agricultural investments,
and an assessment of the expected results of such investments.

Rakowski, Mieczyslaw, ed. EFFICIENCY OF INVESTMENT IN A SOCIALIST
ECONOMY. Translated by Eugene Lepa. New York: Pergamon Press, 1963.
xi, 528 p. Tables, figures, and index.

A compilation of essays, written by Polish economists, concerning
both theoretical problems and actual applications of investment
efficiency calculations.

Raskin, G. "Capital Investments in Agriculture and the Calculation of Their
Effectiveness." PROBLEMS OF ECONOMICS 4 (February 1962): 38-44.
Tables.

A discussion concerning the efficiency of agricultural investments.

Rychlewski, Eugeniusz. "The Investment System of a Socialist Economy."
EASTERN EUROPEAN ECONOMICS 12 (Fall 1973): 3-44. Figures.

A discussion of the organization and functioning of the Polish investment system, including the financing and allocation of investment.

Senchagov, V. "Capital Charges and Their Stimulating Role." PROBLEMS OF
ECONOMICS 15 (June 1972): 80-99.

An examination of the nature of capital charges from the standpoint
of their proposed function as economic incentives.

_____. "Improving the System of Payments for Fixed and Working Capital."
PROBLEMS OF ECONOMICS 15 (October 1972): 41-54.

A survey of the actual role of capital charges in the economy.

Sitarian, S., et al. "Principles of Establishing Norms of Payment for Productive Capital." PROBLEMS OF ECONOMICS 10 (July 1967): 26-33.

A statement concerning the rationale for payment for the use of
productive capital.

Thornton, Judith. "Differential Capital Charges and Resource Allocation in
Soviet Industry." JOURNAL OF POLITICAL ECONOMY 79 (May/June 1971):
545-61. Tables and appendixes.

An estimate of the output loss attributable to differential capital
charges in Soviet industry.

United Nations. Economic Commission for Europe. "A Fifteen-Year Review of In-

vestment and Output in Eastern Europe and the Soviet Union." ECONOMIC BUL-
LETIN FOR EUROPE 18 (November 1966): 31–64. Tables, figures, and appendix.

A survey of the changes in the volume of investment, its composition, and output effects between 1950 and 1965.

Vikhliaev, A.V. "Theoretical and Statistical Problems Concerning the Capital-
Output Ratio for the Social Product." PROBLEMS OF ECONOMICS 15 (May
1972): 48–68. Tables.

An explanation of the economic content of and changes in capital-
output ratios, accompanied by certain international comparisons.

Zauberman, Alfred. "A Note on Soviet Capital Controversy." QUARTERLY
JOURNAL OF ECONOMICS 69 (August 1955): 445–51.

Careful comments on the Soviet debate on investment criteria.

_____. "The Soviet and Polish Quest for a Criterion of Investment Efficiency."
ECONOMICA 29 (August 1962): 234–54.

An analysis of Polish and Soviet investment criteria.

Chapter 8

POPULATION AND LABOR FORCE

Artemev, Vyacheslav. "Labour Camps and Colonies." STUDIES ON THE SO-
VIET UNION 1, no. 4 (1961): 37-42.

A brief review of the history of forced labor in the USSR.

Berent, Jerzy. "Causes of Fertility Decline in Eastern Europe and the Soviet
Union: Part I." POPULATION STUDIES 24 (March 1970): 35-58. Tables.

An investigation of the influence of demographic factors in the
decline of fertility.

_____. "Causes of Fertility Decline in Eastern Europe and the Soviet Union:
Parts II and III." POPULATION STUDIES 24 (July 1970): 247-92. Tables.

An assessment of the role of economic and social factors in the
decline of fertility in the USSR and Eastern Europe.

Brackett, James W. "Demographic Trends and Population Policy in the Soviet
Union." In DIMENSIONS OF SOVIET ECONOMIC POWER, Joint Economic
Committee, 87th Cong., 2d sess., pp. 487-589. Washington, D.C.: Gov-
ernment Printing Office, 1962. Tables, figures, and appendix.

An examination of the size and composition of the Soviet population, population changes during the period of Communist rule, Soviet population policies, and prospective demographic trends through
1980.

Brackett, James W., and DePauw, John W. "Population Policy and Demographic Trends in the Soviet Union." In NEW DIRECTIONS IN THE SOVIET
ECONOMY, Joint Economic Committee, 89th Cong., 2d sess., pp. 593-702.
Washington, D.C.: Government Printing Office, 1966. Tables, figures, and
appendix.

A consideration of the implications of population problems for Soviet population policy, and an analysis of demographic trends between 1950 and 1965 with projections to 1985.

Bradley, Michael E. "Incentives and Labour Supply on Soviet Collective Farms." CANADIAN JOURNAL OF ECONOMICS 4 (August 1971): 342-52.

A theoretical analysis of the household's labor supply function and of the impact on labor supply of quotas and uncertainty.

Bronson, David W. "Scientific and Engineering Manpower in the USSR and Employment in R&D." In SOVIET ECONOMIC PROSPECTS FOR THE SEVEN-TIES, Joint Economic Committee, 93d Cong., 1st sess., pp. 564-93. Washington, D.C.: Government Printing Office, 1973. Tables, figures, and appendixes.

An estimate of the size and trends of Soviet engineering and scientific manpower and its share in R&D activities, and a description of the qualitative and organizational aspects of Soviet R&D manpower, accompanied by some U.S.-USSR comparisons.

Brown, Emily Clark. "Continuity and Change in the Soviet Labor Market." INDUSTRIAL AND LABOR RELATIONS REVIEW 23 (January 1970): 171-90.

An examination of labor supply and utilization in the USSR.

_____. SOVIET TRADE UNIONS AND LABOR RELATIONS. Cambridge, Mass.: Harvard University Press, 1966. ix, 394 p. Index.

An informative work, dealing with the history, structure, government, operation, and role of Soviet labor institutions.

Cohn, Helen Desfosses. "Population Policy in the USSR." PROBLEMS OF COMMUNISM 22 (July-August 1973): 41-55. Tables.

An analysis of the implications of declining birthrates and changes in the Soviet Union's ethnographic balance.

Dewar, Margaret. LABOUR POLICY IN THE USSR: 1917-1928. London: Royal Institute of International Affairs, 1956. viii, 286 p.

A careful examination of Soviet labor policy during the periods of war communism and New Economic Policy.

DeWitt, Nicholas. "Education and the Development of Human Resources: Soviet and American Effort." In DIMENSIONS OF SOVIET ECONOMIC POWER, Joint Economic Committee, 87th Cong., 2d sess., pp. 233-68. Washington, D.C.: Government Printing Office, 1962. Tables and figures.

A comparison of educational aims and the structure and performance of educational systems in the United States and USSR.

_____. "High-Level Manpower in the U.S.S.R." In NEW DIRECTIONS IN THE SOVIET ECONOMY, Joint Economic Committee, 89th Cong., 2d sess., pp. 789-816. Washington, D.C.: Government Printing Office, 1966. Tables.

A study of Soviet educational and manpower policies and of their effect on the supply of highly skilled and professional manpower.

Dodge, Norton T. "Fifty Years of Soviet Labour." STUDIES ON THE SO-VIET UNION 7, no. 1 (1967): 1–34. Tables.

A survey of major labor policy issues and practices in the USSR between 1917 and 1967.

_____. WOMEN IN THE SOVIET ECONOMY. Baltimore: Johns Hopkins Press, 1966. xviii, 331 p. Tables, figures, appendixes, and index.

Information on female industrial employment statistics. Educational achievement, jobs held, and labor force participation of women in the Soviet economy are discussed.

Eason, Warren W. "Comparisons of the United States and Soviet Economies: The Labor Force." In COMPARISONS OF THE UNITED STATES AND SOVIET ECONOMIES, Joint Economic Committee, 86th Cong., 1st sess., pp. 73–93. Washington, D.C.: Government Printing Office, 1959. Tables.

Comparisons of labor force trends, efficiency, and distribution according to various criteria.

_____. "Labor Force." In ECONOMIC TRENDS IN THE SOVIET UNION, edited by Abram Bergson and Simon Kuznets, pp. 38–95. Cambridge, Mass.: Harvard University Press, 1963. Tables and appendix.

An analysis of the quantitative and qualitative dimensions of Soviet labor supply and of the allocation of labor in the Soviet Union.

Elias, Andrew. "Magnitude and Distribution of the Labor Force in Eastern Europe." In ECONOMIC DEVELOPMENTS IN COUNTRIES OF EASTERN EUROPE, Joint Economic Committee, 91st Cong., 2d sess., pp. 149–239. Washington, D.C.: Government Printing Office, 1970. Tables, figures, and appendix.

A description of the changes in the size and distribution of the labor force in Eastern Europe on the basis of two measures: civilian employment and economically active population.

Feshbach, Murray. "Population." In ECONOMIC PERFORMANCE AND THE MILITARY BURDEN OF THE SOVIET UNION, Joint Economic Committee, 91st Cong., 2d sess., pp. 60–70. Washington, D.C.: Government Printing Office, 1970. Tables.

Estimates of vital rates, population growth and distribution between 1913 and 1970, and projected population growth through 1990.

_____. "Soviet Industrial Labor and Productivity Statistics." In SOVIET

ECONOMIC STATISTICS, edited by Vladimir G. Treml and John P. Hardt, pp. 195-228. Durham, N.C.: Duke University Press, 1972. Tables.

An explanation of Soviet industrial labor and productivity statistics.

Feshbach, Murray, and Rapawy, Stephen. "Labor Constraints in the Five Year Plan." In SOVIET ECONOMIC PROSPECTS FOR THE SEVENTIES, Joint Economic Committee, 93d Cong., 1st sess., pp. 485-563. Washington, D.C.: Government Printing Office, 1973.

An investigation of the possible existence of a labor shortage in the Soviet Union during the 1971-75 plan period, and an exploration of its implications for training and manpower utilization.

_____. "Labor and Wages." In ECONOMIC PERFORMANCE AND THE MILITARY BURDEN IN THE SOVIET UNION, Joint Economic Committee, 91st Cong., 2d sess., pp. 71-84. Washington, D.C.: Government Printing Office, 1970. Tables.

Estimates of population, labor force, civilian employment, labor turnover, and money wages.

Galetskaia, R. "The Demographic Situation in Comecon Member Nations." PROBLEMS OF ECONOMICS 17 (December 1974): 80-101. Tables.

A report on the size and growth rate of populations, marriages, divorces, school accommodations, and child support grants.

Gregory, Paul R., and Stuart, Robert C. SOVIET ECONOMIC STRUCTURE AND PERFORMANCE. New York: Harper & Row Publishers, 1974. x, 478 p. Tables, figures, and index. Paperback.

A comprehensive discussion and analysis of issues relevant to the Soviet economy. Included are discussions about war communism and the New Economic Policy, pricing, planning methods and principles, agriculture, growth strategy and performance, foreign trade, monetary and financial controls and policy, and economic reforms.

Hutchings, Raymond. SOVIET ECONOMIC DEVELOPMENT. New York: Barnes & Noble, 1971. xiii, 314 p. Tables, figures, appendix, and index.

An examination of the extent and causes of economic development during World War I, war communism, the New Economic Policy, and the plan era.

Ivanova, R. "Concerning the Development of the Eastern Regions and Their Manpower Supply." PROBLEMS OF ECONOMICS 16 (June 1973): 26-41.

A restatement of the reasons for the development of the eastern regions, with proposals for the assurance of continued manpower supplies for Siberia.

Jasny, Naum. "Labor and Output in Soviet Concentration Camps." JOURNAL OF POLITICAL ECONOMY 59 (October 1951): 405-19. Tables.

Estimates of the number and output of the inmates in Soviet concentration camps during 1940-41.

Kantner, John F. "The Population of the Soviet Union." In COMPARISONS OF THE UNITED STATES AND SOVIET ECONOMIES, Joint Economic Committee, 86th Cong., 1st sess., pp. 31-71. Washington, D.C.: Government Printing Office, 1959. Tables and appendix.

An examination of Soviet population and labor supply, including the role of demographic factors during the first forty years of Soviet development, precedes demographic comparisons between the United States and USSR.

Kuprienko, L. "Influence on the Standard of Living on the Movement of Labor Resources." PROBLEMS OF ECONOMICS 15 (September 1972): 61-77. Tables.

A discussion of wage levels, labor supply, and labor turnover according to branches of the national economy.

Ladenkov, V.N. "Studies of Migration of Skilled Personnel in Agriculture." PROBLEMS OF ECONOMICS 15 (February 1973): 62-80. Tables.

A study of data on agricultural migrants, and a discussion about reasons for migration.

Leedy, Frederick A. "Demographic Trends in The U.S.S.R.." In SOVIET ECONOMIC PROSPECTS FOR THE SEVENTIES, Joint Economic Committee, 93d Cong., 1st sess., pp. 428-84. Washington, D.C.: Government Printing Office, 1973. Tables, figures, and appendix.

A survey of population changes in the Soviet Union since 1950, including total population growth, changes in age and sex distribution, and trends in vital rates. Population projections, by age and sex, are given through the year 2000.

Maikov, A. "Labor Resources in the Ninth Five-Year Plan." PROBLEMS OF ECONOMICS 16 (February 1974): 28-43.

An examination of the territorial distribution and utilization of labor resources and the availability of additional reserves.

Myers, Paul F. "Demographic Trends in Eastern Europe." In ECONOMIC DEVELOPMENTS IN COUNTRIES OF EASTERN EUROPE, Joint Economic Committee, 91st Cong., 2d sess., pp. 68-148. Washington, D.C.: Government Printing Office, 1970. Tables, figures, and appendix.

Analysis of population changes and distribution primarily since 1950 in Eastern Europe, as well as estimates to 1990 of future population growth in the region.

_____. "Population and Labor Force in Eastern Europe: 1950 to 1996." In REORIENTATION AND COMMERCIAL RELATIONS OF THE ECONOMIES OF EASTERN EUROPE, Joint Economic Committee, 93d Cong., 2d sess., pp. 421-78. Washington, D.C.: Government Printing Office, 1974. Tables, figures, and appendix.

>Projections of population and labor force for Bulgaria, Czechoslovakia, East Germany, Hungary, Poland, and Rumania.

Nash, Edmund. "Recent Changes in Labor Controls in the Soviet Union." In NEW DIRECTIONS IN THE SOVIET ECONOMY, Joint Economic Committee, 89th Cong., 2d sess., pp. 849-71. Washington, D.C.: Government Printing Office, 1966. Tables.

>A discussion of measures for the relaxation of labor controls and the labor policies existing between 1956 and 1966.

Oxenfeldt, Alfred R., and Van den Haag, Ernest. "Unemployment in Planned and Capitalist Economies." QUARTERLY JOURNAL OF ECONOMICS 68 (February 1954): 43-60.

>A careful comparison of the problems of unemployment and inflation in market and centrally planned economies.

Prociuk, S.G. "The Manpower Problem in Siberia." SOVIET STUDIES 19 (October 1967): 190-210.

>A description of the excessive manpower fluctuations, the high costs of resettlement, the dissatisfaction of migrants, and the role of women in the Siberian labor force.

Redding, A. David. "Volume and Distribution of Nonagricultural Employment in the USSR, 1928-1955." AMERICAN SLAVIC AND EAST EUROPEAN REVIEW 13 (October 1954): 356-74. Tables and appendix.

>A brief investigation of Soviet employment trends by economic sectors during the plan era.

Rimlinger, Gaston V. "The Trade Union in Soviet Social Insurance: Historical Development and Present Functions." INDUSTRIAL AND LABOR RELATIONS REVIEW 14 (April 1961): 397-418.

>Comments on the organization of social insurance and the role of trade unions in the administration of social insurance programs.

Schroeder, Gertrude E. "An Appraisal of Soviet Wage and Income Statistics." In SOVIET ECONOMIC STATISTICS, edited by Vladimir G. Treml and John P. Hardt, pp. 287-314. Durham, N.C.: Duke University Press, 1972.

>A careful evaluation of Soviet statistics on money and real wages in agriculture and in the nonagricultural sectors.

_____. "Labor Planning in the USSR." SOUTHERN ECONOMIC JOURNAL 32 (July 1965): 63-72. Tables.

An evaluation of manpower planning in the USSR during 1928-60.

Searing, Marjory E. "Education and Economic Growth: The Postwar Experience in Hungary and Poland." In REORIENTATION AND COMMERCIAL RELATIONS OF THE ECONOMIES OF EASTERN EUROPE, Joint Economic Committee, 93d Cong., 2d sess., pp. 479-528. Washington, D.C.: Government Printing Office, 1974. Tables and appendix.

An assessment of the role of education in the economic development of Hungary and Poland.

Shipunov, V. "Effectiveness of Vocational-Technical Training of Workers." PROBLEMS OF ECONOMICS 16 (August 1973): 82-94.

A description of the various types of vocational training and the effects of such training on worker efficiency in the Soviet Union.

Sonin, M., and Zhiltsov, E. "Economic Development and Employment in the Soviet Union." INTERNATIONAL LABOUR REVIEW 96 (July 1967): 67-91. Tables.

A sympathetic examination of Soviet governmental policies on employment.

Stolper, Wolfgang F. "The Labor Force and Industrial Development in Soviet Germany." QUARTERLY JOURNAL OF ECONOMICS 71 (November 1957): 518-45. Tables.

An appraisal of the industrial development of East Germany, accompanied by relevant West German comparisons.

Swianiewicz, S. FORCED LABOUR AND ECONOMIC DEVELOPMENT: AN ENQUIRY INTO THE EXPERIENCE OF SOVIET INDUSTRIALIZATION. New York: Oxford University Press, 1965. ix, 321 p. Tables, appendix, and index.

A close look at the extent and role of forced labor in the economic development of the Soviet Union during 1928-41.

Vais, T., and Degtiar, L. "Collaboration of Comecon Countries in the Utilization of Labor Resources." PROBLEMS OF ECONOMICS 17 (June 1974): 24-34.

Suggestions for the creation of joint enterprises and temporary labor migration as ways of improving labor utilization within the Comecon.

Vermishev, K. "The Stimulation of Population Growth." PROBLEMS OF ECONOMICS 16 (June 1973): 3-13. Tables.

Reflections on the ways to stimulate population growth in the USSR.

Waedekin, Karl-Eugen. "Internal Migration and the Flight from the Land in the USSR, 1939-1959." SOVIET STUDIES 18 (October 1966): 131-52. Tables.

A reexamination of the movement of Soviet rural population between 1939 and 1959.

_____. "Manpower in Soviet Agriculture--Some Post-Krushchev Developments and Problems." SOVIET STUDIES 20 (January 1969): 281-305. Tables.

An examination of Soviet agricultural population and labor supply, wages, mechanization, and land improvement programs.

Weitzman, Murray S., et al. "Employment in the U.S.S.R.: Comparative U.S.S.R.-U.S. Data." In DIMENSIONS OF SOVIET ECONOMIC POWER, Joint Economic Committee, 87th Cong., 2d sess., pp. 591-667. Washington, D.C.: Government Printing Office, 1962. Tables, figures, and appendix.

An examination of labor utilization and management of the labor supply in the Soviet Union is followed by U.S.-USSR employment comparisons.

Wolfe, Bertram D. "Note on the Soviet Slave Labor Reform of 1954-55." RUSSIAN REVIEW 15 (January 1956): 57-59.

Comments on the use of forced labor in the USSR during the 1950s.

Chapter 9

WAGES AND CONSUMER WELFARE

Antosenkov, E.G. "The Availability of Housing and Personnel Turnover."
PROBLEMS OF ECONOMICS 16 (July 1973): 59-76.

A discussion of Soviet housing conditions, ownership, and needs.

Balinky, Alexander S. "Non-Housing Objectives of Soviet Housing Policy."
PROBLEMS OF COMMUNISM 10 (July-August 1961): 17-23.

An illumination of the dual character of Soviet housing policy
and of the impact of this policy on the supply of housing in the
USSR.

Bergson, Abram. THE STRUCTURE OF SOVIET WAGES. Cambridge, Mass.:
Harvard University Press, 1946. xvi, 255 p. Tables, figures, appendixes,
and index.

An analysis of the principles of wage determination and administration, as well as of wage differentiation.

Beskid, Lidia. "Real Wages in Poland During 1956-1967." EASTERN EURO-
PEAN ECONOMICS 7 (Spring 1969): 29-47. Tables.

An investigation of the extent of changes in real wages of manual
and white-collar workers in Poland during 1956-67.

Block, Alexander. "Soviet Housing: Some Town Planning Problems." SO-
VIET STUDIES 6 (July 1964): 1-15.

A study of urban planning and the supply and demand for housing
in the USSR.

_____. "Soviet Housing--The Historical Aspect." SOVIET STUDIES 5 (Jan-
uary 1954): 246-77. Tables.

An evaluation of the amount, cost, and quality of urban housing.

_____. "Soviet Housing--The Historical Aspect: Some Notes on Problems of

Policy--I." SOVIET STUDIES 3 (July 1951): 1-15.

> An examination of the number and types of housing units available
> in the USSR between 1910 and 1920.

_____. "Soviet Housing--The Historical Aspect: Some Notes on Problems of
Policy--II." SOVIET STUDIES 3 (January 1952): 229-57.

> A description of the construction, maintenance, and allocation of
> housing between 1920 and 1950.

Bronson, David W., and Severin, Barbara S. "Recent Trends in Consumption
and Disposable Money Income in the U.S.S.R." In NEW DIRECTIONS IN
THE SOVIET ECONOMY, Joint Economic Committee, 89th Cong., 2d sess.,
pp. 495-529. Washington, D.C.: Government Printing Office, 1966. Tables, figures, and appendixes.

> A survey of trends in consumption and disposable money income
> in the USSR, and an analysis of the implications of the divergence.

_____. "Soviet Consumer Welfare: The Brezhnev Era." In SOVIET ECO-
NOMIC PROSPECTS FOR THE SEVENTIES, Joint Economic Committee, 93d
Cong., 1st sess., pp. 376-403. Washington, D.C.: Government Printing
Office, 1973. Tables and appendixes.

> A detailed consideration of consumer welfare in the Soviet Union
> between 1965 and 1972, and a comparison with consumer welfare
> during the 1956-64 period.

Byrne, Terence E. "Levels of Consumption in Eastern Europe." In ECO-
NOMIC DEVELOPMENTS IN COUNTRIES OF EASTERN EUROPE, Joint Eco-
nomic Committee, 91st Cong., 2d sess., pp. 297-315. Washington, D.C.:
Government Printing Office, 1970. Tables, figures, and appendix.

> An examination of per capita consumption figures and accomplish-
> ments in specific fields of consumption, and the evolution of the
> regimes' policies toward consumption in Czechoslovakia, Hungary,
> and Poland.

Chapman, Janet G. "Consumption." In ECONOMIC TRENDS IN THE SO-
VIET UNION, edited by Abram Bergson and Simon Kuznets, pp. 235-82.
Cambridge, Mass.: Harvard University Press, 1963. Tables and appendix.

> Comparison of the level and pattern of consumption in the USSR
> with past and present levels and patterns of consumption in the
> United States.

_____. REAL WAGES IN SOVIET RUSSIA SINCE 1928. Cambridge, Mass.:
Harvard University Press, 1963. xiv, 395 p. Tables, figures, appendixes,
and index.

> A systematic attempt to measure changes in the cost of living and

in real wages in the USSR between 1928 and 1958 on the basis of Laspeyres and Paasche indexes.

Dalrymple, Dana G. "The Soviet Famine of 1932-1934." SOVIET STUDIES 15 (January 1964): 250-84.

A documented account of the manmade Soviet famine of 1932-34.

DiMaio, Alfred John, Jr. SOVIET URBAN HOUSING: PROBLEMS AND POLICIES. New York: Praeger, 1974. ix, 236 p. Tables.

An examination of the problems, policies, and achievements of urban planning, housing, construction, and allocation.

Erro, Imogene. "Trends in the Production of Consumer Goods." In DIMENSIONS OF SOVIET ECONOMIC POWER, Joint Economic Committee, 87th Cong., 2d sess., pp. 367-89. Washington, D.C.: Government Printing Office, 1962. Tables.

An assessment of the production record and growth problems of Soviet consumer goods industries during 1950-61.

Golden, Rachel E. "Recent Trends in Soviet Personal Income and Consumption." In DIMENSIONS OF SOVIET ECONOMIC POWER, Joint Economic Committee, 87th Cong., 2d sess., pp. 347-66. Washington, D.C.: Government Printing Office, 1962. Tables.

An investigation of the trends in the real personal disposable income of wage and salary earners and collective farmers as well as of changes in the consumption of foodstuffs, nonfood goods, and services during 1950-61.

Goldman, Marshall I. "Consumption Statistics." In SOVIET ECONOMIC STATISTICS, edited by Vladimir G. Treml and John P. Hardt, pp. 315-47. Durham, N.C.: Duke University Press, 1972. Tables.

A careful appraisal of Soviet consumption statistics.

_____. "The Reluctant Consumer and Economic Fluctuations in the Soviet Union." JOURNAL OF POLITICAL ECONOMY 78 (August 1965): 366-80. Tables.

An effort to explain the existence of sales, production, and inventory cycles in the Soviet Union by examining consumption tendencies and production practices.

Hanson, Philip. THE CONSUMER IN THE SOVIET ECONOMY. Evanston, Ill.: Northwestern University Press, 1968. ix, 249 p. Figures, tables, appendixes, and index.

A comparison of consumption trends in economic growth and industrialization, an examination of the causes of the severe constraints on consumption, an analysis of the retail price structure, and an explanation of the mechanism for adjusting supplies to consumer demand.

Holesovsky, Vaclav. "Personal Consumption in Czechoslovakia, Hungary, and Poland, 1950–1960: A Comparison." SLAVIC REVIEW 24 (December 1965): 622–35. Tables.

Comparison of consumption levels as well as rates of change and variability of personal consumption.

Kaplan, Norman M., and Wainstein, Eleanor S. "Comparison of Soviet and American Retail Prices in 1950." JOURNAL OF POLITICAL ECONOMY 64 (December 1956): 470–91. Tables.

A comparison of U.S. and USSR prices and real wages for 1950.

Kapustin, E., and Kuznetsova, N. "Regional Aspects in Raising the Population's Living Standard." PROBLEMS OF ECONOMICS 15 (August 1972): 83–100. Tables.

An examination of regional variations in the cost of market baskets, food expenditures, and expenditures on clothing.

Kirsch, Leonard Joel. SOVIET WAGES: CHANGES IN STRUCTURE AND ADMINISTRATION SINCE 1956. Cambridge, Mass.: MIT Press, 1972. xii, 237 p. Figures, tables, appendixes, and index.

A useful monograph, containing an explanation of the principles governing the determination and administration of Soviet wages, and a discussion of intra- and inter-industry wage differentiation.

Kravis, Irving B., and Mintzes, Joseph. "Food Prices in the Soviet Union, 1936–50." REVIEW OF ECONOMICS AND STATISTICS 32 (May 1950): 164–68. Tables.

A presentation of the difficulties entailed in the construction of consumers' price indexes for the Soviet Union, illustrated by some index number computations.

Kunel'skii, L. "The Principal Trend in the Growth of the Working People's Income." PROBLEMS OF ECONOMICS 11 (September 1968): 32–40.

Comments on the increases in minimum and average wages and the role of wages in the USSR.

Lomberg, Doris Pullman, and Turgeon, Lynn. "The Meaningfulness of Soviet Retail Prices." AMERICAN SLAVIC AND EAST EUROPEAN REVIEW 19 (April 1960): 217–33. Tables.

An analysis of Soviet price and wage structure, with Eastern European comparisons.

Madge, Charles. "Notes on the Standard of Living in Moscow, April 1952." SOVIET STUDIES 4 (January 1953): 229-36.

A comparison of Russian and British prices of food, clothing, and miscellaneous goods and services in 1952.

Madison, Bernice [Q.]. "Social Services for Families and Children in the Soviet Union since 1967." SLAVIC REVIEW 31 (December 1972): 831-52.

A description of the social programs for children in the USSR.

_____. SOCIAL WELFARE IN THE SOVIET UNION. Stanford, Calif.: Stanford University Press, 1968. xxvi, 298 p. Tables, figures, appendixes, and index.

An examination of various aspects of social welfare in the USSR, including family and child welfare, income maintenance, and vocational rehabilitation programs.

Nove, Alec. "Social Welfare in the USSR." PROBLEMS OF COMMUNISM 9 (January-February 1960): 1-10.

A survey of social welfare in the USSR. Health, education, social insurance, and other benefits are discussed and evaluated.

Pozdniakova, N. "On the Distribution of Incomes on Collective Farms." PROBLEMS OF ECONOMICS 15 (January 1973): 90-100. Tables.

Official Soviet figures on gross income and profitability of collective farms and the wages paid to collective farmers.

Prybyla, Jan S. "The Soviet Consumer in Krushchev's Russia." RUSSIAN REVIEW 20 (July 1961): 194-205. Tables.

An examination of trends in Soviet living standards.

Rimlinger, Gaston V. "The Trade Union in Soviet Social Insurance: Historical Development and Present Functions." INDUSTRIAL AND LABOR RELATIONS REVIEW 14 (April 1961): 397-418.

An examination of the organization of social insurance and the role of trade unions in the administration of social insurance programs.

Schroeder, Gertrude E. "An Appraisal of Soviet Wage and Income Statistics." In SOVIET ECONOMIC STATISTICS, edited by Vladimir G. Treml and John P. Hardt, pp. 287-314. Durham, N.C.: Duke University Press, 1972.

A careful evaluation of Soviet statistics on money and real wages in agriculture and in the nonagricultural sectors.

_____. "Consumer Problems and Prospects." PROBLEMS OF COMMUNISM

22 (March–April 1972): 10–24.

A discussion of major current consumer problems and the response of the Soviet leadership to these problems.

_____. "Consumption in the USSR: A Survey." STUDIES ON THE SOVIET UNION 10, no. 4 (1970): 1–40. Tables and appendixes.

A survey of overall consumption trends as well as trends in private, collective, urban, and rural consumption.

_____. "Industrial Wage Differentials in the USSR." SOVIET STUDIES 17 (January 1966): 303–17. Tables.

A discussion of the nature of the Soviet wage and salary system, and estimates of trends in average annual earnings, income inequality, differentials among broad occupational groups and among branches of industry.

Sosnovy, T[imothy]. "The Soviet Urban Housing Problem." AMERICAN SLAVIC AND EAST EUROPEAN REVIEW 11 (December 1952): 288–303. Tables.

A description of Soviet housing conditions prevailing before and during World War II.

_____. "Town Planning and Housing." SURVEY 38 (October 1961): 170–78. Tables.

A review of early Soviet concepts of urbanization, followed by an evaluation of the resulting housing policy.

Stadukhin, D., and Khaverson, M. "Social Consumption Funds and Living Standards of the Population." PROBLEMS OF ECONOMICS 11 (August 1968): 21–25. Tables.

Results of a survey of families of industrial workers in Sverdlovsk, designed to determine the influence on living standards of incomes obtained from social consumption funds.

Turgeon, Lynn. "Future Levels of Living in the U.S.S.R." ECONOMICS OF PLANNING 3 (September 1963): 149–65. Tables.

Information on the promises and prospects for Soviet consumers on the basis of the USSR's Twenty-Year Plan.

_____. "Levels of Living, Wages and Prices in the Soviet and United States Economies." In COMPARISONS OF THE UNITED STATES AND SOVIET ECONOMIES, Joint Economic Committee, 86th Cong., 1st sess., pp. 319–40. Washington, D.C.: Government Printing Office, 1959. Tables.

An examination of Soviet wages, retail prices, and standards of living, accompanied by U.S. comparisons.

Vogel, Heinrich. "Satisfaction of Consumer Needs." In THE DEVELOPMENT OF THE SOVIET ECONOMY: PLAN AND PERFORMANCE, edited by Vladimir G. Treml, pp. 197-212. New York: Frederick A. Praeger, 1968. Tables.

An examination of the changing position of the consumer in the Soviet economy.

Wiles, P[eter]. J.D., and Markowski, Stefan. "Income Distribution under Communism and Capitalism--Some Facts About Poland, the UK, the USA, and the USSR (Part I)." SOVIET STUDIES 22 (January 1971): 344-69. Tables and figures.

Attempts to make firm comparisons, based on identical concepts.

_____. "Income Distribution under Communism and Capitalism--Some Facts about Poland, the UK, the USA, and the USSR (Part II)." SOVIET STUDIES 22 (April 1971): 487-511. Tables and figures.

A study of income distribution, accompanied by intertemporal comparisons.

Yanowitch, Murray. "Changes in the Soviet Money Wage Level since 1940." AMERICAN SLAVIC AND EAST EUROPEAN REVIEW 14 (April 1955): 195-223. Tables.

An analysis of the changes in money wage rates in the USSR between 1940 and 1953.

Chapter 10

EFFICIENCY AND PRODUCTIVITY

Alton, Thad P[aul]. "Economic Growth and Resource Allocation in Eastern Europe." In REORIENTATION AND COMMERCIAL RELATIONS OF THE ECONOMIES OF EASTERN EUROPE, Joint Economic Committee, 93d Cong., 2d sess., pp. 251-98. Washington, D.C.: Government Printing Office, 1974. Tables and appendix.

> An analysis of rates of economic growth, changes in the structure of economic activity, and labor and capital productivity in Bulgaria, Czechoslovakia, East Germany, Hungary, Poland, and Rumania.

_____. "Economic Structure and Growth in Eastern Europe." In ECONOMIC DEVELOPMENTS IN COUNTRIES OF EASTERN EUROPE, Joint Economic Committee, 91st Cong., 2d sess., pp. 41-67. Washington, D.C.: Government Printing Office, 1970. Tables and appendix.

> A statistical approach, using both official data and independent estimates to describe the composition of economic activity, measure its growth, and show trends in labor and capital productivity in Eastern Europe.

Balassa, Bela [A.] "The Dynamic Efficiency of the Soviet Economy." AMERICAN ECONOMIC REVIEW 14 (May 1964): 490-505. Tables and appendix.

> An analysis of the dynamic efficiency of the Soviet economy, accompanied by comparisons with other countries.

Bergson, Abram. "Comparative Productivity and Efficiency in the Soviet Union and the United States." In COMPARISON OF ECONOMIC SYSTEMS: THEORETICAL AND METHODOLOGICAL APPROACHES, edited by Alexander Eckstein, pp. 161-218. Berkeley and Los Angeles: University of California Press, 1971. Tables and figures.

> A presentation of comparative data on U.S. and USSR productivity and an inquiry into the differences in efficiency between socialism (USSR) and capitalism (U.S.).

_____. PLANNING AND PRODUCTIVITY UNDER SOVIET SOCIALISM. New York: Columbia University Press, 1968. 95 p. Tables.

Bergson's 1967 Benjamin F. Fairless Memorial Lectures. He compares the Soviet economic system with the economies of a selected group of Western countries on the basis of static efficiency, dynamic efficiency, and productivity.

Berliner, Joseph S. "The Static Efficiency of the Soviet Economy." AMERICAN ECONOMIC REVIEW 54 (May 1964): 480-90. Tables and appendix.

An analysis of the static efficiency of the Soviet economy.

Boretsky, Michael. "Comparative Progress in Technology, Productivity, and Economic Efficiency: U.S.S.R. Versus U.S.A." In NEW DIRECTIONS IN THE SOVIET ECONOMY, Joint Economic Committee, 89th Cong., 2d sess., pp. 133-256. Washington, D.C.: Government Printing Office, 1966. Tables and appendixes.

Detailed comparisons of key indicators of technical progress, comparisons of growth in factor productivity, and examples of sources of inefficiency in the Soviet economy.

Borisenko, A., and Shastitko, V. "Problems of the Economic Efficiency of Foreign Trade in the Socialist Countries." PROBLEMS OF ECONOMICS 5 (March 1963): 56-62.

A discussion of the major foreign trade efficiency indexes employed by the Soviet-type economies.

Brada, Josef C. "Allocative Efficiency and the System of Economic Management in Some Socialist Countries." KYKLOS 27 (1974): 270-85.

A method for measuring the static efficiency of the export sector; it is found that allocative efficiency is inversely related to the level of development in the Eastern European Soviet-type economies.

Bradley, Michael E., and Clark, M. Gardner. "Supervision and Efficiency in Socialized Agriculture." SOVIET STUDIES 23 (January 1972): 464-76.

An investigation of the causes of low labor productivity on Soviet collective and state farms. Comparisons are made with labor productivity in American agriculture.

Brubaker, Earl R. "A Sectoral Analysis of Efficiency under Market and Plan." SOVIET STUDIES 23 (January 1972): 435-49. Tables and appendix.

Output per man-hour comparisons to examine relative efficiency in the major sectors of origin of national product.

Campbell, Robert W. "A Comparison of Soviet and American Inventory-Output Ratios." AMERICAN ECONOMIC REVIEW 48 (September 1958): 549-65. Tables.

A study and a comparison of measures of inventory and output for the U.S. and Soviet economies.

Cohn, Stanley H. "Soviet Growth Retardation: Trends in Resource Availability and Efficiency." In NEW DIRECTIONS IN THE SOVIET ECONOMY, Joint Economic Committee, 89th Cong., 2d sess., pp. 99-132. Washington, D.C.: Government Printing Office, 1966. Tables and appendixes.

An analysis of Soviet economic structure, trends in GNP, factor availability and productivity, and the future growth prospects of the USSR. Certain comparisons are made with the United States, United Kingdom, West Germany, Japan, France, and Italy.

Czirjak, Laszlo. "Industrial Structure, Growth, and Productivity in Eastern Europe." In ECONOMIC DEVELOPMENTS IN COUNTRIES OF EASTERN EUROPE, Joint Economic Committee, 91st Cong., 2d sess., pp. 434-62. Washington, D.C.: Government Printing Office, 1970. Tables and appendixes.

An examination of rates of growth and the structure of industry on the basis of factor costs, and a survey of trends in factor productivities.

Diamond, Douglas B. "Trends in Output, Inputs and Factor Productivity in Soviet Agriculture." In NEW DIRECTIONS IN THE SOVIET ECONOMY, Joint Economic Committee, 89th Cong., 2d sess., pp. 339-81. Washington, D.C.: Government Printing Office, 1966. Tables and appendixes.

A report on Soviet agricultural output (1950-65) and the use of inputs by the agricultural sector (1950-64), trends in inputs, output, and factor productivity, and the factors contributing to changes in measured productivity.

Diamond, Douglas [B.], and Krueger, Constance. "Recent Developments in Output and Productivity in Soviet Agriculture." In SOVIET ECONOMIC PROSPECTS FOR THE SEVENTIES, Joint Economic Committee, 93d Cong., 1st sess., pp. 316-39. Washington, D.C.: Government Printing Office, 1973. Tables and appendixes.

A review of trends in the output and productivity of Soviet agriculture between 1961-70, followed by an evaluation of the Brezhnev program for 1971-75.

Domar, Evsey D. "On the Measurement of Comparative Efficiency." In COMPARISON OF ECONOMIC SYSTEMS: THEORETICAL AND METHODOLOGICAL APPROACHES, edited by Alexander Eckstein, pp. 219-40. Berkeley and Los Angeles: University of California Press, 1971. Tables.

An analysis of arithmetic and geometric indexes for efficiency comparisons.

Emel'ianov, A., and Krasovskii, V. "Methods of Determining the Economic Effectiveness of Mechanization and Automation." PROBLEMS OF ECONOMICS

3 (March 1961): 29-35.

An illustration of the use of investment efficiency calculations in industry, agriculture, and construction.

Feiwel, George R. THE SOVIET QUEST FOR ECONOMIC EFFICIENCY--IS-SUES, CONTROVERSIES, AND REFORMS. 1967. Exp. and rev. New York: Praeger, 1972. xxiv, 790 p.

A very comprehensive and exhaustive treatment of the issues related to Soviet economic development, planning, efficiency, reform proposals, and implementation.

Goldman, Marshall I. "The Cost and Efficiency of Distribution in the Soviet Union." QUARTERLY JOURNAL OF ECONOMICS 76 (August 1962): 437-53. Tables.

A comparison of U.S. and Soviet distribution markups and explanation of the reasons for the lower Soviet distribution costs.

Hurwicz, Leonid. "Conditions for Economic Efficiency of Centralized and Decentralized Structures." In VALUE AND PLAN--ECONOMIC CALCULATION AND ORGANIZATION IN EASTERN EUROPE, edited by Gregory Grossman, pp. 162-75. Berkeley and Los Angeles: University of California Press, 1960.

A discussion of efficiency, Pareto-optimality, and social welfare functions in centralized and decentralized structures.

Jarkovsky, Vladimir. "The Dynamic Determination of Economically Efficient Capital Investment and New Technology." EASTERN EUROPEAN ECONOMICS 11 (Summer 1973): 86-112. Figures.

An analysis of investment efficiency calculations in Czechoslovakia, including a discussion of the methods and basic considerations of determining economic efficiency, the question of capital asset retirement, and problems of determining the optimum size and life of plants.

Kaplan, Norman M. "The Growth of Output and Inputs in Soviet Transport and Communications." AMERICAN ECONOMIC REVIEW 57 (December 1967): 1154-67. Tables.

After a summary of the results of an attempt to construct and use output indexes for Soviet transport and communication, an exploration of Soviet growth retardation by distinguishing between changes in the rates of increase in factor inputs and in combined factor productivity.

Kvasha, Ia., and Krasovskii, V. "Economic Effectiveness of Capital Investments." PROBLEMS OF ECONOMICS 4 (February 1962): 21-29. Tables.

An investigation of the relation between investment effectiveness and growth rates and ways of increasing the economic efficiency of capital investments.

Lazarcik, Gregor. "Agricultural Output and Productivity in Eastern Europe and Some Comparisons with the U.S.S.R. and U.S.A." In REORIENTATION AND COMMERCIAL RELATIONS OF THE ECONOMIES OF EASTERN EUROPE, Joint Economic Committee, 93d Cong., 2d sess., pp. 328-93. Washington, D.C.: Government Printing Office, 1974. Tables and appendixes.

A discussion of the role of agriculture in East European economies, the growth and structure of agricultural output and inputs, per capita trends and levels of agricultural output, and land and labor productivity trends. Additionally, size comparisons of output are made among Eastern Europe, the Soviet Union, and the United States.

Noren, James H. "Soviet Industry Trends in Output, Inputs, and Productivity." In NEW DIRECTIONS IN THE SOVIET ECONOMY, Joint Economic Committee, 89th Cong., 2d sess., pp. 271-325. Washington, D.C.: Government Printing Office, 1966. Tables, figures, and appendixes.

An authoritative analysis of the growth of Soviet industrial output, inputs, and factor productivity between 1951 and 1965 precedes an analysis of the causes of the decline in industrial growth during the 1950s and 1960s.

Notkin, A. [I.]. "Higher Economic Effectiveness and the Basic Proportions of Development of Social Production under the New Five-Year Plan." PROBLEMS OF ECONOMICS 7 (January 1965): 18-26.

An orthodox approach, stressing the importance of production efficiency and of the maintenance of the relative growth rates of agriculture and industry and of groups A and B (i.e., means of production and means of consumption, respectively) within industry.

Nuti, D[omenico]. M[ario]. "Discounting Methods in Polish Planning." SOVIET STUDIES 23 (October 1971): 309-17.

The efficiency index, adopted for Polish investment planning in 1970, is discussed and assessed.

Rakowski, Mieczyslav, ed. EFFICIENCY OF INVESTMENT IN A SOCIALIST ECONOMY. Translated by Eugene Lepa. New York: Pergamon Press, 1963. xi, 528 p. Tables, figures, and index.

Compilation of essays, written by Polish economists, concerning both theoretical problems and applications of investment efficiency calculations.

Shagalov, G. "The Economic Efficiency of the Socialist Countries' Foreign

Trade." PROBLEMS OF ECONOMICS 8 (December 1965): 49-60. Tables.

An explanation of indexes designed to measure the efficiency of Communist foreign trade.

Siman, Miklos. "Sources of Economic Growth in Hungary, 1967-1972." EASTERN EUROPEAN ECONOMICS 13 (Fall 1974): 25-58. Tables.

Presentation of economic growth statistics by major sectors and branches and appraisal of the role of capital and labor inputs, incomplete investments, capital-output ratios, and productivity changes in the growth of the Hungarian economy.

Snell, Edwin M. "Economic Efficiency in Eastern Europe." In ECONOMIC DEVELOPMENTS IN COUNTRIES OF EASTERN EUROPE, Joint Economic Committee, 91st Cong., 2d sess., pp. 240-96. Washington, D.C.: Government Printing Office, 1970. Tables and appendixes.

A critical examination of the growth of industry, lags in efficiency, terms of trade with the West, capital and labor productivity, and political consequences of economic problems.

Spulber, Nicolas, ed. FOUNDATIONS OF SOVIET STRATEGY FOR ECONOMIC GROWTH; SELECTED SOVIET ESSAYS, 1924-1930. Bloomington: Indiana University Press, 1964. xii, 530 p. Tables, figures, and index.

A compendium of articles (translated from the Russian), written by such notables as Preobrazhenski, Feldman, Shanin, Bazarov, Groman, and Strumilin. Topics include macroeconomic models, growth strategies, and planning theories and methods.

Thornton, Judith. "Value-Added and Factor Productivity in Soviet Industry." AMERICAN ECONOMIC REVIEW 60 (December 1970): 863-71. Tables.

Estimates, in constant and current prices, for Soviet industrial value-added for the period 1955-67.

Vainshtein, B. "The Theory of Effectiveness of Social Production." PROBLEMS OF ECONOMICS 13 (March 1971): 3-21.

An appraisal of various interpretations of the theory of economic effectiveness.

Vergner, Zdenek. "Problems of the Economic Level Already Attained in Czechoslovakia and of Its Future Development." EASTERN EUROPEAN ECONOMICS 1 (Spring 1963): 29-33.

A discussion of problems of economic structure, efficiency, and labor utilization.

Ward, Benjamin [N.]. "Kantorovich on Economic Calculation." JOURNAL OF POLITICAL ECONOMY 68 (December 1960): 545-56.

An instructive, analytical review of Kantorovich's THE BEST USE OF ECONOMIC RESOURCES.

Zauberman, Alfred. "The Soviet and Polish Quest for a Criterion of Investment Efficiency." ECONOMICA 29 (August 1962): 234-54.

An analysis of Polish and Soviet investment criteria.

Chapter 11

SECTORAL PROBLEMS AND ACCOMPLISHMENTS

AGRICULTURE

General

Adams, Arthur E., and Adams, Jan S. MEN VERSUS SYSTEMS: AGRICULTURE IN THE USSR, POLAND, AND CZECHOSLOVAKIA. New York: Free Press, 1971. viii, 327 p. Tables, figures, appendix, and index.

Essays concerning the Soviet agricultural model and its evolution and about agricultural conditions in the USSR, Poland, and Czechoslovakia.

Bazlova, A. "Improving Purchase Prices on Agricultural Output." PROBLEMS OF ECONOMICS 16 (July 1973): 37-58. Tables.

A discussion of the level, regional differentiation, and shortcomings of agricultural purchase prices.

Bradley, Michael E., and Clark, M. Gardner. "Supervision and Efficiency in Socialized Agriculture." SOVIET STUDIES 23 (January 1972): 464-76.

An investigation of the causes of low labor productivity on Soviet collective and state farms. Comparisons with labor productivity in American agriculture.

Bush, Keith. "Agricultural Reforms Since Krushchev." In NEW DIRECTIONS IN THE SOVIET ECONOMY, Joint Economic Committee, 89th Cong., 2d sess., pp. 451-72. Washington, D.C.: Government Printing Office, 1966. Tables.

A survey of the Soviet agricultural reforms which were announced following Krushchev's removal.

_____. "Soviet Agriculture in the 1970s." STUDIES ON THE SOVIET UNION 11, no. 3 (1971): 1-45. Tables.

A survey of agricultural inputs and outputs, prices and incentives, organization, and prospects.

Clarke, Roger A. "Soviet Agricultural Reforms Since Khrushchev." SOVIET STUDIES 20 (October 1968): 159-78. Tables.

A discussion of the changes in Soviet agriculture between 1965 and 1968 and an examination of the results attained.

Conklin, David W. AN EVALUATION OF THE SOVIET PROFIT REFORMS; WITH SPECIAL REFERENCE TO AGRICULTURE. New York: Frederick A. Praeger, 1970. xiii, 192 p. Tables and figures.

An analysis of the shift from traditional, command-type planning to a system which combines centralized and decentralized decisions as they apply to the agricultural sector.

Coogan, James. "Bread and the Soviet Fiscal System." REVIEW OF ECONOMICS AND STATISTICS 35 (May 1953): 161-67. Tables.

An evaluation of assessment and collection techniques of turnover taxes on grain and the importance of the grain economy in the Soviet fiscal structure.

Coulter, Harris L. "The Hungarian Peasantry: 1948-1956." AMERICAN SLAVIC AND EAST EUROPEAN REVIEW 18 (December 1959): 539-54.

A discussion of Hungarian agricultural policy between 1945-56.

Dalrymple, Dana G. "The Soviet Famine of 1932-1934." SOVIET STUDIES 15 (January 1964): 250-84.

A documented account of the manmade Soviet famine of 1932-34.

Diamond, Douglas B. "Trends in Output, Inputs, and Factor Productivity in Soviet Agriculture." In NEW DIRECTIONS IN THE SOVIET ECONOMY, Joint Economic Committee, 89th Cong., 2d sess., pp. 339-81. Washington, D.C.: Government Printing Office, 1966. Tables and appendixes.

A provision of data concerning agricultural output (1950-65) and the use of inputs by the agricultural sector (1950-64); a survey of trends in inputs, output, and factor productivity; and an examination of the factors contributing to changes in measured productivity.

Diamond, Douglas [B.], and Krueger, Constance. "Recent Developments in Output and Productivity in Soviet Agriculture." In SOVIET ECONOMIC PROSPECTS FOR THE SEVENTIES, Joint Economic Committee, 93d Cong., 1st sess., pp. 316-39. Washington, D.C.: Government Printing Office, 1973. Tables and appendixes.

A review of trends in the output and productivity of Soviet

agriculture between 1961-70, followed by an evaluation of the Brezhnev program for 1971-75.

Dobb, Maurice. RUSSIAN ECONOMIC DEVELOPMENT SINCE THE REVOLUTION. New York: E.P. Dutton and Co., 1928. xii, 415 p. Index.

A thorough examination of the periods of war communism and New Economic Policy.

Dumitriu, Dumitru. "Agricultural Organization and Planning in Rumania." In PLANNING AND MARKETS: MODERN TRENDS IN VARIOUS ECONOMIC SYSTEMS, edited by John T. Dunlop and Nikolay P. Fedorenko, pp. 143-54. New York: McGraw-Hill Book Co., 1969.

A description of the functioning and organization of Rumanian agriculture.

Durgin, Frank A., Jr. "Monetization and Policy in Soviet Agriculture since 1952." SOVIET STUDIES 15 (April 1964): 375-407.

An insight into the gradual policy shift from direction in agriculture via commands toward direction via economic and financial levers.

Granberg, A. "Agriculture in the System of Interbranch Balances." PROBLEMS OF ECONOMICS 10 (October 1967): 33-44. Tables.

A description of interbranch relationships of agriculture in output distribution and utilization as well as the intrabranch turnover in agriculture.

Gregory, Paul R., and Stuart, Robert C. SOVIET ECONOMIC STRUCTURE AND PERFORMANCE. New York: Harper & Row Publishers, 1974. x, 478 p. Tables, figures, and index. Paperback.

A comprehensive discussion and analysis of the important issues in the Soviet economy. Included are discussions concerning the economic experiences of the periods of war communism and New Economic Policy, pricing, planning methods and principles, agriculture, growth strategy and performance, foreign trade, monetary and financial controls and policy, and economic reforms.

Hutchings, Raymond. SOVIET ECONOMIC DEVELOPMENT. New York: Barnes & Noble, 1971. xiii, 314 p. Tables, figures, appendix, and index.

An examination of the extent and causes of economic development during World War I, war communism, the New Economic Policy, and the plan era.

Jasny, Naum. THE SOCIALIZED AGRICULTURE OF THE USSR: PLANS AND PERFORMANCE. Stanford, Calif.: Stanford University Press, 1949. xv,

837 p. Tables, figures, appendixes, and index.

A careful and thorough analysis of the development of Soviet agriculture. Topics discussed include prerevolutionary land tenure, peasant farming before collectivization, the collectivization drive, agricultural output, and methods of agricultural planning.

_____. SOVIET INDUSTRIALIZATION, 1928-1952. Chicago: University of Chicago Press, 1961. xviii, 467 p. Tables, figures, appendixes, and index.

A careful and thorough examination of the Soviet experience with industrialization, agriculture, investment, prices, transportation, and retail trade.

Johnson, D. Gale. "Agricultural Production." In ECONOMIC TRENDS IN THE SOVIET UNION, edited by Abram Bergson and Simon Kuznets, pp. 203-34. Cambridge, Mass.: Harvard University Press, 1963. Tables.

Measurement and analysis of the factors associated with changes in Soviet agricultural output.

Johnson, D. Gale, and Kahan, Arcadius. "Soviet Agriculture: Structure and Growth." In COMPARISONS OF THE UNITED STATES AND SOVIET ECONOMIES, Joint Economic Committee, 86th Cong., 1st sess., pp. 201-37. Washington, D.C.: Government Printing Office, 1959. Tables and appendix.

An examination of the growth of agricultural output and changes in imports and average productivity, and explanation of long-run changes in output.

Kabysh, S[ymon]. "The Permanent Crisis in Soviet Agriculture." STUDIES ON THE SOVIET UNION 4, no. 4 (1965): 126-40. Tables.

A discussion of Soviet agricultural issues: scarcity of agricultural inputs, obligatory tasks, and meager compensation of collective farm workers.

_____. "Soviet State Farms." STUDIES ON THE SOVIET UNION 3, no. 1 (1963): 72-82. Tables.

A report on the role, organization, and output of Soviet state farms.

Kahan, Arcadius. "Changes in Labor Inputs in Soviet Agriculture." JOURNAL OF POLITICAL ECONOMY 67 (October 1959): 451-62. Tables.

An analysis of the effects of Soviet institutions and policy during 1926-56 upon agricultural employment, labor inputs, and agricultural productivity.

_____. "The Peasant, the Party and the System." PROBLEMS OF COMMUNISM 9 (July-August 1960): 27-36.

A survey of the state of Soviet agriculture during the 1920s, collectivization, and post-Stalin agricultural policies, including organizational reforms.

Kalvoda, Josef. "Soviet Agricultural Reform and the Future of the Collective Farms." RUSSIAN REVIEW 19 (October 1960): 384-95.

An examination of Khrushchev's agricultural reform.

Karcz, Jerzy F. "Agricultural Reform in Eastern Europe." In PLAN AND MARKET: ECONOMIC REFORM IN EASTERN EUROPE, edited by Morris Bornstein, pp. 207-43. New Haven, Conn.: Yale University Press, 1973. Tables.

A careful, critical examination of agricultural reforms in Bulgaria, Czechoslovakia, East Germany, Hungary, Poland, Rumania, and Yugoslavia.

_____. "Certain Aspects of New Economic Systems in Bulgaria and Czechoslovakia." In AGRARIAN POLICIES AND PROBLEMS IN COMMUNIST AND NON-COMMUNIST COUNTRIES, edited by W.A. Douglas Jackson, pp. 178-204. Seattle: University of Washington Press, 1971.

A discussion of the Czechoslovak and Bulgarian reforms as they pertained to agriculture.

_____. "The New Soviet Agricultural Programme." SOVIET STUDIES 17 (October 1965): 129-61. Tables.

A brief review of the Soviet agricultural problems existing in 1965, followed by a discussion of the Brezhnev-Kosygin agricultural program.

_____. "Seven Years on the Farm: Retrospect and Prospects." In NEW DIRECTIONS IN THE SOVIET ECONOMY, Joint Economic Committee, 89th Cong., 2d sess., pp. 383-450. Washington, D.C.: Government Printing Office, 1966. Tables and appendix.

A detailed and thorough survey of the performance of Soviet agriculture during the Seven-Year Plan (1959-65).

_____. "Soviet Agriculture: A Balance Sheet." STUDIES ON THE SOVIET UNION 6, no. 4 (1967): 108-45. Tables and appendixes.

A critical appraisal of fifty years of Soviet agricultural policy and performance.

_____. "Thoughts on the Grain Problem." SOVIET STUDIES 18 (April 1967): 399-434. Tables.

A detailed reexamination of the Stalin-Nemchinov data on grain marketings and of the 1928 grain procurement crisis.

_____, ed. SOVIET AND EAST EUROPEAN AGRICULTURE. Berkeley and Los Angeles: University of California Press, 1967. xxv, 445 p. Figures, tables, and index.

> A collection of papers on problems of agriculture in the USSR and Eastern Europe, presented by a group of contributors representing several disciplines. A common concern of the papers is the Soviet agrarian reforms of the mid-1960s and their implementation.

Karliuk, I. "Economic Problems in the Development of Agriculture." PROBLEMS OF ECONOMICS 17 (May 1974): 3-21.

> A discussion of the factors influencing agricultural development.

Ladenkov, V.N. "Studies of Migration of Skilled Personnel in Agriculture." PROBLEMS OF ECONOMICS 15 (February 1973): 62-80. Tables.

> Data on agricultural migrants, and a discussion of the reasons for migration.

Laird, Roy D. "Agriculture under Khrushchev." SURVEY 56 (April 1965): 106-17. Tables.

> An assessment of the problems and achievements of Soviet agriculture during the Khrushchev era.

_____. "Prospects for Soviet Agriculture." PROBLEMS OF COMMUNISM 20 (September-October 1971): 31-40. Tables.

> An examination of the problems which confronted Soviet agriculture during the 1960s (underinvestment, overcentralization, etc.), followed by a gloomy forecast for the 1970s.

_____. "Soviet Agriculture in 1973 and Beyond in Light of United States Performance." RUSSIAN REVIEW 33 (October 1974): 372-85. Tables.

> An examination of contemporary as well as probable future problems of Soviet agriculture.

Laird, Roy D., and Laird, Betty A. SOVIET COMMUNISM AND AGRARIAN REVOLUTION, Middlesex, Engl.: Penguin Books, 1970. 158 p. Tables, figures, appendixes, and index. Paperback.

> A concise description and assessment of the problems and accomplishments of Soviet agriculture.

Laird, Roy D., ed. SOVIET AGRICULTURAL AND PEASANT AFFAIRS. Lawrence: University of Kansas Press, 1963. xi, 335 p. Tables, appendix, and index.

> A compendium of essays, written by specialists in their respective fields, concerned with the political setting, output, climatic, and

population problems of Soviet agriculture.

Laird, Roy D., and Crowley, Edward L., eds. SOVIET AGRICULTURE: THE PERMANENT CRISIS. New York: Frederick A. Praeger, 1965. xi, 209 p. Tables, figures, appendixes, and index.

A series of essays dealing with the regional peculiarities, economic advances, and administration of Soviet agriculture.

Lazarcik, Gregor. "Agricultural Output and Productivity in Eastern Europe and Some Comparisons with the U.S.S.R. and U.S.A." In REORIENTATION AND COMMERCIAL RELATIONS OF THE ECONOMIES OF EASTERN EUROPE, Joint Economic Committee, 93d Cong., 2d sess., pp. 328-93. Washington, D.C.: Government Printing Office, 1974. Tables and appendixes.

A survey of the role of agriculture in East European economies, the growth and structure of agricultural output and inputs, per capita trends and levels of agricultural output, and land and labor productivity trends. Additionally, size comparisons of output are made among Eastern Europe, the Soviet Union, and the United States.

Lebed, Andrei. "Causes of Soviet Agricultural Difficulties." STUDIES ON THE SOVIET UNION 2, no. 1 (1962): 32-36.

An outline of the major agricultural fiascoes in the Soviet Union.

Lewin, M. RUSSIAN PEASANTS AND SOVIET POWER. Evanston: Evanston, Ill.: Northwestern University Press, 1968. 539 p. Index.

A thorough examination of the issues and events related to Soviet agriculture during the 1920s, with an emphasis on collectivization.

Manteuffel, Ryszard. "Comparison of State, Cooperative, and Family-Owned Farms in Poland from the Technical and Economic Point of View." EASTERN EUROPEAN ECONOMICS 8 (Spring 1970): 253-77. Tables.

An examination of the problems and achievements of Polish agriculture since World War II, with emphasis on official input and output data for state, collective, and private farms.

Millar, James R. "Financial Innovation in Contemporary Soviet Agricultural Policy." SLAVIC REVIEW 32 (March 1973): 91-114. Tables.

A survey of Soviet financial policies in the collective farm and state farm sectors.

Monov, A. "Agriculture during the Current Five-Year Plan." PROBLEMS OF ECONOMICS 15 (November 1972): 3-19. Tables.

A discussion of agricultural techniques, material inputs, and output.

Nove, Alec. "Soviet Agriculture under Brezhnev." SLAVIC REVIEW 29 (September 1970): 379-410. Tables.

> An interesting and instructive assessment of Khrushchev's agricultural policies and their consequences and the changes inaugurated by Brezhnev, including the changes in input supplies, procurement prices, and peasant incomes.

Osofsky, Stephen. SOVIET AGRICULTURAL POLICY: TOWARD THE ABOLITION OF COLLECTIVE FARMS. New York: Praeger, 1974. xi, 300 p. Appendixes and index.

> A discussion of the salient issues pertaining to Soviet agriculture during the post-Khrushchev era.

Poletaev, P. "Capital Investment in Agriculture." PROBLEMS OF ECONOMICS 14 (February 1972): 19-34.

> An explanation of the further need for agricultural investments and of their expected results.

Prybyla, Jan S. "Problems of Soviet Agriculture." JOURNAL OF FARM ECONOMICS 44 (August 1962): 820-36. Tables.

> An investigation of the reasons for the poor performance of Soviet agriculture.

Raskin, G. "Capital Investments in Agriculture and the Calculation of Their Effectiveness." PROBLEMS OF ECONOMICS 4 (February 1962): 38-44. Tables.

> An essay about the efficiency of agricultural investments.

Romanchenko, G. "Purchase Prices of Agricultural Products and the Planning of Accumulation." PROBLEMS OF ECONOMICS 13 (January 1971): 37-57. Tables.

> A survey of agricultural purchase prices, profitability, capital-output ratios, and accumulation.

Schinke, Eberhard. "Soviet Agricultural Statistics." In SOVIET ECONOMIC STATISTICS, edited by Vladimir G. Treml and John P. Hardt, pp. 237-62. Durham, N.C.: Duke University Press, 1972.

> An assessment of Soviet agricultural statistics.

Schlesinger, Rudolf. "The New Structure of Soviet Agriculture." SOVIET STUDIES 10 (January 1959): 228-51.

> A discussion of agricultural policies in the Soviet collective farm sector after the termination of the compulsory delivery system and the transfer of machinery from the MTS's to the collective farms.

Strauss, Erich E. SOVIET AGRICULTURE IN PERSPECTIVE. New York: Frederick A. Praeger, 1969. 328 p. Tables, appendix, and index.

A discussion of Soviet agricultural policy, the structure and problems of Soviet agriculture, and agricultural productivity and incomes.

Volin, Lazar. "Agricultural Policy of the Soviet Union." In COMPARISONS OF THE UNITED STATES AND SOVIET ECONOMIES, Joint Economic Committee, 86th Cong., 1st sess., pp. 285-318. Washington, D.C.: Government Printing Office, 1959. Tables.

Thoughts' on Soviet agricultural policy pertaining to collective and state farms, farm giantism, Machine Tractor Stations, household plots, government procurement of farm products, capital investment in agriculture, and agricultural planning.

_____. A CENTURY OF RUSSIAN AGRICULTURE: FROM ALEXANDER II TO KHRUSHCHEV. Cambridge, Mass.: Harvard University Press, 1970. viii, 644 p. Tables and index.

A thorough examination of Russian and Soviet agricultural policies, with an emphasis on collectivized agriculture.

_____. "Khrushchev's Economic Neo-Stalinism." AMERICAN SLAVIC AND EAST EUROPEAN REVIEW 14 (December 1955): 445-64.

Comments on Soviet agricultural policy in the immediate post-Stalin period.

_____. "Soviet Agriculture under Khrushchev." AMERICAN ECONOMIC REVIEW 49 (May 1959): 15-32.

A discussion of the impact on Soviet agriculture of the changes which occurred under Khrushchev's leadership.

Waedekin, Karl-Eugen. "Kolkhoz, Sovkhoz, and Private Production in Soviet Agriculture." In AGRARIAN POLICIES AND PROBLEMS IN COMMUNIST AND NON-COMMUNIST COUNTRIES, edited by W.A. Douglas Jackson, pp. 106-37. Seattle: University of Washington Press, 1971. Tables.

An examination of the relative importance in Soviet agriculture of collective farms, state farms, and the private sector.

_____. "Manpower in Soviet Agriculture--Some Post-Khrushchev Developments and Problems." SOVIET STUDIES 20 (January 1969): 281-305. Tables.

An instructive approach to Soviet agricultural population and labor supply, wages, mechanization, and land improvement programs.

_____. THE PRIVATE SECTOR IN SOVIET AGRICULTURE. Translated by

Keith Bush. Berkeley and Los Angeles: University of California Press, 1973. xi, 407 p. Tables and index.

> A thorough examination of the characteristics and performance of the private sector of Soviet agriculture and of the official policy toward the private sector between 1953 and 1971.

Weber, Adolf. "Agricultural Modernization in Market and Planned Economies: The German Experience." STUDIES IN COMPARATIVE COMMUNISM 6 (Autumn 1973): 280-300. Tables.

> An assessment of the relationship between industry and agriculture in prewar Germany and in the two postwar Germanys, including a discussion of the postwar financing of farm reorganizations and investments.

Whitehouse, F. Douglas, and Havelka, Joseph F. "Comparisons of Farm Output in the US and USSR, 1950-1971." In SOVIET ECONOMIC PROSPECTS FOR THE SEVENTIES, Joint Economic Committee, 93d Cong., 1st sess., pp. 340-74. Washington, D.C.: Government Printing Office, 1973. Tables, figures, and appendixes.

> A comparison of the volume growth of agricultural output and its major components in the USSR and in the United States for the time period 1950-71.

Wilber, Charles K. "The Role of Agriculture in Soviet Economic Development." LAND ECONOMICS 45 (February 1969): 87-96. Tables.

> An essay on the contribution of the agricultural sector to Soviet economic development.

Zoerb, Carl R. "From the Promise of Land and Bread to the Reality of the State Farm." STUDIES ON THE SOVIET UNION 6, no. 4 (1967): 89-107. Tables.

> An appraisal of the development of the Soviet state farm system.

Collective Farms

Bashkin, P. "Differential Ground Rent in Soviet Collective Farm Production." PROBLEMS OF ECONOMICS 4 (November 1961): 42-49. Tables.

> A discussion of the functions of and justification for ground rent in the production of collective farms.

Batra, Raveendra N. "Technological Change in the Soviet Collective Farm." AMERICAN ECONOMIC REVIEW 64 (September 1974): 594-603. Figures.

> A theoretical analysis of the Soviet-type collective farm, with special attention to technological change and consumption effects.

Bradley, Michael E. "Incentives and Labour Supply on Soviet Collective Farms." CANADIAN JOURNAL OF ECONOMICS 4 (August 1971): 342-52.

A theoretical analysis of the household's labor supply function and of the impact on labor supply of quotas and uncertainty.

DePauw, John W. "The Private Sector in Soviet Agriculture." SLAVIC REVIEW 28 (March 1969): 63-71.

An assessment of the importance of private plots in Soviet agricultural production.

Dohrs, Fred E. "Incentives in Communist Agriculture: The Hungarian Models." SLAVIC REVIEW 27 (March 1968): 23-38.

A description of the incentive systems used on Hungarian collective farms.

Domar, Evsey D. "The Soviet Collective Farm as a Producer Cooperative." AMERICAN ECONOMIC REVIEW 56 (September 1966): 734-57. Tables, figures, and appendix.

A theoretical analysis of the functioning of a Soviet collective farm.

Draganov, Rashko. "The Auxiliary Plot of the Cooperative Farmers." EASTERN EUROPEAN ECONOMICS 3 (Fall 1964): 50-59. Tables.

An examination of the structure of production on collective farms and private plots, as well as of the output produced on the private plots of Bulgarian collective farm members.

Ellison, Herbert J. "The Decision to Collectivize Agriculture." SLAVIC REVIEW 20 (April 1961): 189-202.

An analysis of the reasons for the collectivization of Soviet agriculture.

Fallenbuchl, Z[bigniew]. M. "Collectivization and Economic Development." CANADIAN JOURNAL OF ECONOMICS AND POLITICAL SCIENCE 33 (February 1967): 1-15.

An examination, in light of the Soviet-bloc experience, of the possible connection between collectivization and economic development.

Jasny, Naum. THE SOCIALIZED AGRICULTURE OF THE USSR: PLANS AND PERFORMANCE. Stanford, Calif.: Stanford University Press, 1949. xv, 837 p. Tables, figures, appendixes, and index.

A careful and thorough analysis of the development of Soviet agriculture. Topics discussed include prerevolutionary land tenure, precollectivization peasant farming, the collectivization drive, agricultural output, and methods of agricultural planning.

Kabysh, S[ymon]. "The Permanent Crisis in Soviet Agriculture." STUDIES ON THE SOVIET UNION 4, no. 4 (1965): 126-40. Tables.

A discussion of important features of Soviet agriculture: scarcity of agricultural inputs, obligatory tasks, and meager compensation of collective farm workers.

Kahan, Arcadius. "The Collective Farm System in Russia: Some Aspects of Its Contribution to Soviet Economic Development." In AGRICULTURE IN ECONOMIC DEVELOPMENT, edited by Carl Eicher and Lawrence Witt, pp. 251-71. New York: McGraw-Hill Book Co., 1964. Tables.

A survey of the role of collective farms in the implementation of Soviet growth strategy.

Karcz, Jerzy F. "Quantitative Analysis of the Collective Farm Market." AMERICAN ECONOMIC REVIEW 54 (June 1964): 315-34. Figures and tables.

Official data and calculated estimates for prices and the volume of sales on Soviet collective farm markets.

Laird, Roy D. "Collectivization: New and Old Myths." STUDIES ON THE SOVIET UNION 6, no. 4 (1967): 78-88.

A reexamination of Soviet views concerning the reasons for collectivization.

Lewin, M. "The Immediate Background of Soviet Collectivization." SOVIET STUDIES 17 (October 1965): 162-97.

An interesting discussion of the economic performance and of the great debates preceding the Soviet collectivization drive.

_____. RUSSIAN PEASANTS AND SOVIET POWER. Evanston, Ill.: Northwestern University Press, 1968. 539 p. Index.

A thorough examination of the issues and events related to Soviet agriculture during the 1920s, with an emphasis on collectivization.

Manteuffel, Ryszard. "Comparison of State, Cooperative, and Family-Owned Farms in Poland from the Technical and Economic Point of View." EASTERN EUROPEAN ECONOMICS 8 (Spring 1970): 253-77. Tables.

An examination of the problems and achievements of Polish agriculture since World War II, with emphasis on official input and output data for state, collective, and private farms.

Mertsalov, V. "Collectivisation in the USSR." STUDIES ON THE SOVIET UNION, no. 1 (1957): 37-57. Tables.

Comments on the reasons, method, and impact of collectivization in the USSR, as well as on collective farm policy in the post-Stalin period.

Narkiewicz, O.A. "Stalin, War Communism, and Collectivization." SO-VIET STUDIES 18 (July 1966): 20-37.

An interesting account of Stalin's role in the collectivization drive of 1929-30.

Nimitz, Nancy. "Soviet Agricultural Prices and Costs." In COMPARISONS OF THE UNITED STATES AND SOVIET ECONOMIES, Joint Economic Committee, 86th Cong., 1st sess., pp. 239-84. Washington, D.C.: Government Printing Office, 1959. Tables and appendix.

An examination of agricultural procurement prices and realized prices and collective farm costs of production.

Nove, Alec. "The Decision to Collectivize." In AGRARIAN POLICIES IN COMMUNIST AND NON-COMMUNIST COUNTRIES, edited by W.A. Douglas Jackson, pp. 69-97. Seattle: University of Washington Press, 1971. Tables.

An examination of the collectivization decision and its implementation.

_____. "Rural Taxation in the USSR." SOVIET STUDIES 5 (October 1953): 159-66.

An appraisal of the weight of taxation borne by the collectivized sector of the Soviet economy.

Oi, Walter Y., and Clayton, Elisabeth M. "A Peasant's View of a Soviet Collective Farm." AMERICAN ECONOMIC REVIEW 58 (March 1968): 37-59. Tables, figures, and appendix.

A theoretical analysis of how the welfare (per capita income) of peasants in a Soviet collective farm is affected by the separation of crops on private and collective lands, arbitrary allocations of land to private plots, and prescribed crop quotas accompanied by a discriminatory pricing system.

Osofsky, Stephen. SOVIET AGRICULTURAL POLICY: TOWARD THE ABOLI-TION OF COLLECTIVE FARMS. New York: Praeger, 1974. xi, 300 p. Appendixes and index.

A discussion of the major agricultural issues of the post-Khrushchev era.

Postyshev, A. "The Labor Theory of Value and Optimal Planning." PROB-
LEMS OF ECONOMICS 10 (December 1967): 3-15.

A look at mathematical programming and the theory of value, as
well as the prospects for the use of mathematics in planned price
formation.

Stuart, Robert C. "The Changing Role of the Collective Farm in Soviet Agriculture." CANADIAN SLAVONIC PAPERS 16 (Summer 1974): 145-59. Tables.

An assessment of the declining role of collective farms in Soviet
agriculture between the early 1950s and early 1970s.

_____. THE COLLECTIVE FARM IN SOVIET AGRICULTURE. Lexington,
Mass.: D.C. Heath, 1972. xx, 254 p. Figures, tables, appendixes, and
index.

A description of the role, organization, and methods of operation
of collective farms in the Soviet economy.

_____. "Managerial Incentives in Soviet Collective Agriculture During the
Khrushchev Era." SOVIET STUDIES 22 (April 1971): 539-55. Tables.

General remarks on the structure of rewards for Soviet collective
farm chairmen during the period 1952-64.

Venzher, V[ladimir]. G. "Characteristics of the Collective-Farm Economy and
Problems of Its Development." PROBLEMS OF ECONOMICS 9 (January-Feb-
ruary-March 1967): 149-74.

A discussion concerning the nature of collective farm production
and problems of marketing, procurement, and price formation on
collective farms.

_____. "Subsidiary Plots--An Additional Source of Output of Agricultural
Products." PROBLEMS OF ECONOMICS 5 (December 1962): 30-39. Tables.

An assessment of the function of private plots in Soviet agricultural
production.

Volin, Lazar. A CENTURY OF RUSSIAN AGRICULTURE: FROM ALEXANDER
II TO KHRUSHCHEV. Cambridge, Mass.: Harvard University Press, 1970.
xiii, 644 p. Tables and index.

A thorough examination of Russian and Soviet agricultural policies,
with an emphasis on collectivized agriculture.

Whitman, John T. "The Kolkhoz Market." SOVIET STUDIES 7 (April 1956):
384-408. Tables.

A historical survey of the value of sales on collective farm markets and of the incomes generated from such sales.

INDUSTRY

Cook, Paul K. "The Administration and Distribution of Soviet Industry." In DIMENSIONS OF SOVIET ECONOMIC POWER, Joint Economic Committee, 87th Cong., 2d sess., pp. 181–210. Washington, D.C.: Government Printing Office, 1962. Tables and figures.

> An examination of Soviet industrial administration and the geographical distribution of Soviet industry.

Czirjak, Laszlo. "Industrial Structure, Growth, and Productivity in Eastern Europe." In ECONOMIC DEVELOPMENTS IN COUNTRIES OF EASTERN EUROPE, Joint Economic Committee, 91st Cong., 2d sess., pp. 434–62. Washington, D.C.: Government Printing Office, 1970. Tables and appendixes.

> A survey of rates of growth and the structure of industry on the basis of factor costs, and of trends in factor productivities.

Dobb, Maurice. "Rates of Growth under the Five-Year Plans." SOVIET STUDIES 4 (April 1953): 364–85.

> An analysis of Soviet growth rates under the five-year plans on the basis of four selected indicators: steel, coal, oil, and electricity.

_____. RUSSIAN ECONOMIC DEVELOPMENT SINCE THE REVOLUTION. New York: E.P. Dutton and Co., 1928. xii, 415 p. Index.

> A thorough examination of the periods of war communism and New Economic Policy.

Dockstader, Robert A. "Developments in Soviet Industry." In ECONOMIC PERFORMANCE AND THE MILITARY BURDEN IN THE SOVIET UNION, Joint Economic Committee, 91st Cong., 2d sess., pp. 18–25. Washington, D.C.: Government Printing Office, 1970. Tables.

> A survey of changes in civilian industrial output, factor inputs, and factor productivity.

Granick, David. "Technological Policy and Economic Calculation in Soviet Industry." In VALUE AND PLAN--ECONOMIC CALCULATION AND ORGANIZATION IN EASTERN EUROPE, edited by Gregory Grossman, pp. 271–94. Berkeley and Los Angeles: University of California Press, 1960. Tables.

> Thoughts on the rationality of economic decisions in the Soviet metalworking industries.

Gregory, Paul [R.]. SOCIALIST AND NONSOCIALIST INDUSTRIALIZATION

PATTERNS. New York: Frederick A. Praeger, 1970. xxvi, 209 p. Tables, figures, and appendixes.

> An examination of Soviet and Eastern European industrial structure and comparison of Soviet and Eastern European industrialization patterns with Western patterns.

Hoeffding, Oleg. "The Soviet Industrial Reorganization of 1957." AMERICAN ECONOMIC REVIEW 49 (May 1959): 65-77.

> A discussion of selected aspects of the Soviet industrial reorganization of 1957.

Hutchings, Raymond. SOVIET ECONOMIC DEVELOPMENT. New York: Barnes & Noble, 1971. xiii, 314 p. Tables, figures, appendix, and index.

> An examination of the extent and causes of economic development during World War I, war communism, the New Economic Policy, and the plan era.

Jasny, Naum. "Prospects of the Soviet Iron and Steel Industry." SOVIET STUDIES 14 (January 1963): 275-94. Tables.

> A discussion of the prospects, through 1980, for the Soviet iron and steel industry.

_____. SOVIET INDUSTRIALIZATION, 1928-1952. Chicago: University of Chicago Press, 1961. xviii, 467 p. Tables, figures, appendixes, and index.

> A careful and thorough examination of the Soviet experience with industrialization, agriculture, investment, prices, transportation, and retail trade.

Kaplan, Norman M., and Moorsteen, Richard H. "An Index of Soviet Industrial Output." AMERICAN ECONOMIC REVIEW 50 (June 1960): 295-318. Tables.

> A presentation and analysis of Soviet industrial output indexes.

Karagedov, R.[G]. "Problems of Increasing the Stimulating Role of Profits in Industry." PROBLEMS OF ECONOMICS 7 (July 1964): 38-48.

> An examination of the role of profit in Soviet industry.

Kaufman, Adam. SMALL-SCALE INDUSTRY IN THE SOVIET UNION. New York: National Bureau of Economic Research, 1962. xvi, 95 p. Figures, tables and appendix.

> A discussion of the importance of small-scale industry in the Soviet Union prior to the plan era, and the absorption of small scale industry during the plan period.

Koropeckyj, Iwan S. "Soviet Industrial Location in Practice." STUDIES ON

THE SOVIET UNION 1, no. 1 (1961): 38-46.

A description of principles and practices of industrial location in the USSR.

Kozlov, I., et al. "Collaboration of Comecon Countries in the Key Branches of Industry." PROBLEMS OF ECONOMICS 17 (September 1974): 20-38.

An essay on the collaboration among Comecon countries in electric power production, chemistry, machine building, and ferrous metallurgy.

Lamet, Stefan. "A Survey of the Soviet Engineering Industries." SOVIET STUDIES 5 (April 1954): 335-56. Tables.

A survey of the growth of output, effects of the war, and postwar development, including an enumeration of the various types of equipment produced.

Lee, Pong S. "Structural Changes in Rumanian Industry, 1938-63." SOVIET STUDIES 20 (October 1968): 219-28. Tables.

An examination of the changes in Rumanian industrial structure and of the divergence of this change from what might be expected from a non-Communist country in a similar stage of development.

Lydolph, Paul E. "The Soviet Reorganization of Industry." AMERICAN SLAVIC AND EAST EUROPEAN REVIEW 17 (October 1958): 293-301.

A discussion of the antecedents and main features of the Soviet industrial reorganization of 1957.

Mieczkowski, Z. "The Economic Regionalization of the Soviet Union in the Lenin and Stalin Period." CANADIAN SLAVONIC PAPERS 8 (1966): 89-124. Figures.

A survey of Goelro and Gosplan regionalization efforts.

Montias, John M[ichael]. "Socialist Industrialization and Trade in Machinery Products: An Analysis Based on the Experience of Bulgaria, Poland, and Rumania." In INTERNATIONAL TRADE AND CENTRAL PLANNING--AN ANALYSIS OF ECONOMIC INTERACTIONS, edited by Alan A. Brown and Egon Neuberger, pp. 130-59. Berkeley and Los Angeles: University of California Press, 1968. Tables.

A discussion of both theoretical and empirical aspects of the volume and commodity composition of trade and balance of payments position of Bulgaria, Poland, and Rumania. A twenty-six variable, six-sector simulation model is also presented.

Noren, James H., and Whitehouse, Douglas E. "Soviet Industry in the 1971-75 Plan." In SOVIET ECONOMIC PROSPECTS FOR THE SEVENTIES, Joint

Economic Committee, 93d Cong., 1st sess., pp. 206-45. Washington, D.C.: Government Printing Office, 1973. Tables, figures, and appendixes.

An investigation of the purpose and special features, consistency and feasibility for output and material inputs, regional aspects, branch targets, as well as policy implications of the 1971-75 industrial plan.

Richman, Barry M. SOVIET MANAGEMENT; WITH SIGNIFICANT AMERICAN COMPARISONS. Englewood Cliffs, N.J.: Prentice-Hall, 1965. vii, 279 p. Figures, tables, and appendixes.

A description of the organizational structure of Soviet industry and its enterprises, the industrial planning process, and some fundamental problems of the Soviet administrative-economic system to 1962. Comparisons are made between Soviet and American managers.

Ronimmois, H.E. "The Cost-Profit-Output Relationship in a Soviet Industrial Firm." CANADIAN JOURNAL OF ECONOMICS AND POLITICAL SCIENCE 18 (May 1952): 173-83. Figures.

An analysis of cost, production, and profit in the Soviet industrial enterprise.

Shabad, Theodore. BASIC INDUSTRIAL RESOURCES OF THE U.S.S.R. New York: Columbia University Press, 1969. xiii, 393 p. Tables, figures, and index.

A detailed description, by regions, of the various Soviet industries.

Smolinski, Leon. "The Scale of Soviet Industrial Establishments." AMERICAN ECONOMIC REVIEW 52 (May 1962): 138-48. Tables.

A survey of the scale of Soviet industrial establishments between 1913 and 1960 and a discussion of the impact of scale of plant on industrial growth in the USSR.

_____. "Towards a Socialist Corporation: Soviet Industrial Reorganization of 1973." SURVEY 20 (Winter 1974): 24-35.

An explanation of the 1973 Soviet industrial reorganization.

Spigler, Iancu. ECONOMIC REFORMS IN RUMANIAN INDUSTRY. Economic Reforms in East European Industry Series. London: Oxford University Press, 1973. xx, 176 p. Tables, figures, and index.

A survey of the origins, provisions, and results of the Rumanian industrial planning reforms of the 1960s.

Sutton, Antony C. WESTERN TECHNOLOGY AND SOVIET ECONOMIC DEVELOPMENT, 1930 TO 1945. Stanford, Calif.: Hoover Institution Press,

1971. xxiv, 401 p. Tables, figures, appendixes, and index.

An examination of the role of Western technology in Soviet industrial development.

Thornton, Judith. "Differential Capital Charges and Resource Allocation in
Soviet Industry." JOURNAL OF POLITICAL ECONOMY 79 (May/June 1971):
545-61. Tables and appendixes.

Estimates of the output loss attributable to differential capital
charges in Soviet industry.

_____. "Value-Added and Factor Productivity in Soviet Industry." AMERI-
CAN ECONOMIC REVIEW 60 (December 1970): 863-71. Tables.

Estimates, in constant and current prices, for Soviet industrial
value-added for the period 1955-67.

Treml, Vladimir G., et al. "Interindustry Structure of the Soviet Economy:
1959 and 1966." In SOVIET ECONOMIC PROSPECTS FOR THE SEVENTIES,
Joint Economic Committee, 93d Cong., 1st sess., pp. 246-69. Washington,
D.C.: Government Printing Office, 1973. Tables and appendixes.

Reconstruction of the Soviet input-output tables for 1959 and 1966
in a comparable format.

Turgeon, Lynn. "Cost-Price Relationships in Basic Industries During the Soviet
Planning Era." SOVIET STUDIES 9 (October 1957): 143-77. Tables.

An account of the relative trends of prices and production costs
in Soviet basic industries between 1928 and 1955.

Vvedensky, George. "The Major Industries." STUDIES ON THE SOVIET
UNION 8, no. 1 (1968): 1-8. Tables.

A bird's eye view of the major industries in the USSR.

_____. "The Twenty-Year Plan for Soviet Heavy Industry." STUDIES ON
THE SOVIET UNION 2, no. 4 (1963): 35-49.

A survey of Soviet plans for the growth of heavy industry through
1980.

TRANSPORT AND COMMUNICATION

Hunter, Holland. "Costs, Freight Rates, and Location Decisions in the
U.S.S.R." In VALUE AND PLAN--ECONOMIC CALCULATION AND OR-
GANIZATION IN EASTERN EUROPE, edited by Gregory Grossman, pp. 322-
37. Berkeley and Los Angeles: University of California Press, 1960. Tables.

An examination of short-run and long-run issues in freight rates
and location decisions.

_____. SOVIET TRANSPORT EXPERIENCE: ITS LESSONS FOR OTHER COUNTRIES. Washington, D.C.: Brookings Institution, 1968. xiii, 194 p. Figures, tables, appendixes, and index.

A consideration of the problems and achievements of various forms of transportation, followed by conclusions that may be of value to the developing nations.

_____. "Soviet Transportation Policies--A Current View." In COMPARISONS OF THE UNITED STATES AND SOVIET ECONOMIES, Joint Economic Committee, 86th Cong., 1st sess., pp. 189-99. Washington, D.C.: Government Printing Office, 1959. Tables.

A discussion of Soviet transportation policies and practices of the 1950s.

_____. "The Soviet Transport Sector." In NEW DIRECTIONS IN THE SOVIET ECONOMY, Joint Economic Committee, 89th Cong., 2d sess., pp. 569-91. Washington, D.C.: Government Printing Office, 1966. Tables and figures.

An evaluation of the overall performance of the Soviet transport sector and a discussion of policy and problems in freight and passenger transport.

_____. "Transport in Soviet and Chinese Development." ECONOMIC DEVELOPMENT AND CULTURAL CHANGE 14 (October 1965): 71-84. Tables.

An inquiry into the role of the transport sector in Soviet and Chinese economic development.

Jasny, Naum. SOVIET INDUSTRIALIZATION, 1928-1952. Chicago: University of Chicago Press, 1961. xviii, 467 p. Tables, figures, appendixes, and index.

A careful examination of the Soviet experience with industrialization, agriculture, investment, prices, transportation, and retail trade.

Kaplan, Norman M. "The Growth of Output and Inputs in Soviet Transport and Communications." AMERICAN ECONOMIC REVIEW 57 (December 1967): 1154-67. Tables.

After a summary of an attempt to construct and use output indexes for Soviet transport and communication, an exploration of growth retardation by distinguishing between changes in the rates of increase in factor inputs and in combined factor productivity.

Redding, A. David. "Employment and Labor Productivity in USSR Railroads,

1928-1950." SOVIET STUDIES 5 (July 1953): 32-43. Tables.

A discussion of changes in employment, traffic volume, and labor productivity.

Sutton, Antony C. WESTERN TECHNOLOGY AND SOVIET ECONOMIC DEVELOPMENT, 1930 TO 1945. Stanford, Calif.: Hoover Institution Press, 1971. xxiv, 401 p. Tables, figures, appendixes, and index.

An examination of the role of Western technology in Soviet industrial development.

Williams, Ernest W., Jr. FREIGHT TRANSPORTATION IN THE SOVIET UNION. Princeton, N.J.: Princeton University Press, 1962. xxi, 221 p. Tables, figures, appendixes, and index.

A thorough examination of the development and growth of the Soviet transport sector, with special emphasis on rail transport.

_____. "Some Aspects of the Structure and Growth of Soviet Transportation." In COMPARISONS OF THE UNITED STATES AND SOVIET ECONOMIES, Joint Economic Committee, 86th Cong., 1st sess., pp. 177-87. Washington, D.C.: Government Printing Office, 1959. Tables.

Assessment of Soviet transportation development and rail operations, and comparison of U.S. and Soviet freight traffic.

ENERGY AND OTHER NATURAL RESOURCES

Campbell, Robert W. THE ECONOMICS OF SOVIET OIL AND GAS. Baltimore: Johns Hopkins Press, 1968. xv, 279 p. Tables, figures, and index.

An interesting account of the exploration, drilling, production, transport, and pricing of Soviet oil and natural gas, a comparison of Soviet and Western energy sectors, and an analysis of the reasons for the structure of consumption of liquid fuels in the USSR.

_____. "Some Issues In Soviet Energy Policy for the Seventies." In SOVIET ECONOMIC PROSPECTS FOR THE SEVENTIES, Joint Economic Committee, 93d Cong., 1st sess., pp. 45-55. Washington, D.C.: Government Printing Office, 1973.

A discussion of present and projected Soviet energy supplies and demands.

Dienes, Leslie. "Issues in Soviet Energy Policy and Conflicts Over Fuel Costs in Regional Development." SOVIET STUDIES 23 (July 1971): 26-58. Tables and figures.

An examination of the spatial allocation and economic evaluation of fuel and hydrocarbon resources in the Soviet Union, including the subject of how evaluation and costing affect the competitive position for economic development of the various regions. Some of the Soviet proposals concerning resource use are also considered.

Dobb, Maurice. "Rates of Growth under the Five-Year Plans." SOVIET STUDIES 4 (April 1953): 364-85.

An analysis of Soviet growth rates under the five-year plans on the basis of four selected indicators: steel, coal, oil, and electricity.

Gantman, Ia. "Structural Changes in the Fuel Balance of the USSR." PROBLEMS OF ECONOMICS 15 (August 1972): 63-71.

A description of the geographical distribution of energy sources, as well as the transportation and use of energy.

Gerasimov, I.P., et al., eds. NATURAL RESOURCES OF THE SOVIET UNION: THEIR USE AND RENEWAL. Translated by Jacek I. Romanowski. San Francisco: W.H. Freeman and Co., 1971. xiii, 349 p. Tables, figures, and index.

An examination of water resources, climatic conditions, land, vegetation, game resources, and fisheries.

Hardt, John P. "West Siberia: The Quest for Energy." PROBLEMS OF COMMUNISM 22 (May-June 1973): 25-36.

A study of Soviet energy concerns in the 1970s, changes in the Soviet energy balance, and the role of West Siberia as a source of additional oil and gas.

Khachaturov, T. "Natural Resources and National Economic Planning." PROBLEMS OF ECONOMICS 16 (March 1972): 3-28.

Determination of the availability and need for natural resources and planning tasks with respect to natural resources.

Lamet, Stefan. "Soviet Fuel and Power." SOVIET STUDIES 4 (July 1952): 1-14. Tables.

An examination of the expansion of the production and consumption of energy in the Soviet Union.

Lee, Richard J. "Petroleum Supply Problems in Eastern Europe." In REORIENTATION AND COMMERCIAL RELATIONS OF THE ECONOMIES OF EASTERN EUROPE, Joint Economic Committee, 93d Cong., 2d sess., pp. 406-20. Washington, D.C.: Government Printing Office, 1974. Tables and appendix.

Estimates of crude oil and natural gas requirements and availabilities, as well as the future energy prospects of Eastern Europe.

_____. "The Soviet Petroleum Industry: Promise and Problems." In SOVIET ECONOMIC PROSPECTS FOR THE SEVENTIES, Joint Economic Committee, 93d Cong., 1st sess., pp. 283-90. Washington, D.C.: Government Printing Office, 1973. Tables.

Estimates for Soviet crude oil and natural gas reserves and for current production.

Polach, J.G. "The Development of Energy in East Europe." In ECONOMIC DEVELOPMENTS IN COUNTRIES OF EASTERN EUROPE, Joint Economic Committee, 91st Cong., 2d sess., pp. 348-432. Washington, D.C.: Government Printing Office, 1970. Tables, figures, and appendixes.

An analysis of the role of energy in the economies of Eastern Europe by examining patterns of energy supply and demand, the origin and direction of energy commodity trade, and the structure of energy resource base.

Smyshliaeva, L. "The Development of the Gas Industry and the Use of Gas in the USSR." PROBLEMS OF ECONOMICS 3 (April 1961): 24-31. Tables.

A brief survey of the production, distribution, and consumption of natural gas in the USSR, accompanied by U.S.-USSR comparisons.

Sutton, Antony C. WESTERN TECHNOLOGY AND SOVIET ECONOMIC DE-VELOPMENT, 1917 TO 1930. Stanford, Calif.: Hoover Institution Press, 1968. xx, 381 p. Tables, figures, appendixes, and index.

An examination of foreign concessions and technological transfers and of their significance for Soviet economic development.

_____. WESTERN TECHNOLOGY AND SOVIET ECONOMIC DEVELOP-MENT, 1930 TO 1945. Stanford, Calif.: Hoover Institution Press, 1971. xxiv, 401 p. Tables, figures, appendixes, and index.

An examination of the role of Western technology in Soviet industrial development.

Voinov, A., and Semenov, I. "The Socialist Division of Labor in the Fuel and Power Branches of Industry." PROBLEMS OF ECONOMICS 3 (April 1961): 32-40. Tables.

A glance at the energy reserves and production of the Soviet-bloc countries.

Wasowski, Stanislaw. "The Fuel Situation in Eastern Europe." SOVIET STUDIES 21 (July 1969): 35-51. Tables.

A discussion of the oil requirements of Eastern Europe, the availabilities of oil in Eastern Europe and in the Soviet Union, and the alternatives available to the Eastern European countries to cope with their oil shortage.

Zybenko, Roman. "Fuel and Power Resources." STUDIES ON THE SOVIET UNION 8, no. 1 (1968): 9-13.

 A survey of Soviet energy resources.

SERVICES

Dikhtiar, G. "Soviet Trade in the Period of the Full-Scale Building of Communism." PROBLEMS OF ECONOMICS 5 (August 1962): 45-52.

 An examination of the functioning and future tasks of wholesale and retail trade organizations.

Goldman, Marshall I. "The Cost and Efficiency of Distribution in the Soviet Union." QUARTERLY JOURNAL OF ECONOMICS 76 (August 1962): 437-53. Tables.

 A comparison of U.S. and Soviet distribution markups and explanation of the reasons for the lower Soviet distribution costs.

_____. "The Marketing Structure in the Soviet Union." JOURNAL OF MARKETING 25 (July 1961): 7-14. Figures.

 An inquiry into the organization and functioning of the Soviet distribution network.

_____. "The Reluctant Consumer and Economic Fluctuations in the Soviet Union." JOURNAL OF POLITICAL ECONOMY 78 (August 1965): 366-80. Tables.

 An illustration of consumption tendencies and production practices in an effort to explain the existence of sales, production, and inventory cycles in the Soviet Union.

_____. SOVIET MARKETING: DISTRIBUTION IN A CONTROLLED ECONOMY. New York: Free Press of Glencoe, 1963. 229 p. Tables, figures, appendix, and index.

 An examination of the Soviet distribution sector, including a discussion of the organization of domestic trade, planning, pricing, and distribution of consumer goods, and the costs of distribution.

Hanson, Philip. "The Assortment Problem in Soviet Retail Trade." SOVIET STUDIES 14 (April 1963): 347-64.

 A discussion of the Soviet retail distribution system and of Soviet views concerning its improvement.

_____. THE CONSUMER IN THE SOVIET ECONOMY. Evanston, Ill.: Northwestern University Press, 1968. ix, 249 p. Figures, tables, appendixes, and index.

A comparison of trends in consumption with trends in economic
growth and industrialization, accompanied by a close look at
the severe constraints on consumption, the retail price structure,
and the mechanism for adjusting supplies to consumer demand.

_____. "The Structure and Efficiency of Soviet Retailing and Wholesaling."
SOVIET STUDIES 16 (October 1964): 186-208. Tables and appendix.

A discussion of the density, development, location, and efficiency
of the Soviet distributive network.

Komarov, V. "The Service Sphere and Its Structure." PROBLEMS OF ECO-
NOMICS 16 (July 1973): 3-21. Tables.

A description of the output, growth, and structure of the Soviet
Union's service sector.

Ofer, Gur. THE SERVICE SECTOR IN SOVIET ECONOMIC GROWTH.
Cambridge, Mass.: Harvard University Press, 1973. xi, 202 p. Tables,
figures, appendixes, and index.

An explanation of why the service sector occupies such a small
place in the highly developed economy of the Soviet Union.

Prosandeev, A. "Indices of the Effectiveness of Soviet Trade." PROBLEMS
OF ECONOMICS 13 (September 1970): 58-69. Tables.

Review of the volume of trade turnover, profits, and subsidies in
trade enterprises. Profit is considered as an important index of
the work of such enterprises.

Rutgaizer, V. "A Comprehensive Plan for the Development of the Service
Sector." PROBLEMS OF ECONOMICS 16 (September 1973): 41-59. Tables.

Methodological questions concerning long-range planning in the
service sector.

Skurski, Roger. "The Buyers' Market and Soviet Consumer Goods Distribution."
SLAVIC REVIEW 31 (December 1972): 817-30. Tables.

A report on inventory, sales, and labor productivity trends in
Soviet retailing.

_____. "The Factor Proportions Problem in Soviet Internal Trade." SOVIET
STUDIES 23 (January 1972): 450-64. Tables.

Estimates of capital and labor inputs in the Soviet trade sector,
and a comparison with factor shares in other sectors of the economy.
Comparisons are made also between factor proportions in U.S. and
Soviet domestic trade.

Sukharevskii, B. "Development of the Sphere of Services and the Building of Communism." PROBLEMS OF ECONOMICS 7 (February 1965): 21-30.

An examination of the volume and role of public services and the proportions between material production and services in the Soviet economy.

Chapter 12

MONETARY AND FISCAL THEORY, PRACTICES, AND INSTITUTIONS

Aleksandrov, A., and Rabinovich, G. "Once More on the Nature of the Turnover Tax." PROBLEMS OF ECONOMICS 6 (March 1964): 30-35.

A reexamination of the economic nature of the turnover tax.

Ames, Edward. "Soviet Bloc Currency Conversions." AMERICAN ECONOMIC REVIEW 44 (June 1954): 339-53. Tables.

A description of the background of the currency conversions which occurred between 1947 and 1953 in Poland, Rumania, Bulgaria, and Czechoslovakia, and an analysis of currency conversion operations.

_____. SOVIET ECONOMIC PROCESSES. Homewood, Ill.: Richard D. Irwin, 1965. 257 p. Tables, figures, and index. Paperback.

An excellent overview of the Soviet economy, with particular attention to economic organization, planning on the macro and micro levels, fiscal and monetary policy, international trade, and economic performance.

Andreassen, Knut. "Features of Banking Organization, Monetary and Credit Policy in the Soviet Union." ECONOMICS OF PLANNING 3 (April 1963): 41-52.

A discussion of the organization of the banking system, control by the ruble, and the role of short and long-term credit and interest.

Arnold, Arthur Z. BANKS, CREDIT AND MONEY IN SOVIET RUSSIA. New York: Columbia University Press, 1937. xxiii, 559 p. Tables and index.

A thorough, exhaustive discussion and explanation of Soviet financial and banking operations and inflationary pressures during 1917-37.

Babitchev, Eugene. "The International Bank for Economic Cooperation." In MONEY AND PLAN--FINANCIAL ASPECTS OF EAST EUROPEAN ECONOMIC

REFORMS, edited by Gregory Grossman, pp. 129-52. Berkeley and Los Angeles: University of California Press, 1968.

> An examination of the functions, organization, and operation of the International Bank for Economic Cooperation.

Batyrev, V. "The Economic Reform and the Increasing Role of Credit." PROBLEMS OF ECONOMICS 9 (September 1966): 50-58.

> An analysis of the role of credit in the Soviet economy after the announcement of reforms in 1965.

_____. "Some Theoretical and Practical Problems of Credit in the USSR." PROBLEMS OF ECONOMICS 9 (March 1960): 19-24.

> A description of the prevailing and proposed functions and uses of credit.

Berliner, Joseph S. "Monetary Planning in the USSR." AMERICAN SLAVIC AND EAST EUROPEAN REVIEW 9 (December 1950): 237-54.

> A view of Soviet monetary planning from the standpoint of the alternatives open to the planners.

Birman, A. "The USSR State Budget in the Perspective of Economic Development." PROBLEMS OF ECONOMICS 16 (March 1974): 74-87.

> A study of the various components of state revenues and the use of budget expenditures for developmental purposes.

Borisov, V. "The Growth of Saving in the USSR." PROBLEMS OF ECONOMICS 10 (September 1967): 37-46. Tables.

> An examination of income and saving relationships and savings bank deposits.

Brzeski, Andrzej. "Forced-Draft Industrialization with Unlimited Supply of Money: Poland, 1945-1964." In MONEY AND PLAN--FINANCIAL ASPECTS OF EAST EUROPEAN ECONOMIC REFORMS, edited by Gregory Grossman, pp. 17-37. Berkeley and Los Angeles: University of California Press, 1968. Appendix.

> Reflections on the supply and demand for money, inflation, and economic growth in postwar Poland.

Condoide, Mikhail V. THE SOVIET FINANCIAL SYSTEM: ITS DEVELOPMENT AND RELATIONS WITH THE WESTERN WORLD. Columbus: Ohio State University, Bureau of Business Research, 1951. xiii, 230 p. Tables, appendixes, and index.

> An examination of the Soviet banking and credit system, the nature and functions of money in the Soviet economy, Soviet bud-

getary revenues and expenditures, and the international financial relations of the USSR.

Coogan, James. "Bread and the Soviet Fiscal System." REVIEW OF ECONOMICS AND STATISTICS 35 (May 1953): 161-67. Tables.

An evaluation of the assessment and collection techniques of turn-over taxes on grain and the importance of the grain-economy in the Soviet fiscal structure.

Csikos-Nagy, Bela. SOCIALIST ECONOMIC POLICY. New York: St. Martin's Press, 1973. 238 p. Index.

A discussion of Soviet-type economic organization, planning, financial policies, price and income policies, and distribution and foreign trade policies.

Davies, R.W. THE DEVELOPMENT OF THE SOVIET BUDGETARY SYSTEM. Cambridge: At the University Press, 1958. xxi, 373 p. Tables, figures, and index.

A detailed study of the development of the Soviet budgetary and financial system from the period of war communism until the end of World War II.

_____. "Short-Term Credit in the USSR: Some Post-war Problems." SOVIET STUDIES 5 (July 1953): 18-31.

An account of short-term credit problems in the Soviet Union.

Dobb, Maurice. RUSSIAN ECONOMIC DEVELOPMENT SINCE THE REVOLUTION. New York: E.P. Dutton and Co., 1928. xii, 415 p. Index.

A thorough examination of the periods of war communism and New Economic Policy.

_____. SOVIET ECONOMIC DEVELOPMENT SINCE 1917. New York: International Publishers, 1948. vii, 475 p. Tables and index.

A detailed, sympathetic account of the unfolding Soviet economic organization and development strategy. Topics discussed include the periods of war communism and NEP, the growth of industry and agriculture, the financial system, and the five-year plans.

Francuz, Henryk. "The International Bank for Economic Cooperation." INTERNATIONAL MONETARY FUND STAFF PAPERS 16 (November 1969): 489-503. Tables.

A discussion of IBEC's organization, structure, operations, and impact on the foreign trade of CMEA member countries.

Garbuzov, V.F. "The Development of Currency and Financial Relations of

Comecon Member Nations." SOVIET AND EASTERN EUROPEAN FOREIGN TRADE 9 (Summer 1973): 74-82. Table and figure.

> An assessment of the role of the International Investment Bank and International Bank for Economic Cooperation in economic relations within the CMEA.

_____. "Economic Reform and Finance." PROBLEMS OF ECONOMICS 11 (December 1968): 47-56. Tables.

> A description of the role of the turnover tax and the use of credits and various enterprise funds.

_____. "Finances and Economic Stimuli." PROBLEMS OF ECONOMICS 8 (February 1966): 3-10. Figures.

> A discussion of the role of credit, prices, and profit under the Soviet economic reform of 1965.

Garvy, George. "East European Credit and Finance in Transition." In MONEY AND PLAN--FINANCIAL ASPECTS OF EAST EUROPEAN ECONOMIC REFORMS, edited by Gregory Grossman, pp. 153-82. Berkeley and Los Angeles: University of California Press, 1968.

> An examination of the new role of money, prices, interest rates, and profits in Eastern Europe.

_____. MONEY, BANKING, AND CREDIT IN EASTERN EUROPE. New York: Federal Reserve Bank of New York, 1966. 167 p. Tables. Paperback.

> A close look at the financial characteristics of the centrally planned economies, the structure of the various banking systems, monetary and credit policies, as well as financial operations in the foreign sectors of the Eastern European countries.

_____. "The Role of the State Bank in Soviet Planning." In SOVIET PLANNING: ESSAYS IN HONOUR OF NAUM JASNY, edited by Jane Degras and Alec Nove, pp. 46-76. Oxford: Basil Blackwell, 1964. Tables.

> A discussion of Soviet monetary plans, the principle of "control by the ruble," and the activities of Gosbank.

Gekker, Paul. "The Soviet Bank for Foreign Trade and Soviet Banks Abroad: A Note." ECONOMICS OF PLANNING 7, no. 2 (1967): 183-97. Tables.

> A description of the functions and activities of the Soviet Foreign Trade Bank and of Soviet-owned banks abroad.

Grossman, Gregory. "Union of Soviet Socialist Republics." In BANKING SYSTEMS, edited by Benjamin Haggott Beckhart, pp. 733-68. New York: Columbia University Press, 1954. Tables.

> A brief survey of the Soviet banking system, including a discussion

of financial organization, monetary stability, the functions of
Gosbank, and control by the ruble.

Herman, Leon M. "Taxes and the Soviet Citizen." PROBLEMS OF COM-
MUNISM 8 (September-October 1959): 21-26.

An examination of the functions of taxation in the USSR, methods
of collection, and the size of the turnover tax.

Hodgman, Donald R. "Soviet Monetary Controls Through the Banking System."
In VALUE AND PLAN--ECONOMIC CALCULATION AND ORGANIZATION
IN EASTERN EUROPE, edited by Gregory Grossman, pp. 105-24. Berkeley
and Los Angeles: University of California Press, 1960. Tables.

Comments on short-term credit, monetary controls, and the role of
the State Bank.

Holesovsky, Vaclav. "Financial Aspects of the Czechoslovak Economic Re-
form." In MONEY AND PLAN--FINANCIAL ASPECTS OF THE EAST EURO-
PEAN ECONOMIC REFORMS, edited by Gregory Grossman, pp. 80-105.
Berkeley and Los Angeles: University of California Press, 1968.

Thoughts on money and finance in the 1967 economic model.

Holzman, F[ranklyn]. D. "The Burden of Soviet Taxation." AMERICAN
ECONOMIC REVIEW 43 (September 1953): 548-71. Tables.

A measure of the changes in the burden of Soviet taxation between
1925-26 and 1950, and a comparison between the burden of taxation in the United States and in the USSR.

_____. "Commodity and Income Taxation in the Soviet Union." JOURNAL
OF POLITICAL ECONOMY 58 (October 1950): 425-33.

An illustration of the approaches open to the decision makers in
the USSR in solving the problem of inflation.

_____. "Some Financial Aspects of Soviet Foreign Trade." In COMPARI-
SONS OF THE UNITED STATES AND SOVIET ECONOMIES, Joint Economic
Committee, 86th Cong., 1st sess., pp. 427-43. Washington, D.C.: Govern-
ment Printing Office, 1959. Tables and appendix.

A discussion of the trends in the official ruble exchange rate, and
examination of Soviet international price policy and the impact of
Soviet foreign trade on internal financial stability.

_____. "Soviet Inflationary Pressures, 1928-1957: Causes and Cures."
QUARTERLY JOURNAL OF ECONOMICS 74 (May 1960): 167-88. Tables.

An analysis of Soviet price and wage trends.

_____ . SOVIET TAXATION: THE FISCAL AND MONETARY PROBLEMS OF A PLANNED ECONOMY. Cambridge, Mass.: Harvard University Press, 1955. xix, 375 p. Tables, appendix, and index.

An examination of the theory, alternative methods, and actual burden and functions of Soviet taxation.

Hutchings, Raymond. SOVIET ECONOMIC DEVELOPMENT. New York: Barnes & Noble, 1971. xiii, 314 p. Tables, figures, appendix, and index.

A discussion of the extent and causes of economic development during World War I, war communism, the New Economic Policy, and the plan era.

Ivanov, Iu. A. "Improving the Foreign Exchange Relations of Comecon Member Nations." PROBLEMS OF ECONOMICS 17 (September 1974): 39-49.

A description of the role and functioning of the International Bank for Economic Cooperation (IBEC), the International Investment Bank (IIB), and the transferable ruble.

Ivensen, T. "Problems in Forecasting the Monetary Savings of the Population." PROBLEMS OF ECONOMICS 17 (June 1974): 65-75. Tables.

An emphasis on the need for identifying the factors which increase and decrease the volume of savings.

Jasny, Naum. "The Soviet Price System." AMERICAN ECONOMIC REVIEW 40 (December 1950): 845-62. Tables.

An analysis of Soviet wage-price relationships, taxes, inflation, and budgetary expenditures.

Karpich, V. "The Development of Currency and Financial Relations among Comecon Countries." SOVIET AND EASTERN EUROPEAN FOREIGN TRADE 6 (Summer 1970): 103-24.

Familiarization with Comecon credits, payment relations, multilateral clearinghouse operations, and so on.

Konnik, I. "The Problem of the Ruble's Rate of Exchange." PROBLEMS OF ECONOMICS 6 (September 1963): 39-46.

An orthodox view on the alleged relationship between the defined gold content and the exchange rate of the ruble.

Lavrov, V. "The Budget and Accumulations." PROBLEMS OF ECONOMICS 10 (June 1967): 29-33. Tables.

An explanation of budgetary incomes and expenditures.

Markovskaia, K., and Voronov, A. "Balance of Money Incomes and Expenditures of the Urban and Rural Populations." PROBLEMS OF ECONOMICS 14 (February 1972): 37-50.

A description of the methods for calculating the balance of money incomes and expenditures.

Millar, James R. "Financial Innovation in Contemporary Soviet Agricultural Policy." SLAVIC REVIEW 32 (March 1973): 91-114. Tables.

A survey of Soviet financial policies in the collective farm and state farm sectors.

Montias, John M[ichael]. "Bank Lending and Fiscal Policy in Eastern Europe." In MONEY AND PLAN--FINANCIAL ASPECTS OF EAST EUROPEAN ECONOMIC REFORMS, edited by Gregory Grossman, pp. 38-56. Berkeley and Los Angeles: University of California Press, 1968. Tables.

Presentation of a model, showing the calculation of a budget surplus consistent with aggregate market equilibrium for a volume of bank lending to enterprises corresponding to given rates of inventory accumulation.

Nosko, P., and Poliakov, M. "The Currency Monopoly and the USSR's International Accounts." PROBLEMS OF ECONOMICS 11 (August 1968): 35-42.

A description of the financial aspects of Soviet foreign trade: definition of exchange rates, financing of international transactions, the role of the transferable ruble, and the functions of the International Bank for Economic Cooperation and of other banks involved in foreign trade.

Nove, A[lec]. "Rural Taxation in the USSR." SOVIET STUDIES 5 (October 1953): 159-66.

An assessment of the weight of taxation borne by the collectivized sector of the Soviet economy.

_____. "Soviet Budgets after Stalin." REVIEW OF ECONOMICS AND STATISTICS 36 (November 1954): 415-24. Tables.

A comparison of pre- and post-Stalin Soviet budgets.

Pessel', M. "Credit and Its Development under Current Conditions." PROBLEMS OF ECONOMICS 15 (April 1973): 86-99. Tables.

Remarks on the importance and functions of credit in the Soviet economy.

_____. "Profit, Capital Charges, and Interest." PROBLEMS OF ECONOMICS 15 (October 1972): 55-66.

Observations on the part played by profit, incentive funds, capital charges, and interest in the financial and credit mechanism.

Powell, Raymond P. "Monetary Statistics." In SOVIET ECONOMIC STATIS-TICS, edited by Vladimir G. Treml and John P. Hardt, pp. 397-432. Durham, N.C.: Duke University Press, 1972. Tables.

A discussion of Soviet monetary statistics by examination of the accounts of various Soviet financial institutions.

Pryor, Frederic L. PUBLIC EXPENDITURES IN COMMUNIST AND CAPITAL-IST NATIONS. Homewood, Ill.: Richard D. Irwin, 1968. 543 p. Tables, figures, appendixes, and index.

An analysis of public consumption expenditures for defense, health, education, and welfare.

Sher, I. "Long-Term Credit for Industry." PROBLEMS OF ECONOMICS 13 (December 1970): 43-60.

An explanation of Soviet policy regarding long-term industrial loans, including coverage and repayment terms and conditions.

Sitarian, S. "The Budget and Changes in Profits and the Turnover Tax." PROBLEMS OF ECONOMICS 7 (May 1964): 12-20. Tables.

An assessment of the trends in the relationships between the Soviet budget and its two main revenue sources: deductions from profits and the turnover tax.

Tucek, Miroslav. "Monetary Equilibrium and Future Economic Growth in Czechoslovakia." EASTERN EUROPEAN ECONOMICS 6 (Summer 1968): 3-12.

Evaluation of the basic concepts of the mechanism of monetary equilibrium in Czechoslovakia, followed by an appraisal of the relationship between monetary equilibrium and future economic growth.

Vasil'ev, P. and Shirkevich, N. "Budgetary Revenues of the Union Republics and Their Allocation." PROBLEMS OF ECONOMICS 7 (September 1964): 18-28. Tables.

An explanation of the sources and uses of the union republics' budget revenues.

Wilczynski, J. SOCIALIST ECONOMIC DEVELOPMENT AND REFORMS. New York: Praeger, 1972. xvii, 350 p. Tables and index.

A discussion of growth strategy, orthodox planning practices, prices, financial and monetary policies, foreign trade criteria and practices, reforms, and growth performance in the Soviet-type economies.

Wiles, P[eter]. J.D. COMMUNIST INTERNATIONAL ECONOMICS. New York: Frederick A. Praeger, 1969. xvi, 566 p. Tables and index.

Stimulating discussions of inflation in a Soviet-type economy, balance of payments and exchange rates, international integration, and problems of bilateralism, multilateralism, and international finance.

Wyczalkowski, Marcin R. "Communist Economics and Currency Convertibility." INTERNATIONAL MONETARY FUND STAFF PAPERS 8 (July 1966): 155-97.

Consideration of the pre-1956 financial system of the Soviet bloc countries, followed by an outline of the financial reform discussions, current issues of "convertibility" and "multilateralism" within the CMEA, and the economic conditions for meaningful multilateralism and convertibility.

_____. "The Soviet Price System and the Ruble Exchange Rate." INTERNATIONAL MONETARY FUND STAFF PAPERS 1 (September 1950): 203-23.

Observations on Soviet price formation in 1950, the meaning of the ruble exchange rate, and the significance of ruble revaluation.

Zahalka, Vaclav. "Banks and Foreign Trade." SOVIET AND EASTERN EUROPEAN FOREIGN TRADE 8 (Summer 1972): 155-73.

An examination of the role of financial and banking institutions, including those within the CMEA, in the promotion of foreign trade.

Zauberman, Alfred. "Gold in Soviet Economic Theory and Policies." AMERICAN ECONOMIC REVIEW 41 (December 1951): 879-90.

A survey of Soviet economic thought on the role of gold up to 1951.

Zverev, A. "Role of the State Budget in the Distribution of the Social Product and National Income." PROBLEMS OF ECONOMICS 7 (December 1964): 28-35. Tables.

A discussion of the role of the budget in the furtherance of politico-economic objectives.

Zwass, Adam. "CMEA Monetary Institutions and Steering Instruments." SOVIET AND EASTERN EUROPEAN FOREIGN TRADE 10 (Fall-Winter 1974-75): 97-158. Tables.

Consideration of the formal organization of the CMEA, credits, prices, and clearing arrangements in intra-CMEA trade, and the role of the International Investment Bank and International Bank for Economic Cooperation.

_____. "Currency in the Foreign Trade of the CMEA Countries." SOVIET AND EASTERN EUROPEAN FOREIGN TRADE 10 (Fall-Winter 1974-75): 46-96. Tables.

General remarks on the foreign trade of planned economies, the concepts of currency and exchange monopoly, functions of the exchange rate, and reforms in the foreign trade system of Soviet-type economies.

_____. "The International Investment Bank and the Council for Mutual Economic Assistance." SOVIET AND EASTERN EUROPEAN FOREIGN TRADE 9 (Spring 1973): 3-50. Tables.

A description of the organization, functions, capital, and other monetary reserves of the International Investment Bank, as well as some discussion concerning the functioning of the International Bank for Economic Cooperation.

_____. "Monetary Steering Instruments of East-West Trade." SOVIET AND EASTERN EUROPEAN FOREIGN TRADE 10 (Fall-Winter 1974-75): 159-233. Tables.

Careful examination of the following aspects of East-West trade: Communist foreign trade relations with nonconvertible currencies; Comecon and the international monetary and credit institutions; settlement, payments procedures, and credit in East-West trade; and the role of Eastern European banks in the West and that of Western banks in Eastern Europe.

_____. "Money and Credit in the USSR and Eastern Europe in the Light of Economic Reforms." SOVIET AND EASTERN EUROPEAN FOREIGN TRADE 10 (Fall-Winter 1974-75): 1-45. Tables and appendix.

An assessment of the functions of money, credit, and banks, and aspects of credit policy.

Chapter 13

FOREIGN TRADE

Allen, Robert Loring. "Economic Motives in Soviet Foreign Trade Policy." SOUTHERN ECONOMIC JOURNAL 25 (October 1958): 189-201. Tables.

An examination of Soviet foreign trade trends between 1928-55.

_____. "A Note on Soviet Foreign Trade Statistics." SOVIET STUDIES 10 (April 1959): 360-69. Tables.

A brief discussion of the discrepancies and inconsistencies which exist in Soviet foreign trade data.

Ames, Edward. "International Trade Without Markets--The Soviet Bloc Case." AMERICAN ECONOMIC REVIEW 44 (December 1954): 791-807.

An analysis of direct controls in determining the composition of exports and imports and ensuring external equilibrium.

_____. SOVIET ECONOMIC PROCESSES. Homewood, Ill.: Richard D. Irwin, 1965. 257 p. Tables, figures, and index. Paperback.

An excellent overview of the Soviet economy, with particular attention to economic organization, planning on the macro and micro levels, fiscal and monetary policy, international trade, and economic performance.

Augustinovics, M. "Linear Inquiries into Foreign Trade." In PLANNING AND MARKETS: MODERN TRENDS IN VARIOUS ECONOMIC SYSTEMS, edited by John T. Dunlap and Nikolay P. Fedorenko, pp. 329-50. New York: McGraw-Hill Book Co., 1969.

An analysis of the effects of foreign trade on the volume of and structural relationships among gross output, final product, and primary inputs.

Baykov, Alexander. SOVIET FOREIGN TRADE. Princeton, N.J.: Princeton University Press, 1946. x, 125 p. Tables and appendix.

An examination of the evolution and organization of the Soviet foreign trade system.

Boltho, Andrea. FOREIGN TRADE CRITERIA IN SOCIALIST ECONOMIES. Cambridge: At the University Press, 1971. viii, 176 p. Tables, figures, appendix, and index.

A thorough examination of the theories and methods employed by the Soviet-type economies to implement their decisions concerning foreign trade. The Marxist approach to the foreign trade problem, the orthodox Soviet model of foreign trade planning, intra-CMEA specialization, and global and sectoral foreign trade models are among the topics discussed.

Borisenko, A., and Shastitko, V. "Problems of the Economic Efficiency of Foreign Trade in the Socialist Countries." PROBLEMS OF ECONOMICS 5 (March 1963): 56-62.

A survey of the major foreign trade efficiency indexes employed by the Soviet-type economies.

Bozyk, Pawel. "Functions of Planning and Forecasting in International Trade." SOVIET AND EASTERN EUROPEAN FOREIGN TRADE 9 (Winter 1973-74): 3-18.

A discussion of foreign trade planning, particularly as related to the Polish economy.

Brada, Josef C. "Allocative Efficiency and the System of Economic Management in Some Socialist Countries." KYKLOS 27 (1974): 270-85.

A method for measuring the static efficiency of the export sector. The author demonstrates that allocative efficiency is inversely related to the level of development in the Eastern European Soviet-type economies.

Brown, Alan A. "Towards a Theory of Centrally Planned Foreign Trade." In INTERNATIONAL TRADE AND CENTRAL PLANNING--AN ANALYSIS OF ECONOMIC INTERACTIONS, edited by Alan A. Brown and Egon Neuberger, pp. 57-93. Berkeley and Los Angeles: University of California Press, 1968. Appendix.

A thoughtful integration of static and dynamic equilibrium analysis of certain aspects of centrally planned foreign trade.

Brown, Alan A., and Marer, Paul. "Foreign Trade in the East European Reforms." In PLAN AND MARKET: ECONOMIC REFORM IN EASTERN EUROPE, edited by Morris Bornstein, pp. 153-205. New Haven, Conn.: Yale University Press, 1973. Tables, figures, and appendixes.

Observations concerning the role of foreign trade in centrally planned economies, primarily on the basis of Hungary's experiences. Relationships between foreign trade and economic reform.

Bystrov, Feodor. "Soviet International Credit Relations." PROBLEMS OF ECONOMICS 5 (August 1962): 39-44.

A brief survey of Soviet foreign credit policy.

Caiola, Marcello. "Balance of Payments of the U.S.S.R., 1955-58." INTERNATIONAL MONETARY FUND STAFF PAPERS 9 (March 1962): 1-36. Tables.

An assemblage of the financial transactions of the USSR with the rest of the world for 1955-58.

_____. "Balance of Payments of the U.S.S.R., 1959-60." INTERNATIONAL MONETARY FUND STAFF PAPERS 10 (July 1963): 321-44. Tables and appendixes.

An assemblage of Soviet transactions with the Soviet area and with the rest of the world during 1959-60.

Carter, F.W. "Bulgaria's Economic Ties with her Immediate Neighbors and Prospects for Future Development." EAST EUROPEAN QUARTERLY 4 (June 1970): 209-24. Tables and.figures.

An explanation of the expansion of Bulgaria's postwar trade with the Balkan countries.

Csikos-Nagy, Bela. SOCIALIST ECONOMIC POLICY. New York: St. Martin's Press, 1973. 238 p. Index.

A discussion of Soviet-type economic organization, planning, financial policies, price and incomes policies, and distribution and foreign trade policies.

Donaldson, Loraine. "The Underdeveloped Countries and Soviet Bloc Trade." EAST EUROPEAN QUARTERLY 2 (January 1969): 439-60. Figures.

An analysis of the disadvantages for underdeveloped countries of foreign trade integration with the Soviet bloc.

Elias, Andrew, and Searing, Marjory. "A Quantitative Assessment of U.S. Constraints on Trade with Eastern Europe and the U.S.S.R." In REORIENTATION AND COMMERCIAL RELATIONS OF THE ECONOMIES OF EASTERN EUROPE, Joint Economic Committee, 93d Cong., 2d sess., pp. 599-661. Washington, D.C.: Government Printing Office, 1974. Tables, figures, and appendix.

An examination of U.S. trade barriers to imports from Bulgaria, Czechoslovakia, East Germany, Hungary, Rumania, and the USSR, accompanied by quantitative estimates of foreign exchange losses to these countries because of trade barriers. The volume of U.S. imports in 1976 and 1980 is projected on the assumption of "normalized" trade relations.

Fallenbuchl, Z[bigniew]. M. "The Role of International Trade in the Czechoslovak Economy." CANADIAN SLAVONIC PAPERS 10 (Winter 1968): 451-78. Tables.

> A discussion of the direction, commodity composition, and growth of Czechoslovakia's foreign trade, accompanied by comparisons with selected countries.

Gekker, Paul. "The Soviet Bank for Foreign Trade and Soviet Banks Abroad: A Note." ECONOMICS OF PLANNING 7 (1967): 183-97. Tables.

> A description of the functions and activities of the Soviet Foreign Trade Bank and of Soviet-owned banks abroad.

Glovinsky, Evgeny. "The Economic Relations of the USSR with Latin America." STUDIES ON THE SOVIET UNION 1, no. 3 (1962): 64-79. Tables.

> A chronological survey of the USSR's economic relations with Latin America, with emphasis on the 1950s.

Glowacki, Jerzy. "Problems of Optimizing the Directions of International Trade in a Planned Economy." ECONOMICS OF PLANNING 6 (1966): 27-42. Tables.

> A presentation and interpretation of a dual program for foreign trade optimization, with explanations as to its relationship with practical decisions.

Granick, David. "The Pattern of Foreign Trade in Eastern Europe and Its Relation to Economic Development Policy." QUARTERLY JOURNAL OF ECONOMICS 68 (August 1954): 377-400. Tables.

> A survey of the economic development and trade patterns in Eastern Europe. Hypotheses are advanced regarding internal development and foreign trade patterns in the Soviet bloc.

Gregory, Paul R., and Stuart, Robert C. SOVIET ECONOMIC STRUCTURE AND PERFORMANCE. New York: Harper & Row Publishers, 1974. x, 478 p. Tables, figures, and index. Paperback.

> A comprehensive discussion and analysis of the issues relevant to the Soviet economy. Included are discussions concerning the economic experiences of the periods of war communism and New Economic Policy, pricing, planning methods and principles, agriculture, growth strategy and performance, foreign trade, monetary and financial controls and policy, and economic reforms.

Gross, George. "Rumania: The Fruits of Autonomy." PROBLEMS OF COMMUNISM 15 (January-February 1966): 16-27.

> A delineation of the rise of Rumanian autonomy within the bloc and the consequent partial reorientation in Rumania's foreign trade from East to West.

Heiss, Hertha W. "The Soviet Union in the World Market." In NEW DI-
RECTIONS IN THE SOVIET ECONOMY, Joint Economic Committee, 89th
Cong., 2d sess., pp. 917-33. Washington, D.C.: Government Printing Of-
fice, 1966. Tables.

A survey of trends in the volume, geographical distribution, and
commodity composition of Soviet foreign trade and in the balance
of payments.

Herman, L[eon]. M. "A Dollar Estimate of Soviet Foreign Trade, 1947-1951."
REVIEW OF ECONOMICS AND STATISTICS 36 (November 1954): 437-43.
Tables and appendix.

An analysis of the altered direction of Soviet trade and the nature
of intra-bloc trade.

_____. "The Promises of Economic Self-Sufficiency under Soviet Socialism."
STUDIES ON THE SOVIET UNION 7, no. 1 (1967): 67-102. Tables.

Issues in Soviet foreign trade theory and policy from the revolution
until the 1960s.

Hoeffding, Oleg. "Recent Structural Changes and Balance-of-Payments Adjust-
ments in Soviet Foreign Trade." In INTERNATIONAL TRADE AND CENTRAL
PLANNING--AN ANALYSIS OF ECONOMIC INTERACTIONS, edited by
Alan A. Brown and Egon Neuberger, pp. 312-37. Berkeley and Los Angeles:
University of California Press, 1968. Tables.

An illuminating analysis of how Soviet planners solved the USSR's
balance of payments problem during 1963-65.

Holzman, Franklyn D. "Foreign Trade." In ECONOMIC TRENDS IN THE
SOVIET UNION, edited by Abram Bergson and Simon Kuznets, pp. 283-32.
Cambridge, Mass.: Harvard University Press, 1963. Figure, tables, and ap-
pendix.

An explanation of the major trends in Soviet foreign trade and
appraisal of the importance of foreign trade for Soviet industrial
growth.

_____. "More on Soviet Bloc Trade Discrimination." SOVIET STUDIES 17
(July 1965): 44-65. Tables.

A concise, critical review of the argument concerning whether the
USSR engaged in price discrimination toward its satellites during
the 1950s.

_____. "The Ruble Exchange Rate and Soviet Foreign Trade Pricing Policies,
1929-1961." AMERICAN ECONOMIC REVIEW 58 (September 1968): 803-
25.

An empirical investigation of Soviet practices between 1929 and

and 1961 as they pertained to export and import pricing policies and the ruble exchange rate.

_____. "Some Financial Aspects of Soviet Foreign Trade." In COMPARISONS OF THE UNITED STATES AND SOVIET ECONOMIES, Joint Economic Committee, 86th Cong., 1st sess., pp. 427-43. Washington, D.C.: Government Printing Office, 1959. Tables and appendix.

A discussion of the trends in the official ruble exchange rate, and examination of Soviet international price policy and the impact of Soviet foreign trade on internal financial stability.

_____. "Soviet Central Planning and Its Impact on Foreign Trade Behavior and Adjustment Mechanisms." In INTERNATIONAL TRADE AND CENTRAL PLANNING--AN ANALYSIS OF ECONOMIC INTERACTIONS, edited by Alan A. Brown and Egon Neuberger, pp. 280-305. Berkeley and Los Angeles: University of California Press, 1968.

An analytical exposition of the impact of central planning on foreign trade behavior by examining the operation of certain adjustment mechanisms (price, income, and exchange rate adjustment) in the USSR.

_____. "Soviet Foreign Trade Pricing and the Question of Discrimination: A 'Customs Union' Approach." REVIEW OF ECONOMICS AND STATISTICS 44 (May 1962): 134-47. Tables.

An examination, via a "customs union" approach, of intra-bloc foreign trade pricing and price discrimination by the Soviet Union.

Kiss, Tibor. INTERNATIONAL DIVISION OF LABOR IN OPEN ECONOMIES, WITH SPECIAL REGARD TO THE CMEA. Translated by J. Racz. Budapest: Akademiai Kiado, 1971. 322 p. Tables and figures.

A basic introduction to the principles which govern foreign trade and economic growth. The author concentrates on the economic and financial aspects of CMEA integration and on certain problems of Socialist world market prices.

Kohler, Heinz. "East Germany's Terms of Trade: 1950-1961." KYKLOS 16 (1963): 286-302. Tables.

Estimates of the gross and net barter terms of trade for East Germany for the period 1950-61.

_____. ECONOMIC INTEGRATION IN THE SOVIET BLOC: WITH AN EAST GERMAN CASE STUDY. New York: Frederick A. Praeger, 1965. xxi, 402 p. Tables and appendixes.

A thorough discussion of the foreign trade relations of East Germany, including the volume and direction of the GDR's trade, the country's economic integration into the Soviet bloc, as well as the importance of foreign trade to East Germany.

Kovach, Robert S., and Farrell, John T. "Foreign Trade of the USSR." In ECONOMIC PERFORMANCE AND MILITARY BURDEN IN THE SOVIET UNION, Joint Economic Committee, 91st Cong., 2d sess., pp. 100-116. Washington, D.C.: Government Printing Office, 1970. Tables and appendix.

> Analyzes useful information about the distribution and composition of Soviet foreign trade between 1960 and 1969.

Lawson, C.W. "An Empirical Analysis of the Structure and Stability of Communist Foreign Trade, 1960-68." SOVIET STUDIES 26 (April 1974): 224-38. Tables.

> An analysis of the stability of Communist and non-Communist trade patterns, the relative stability of exports and imports, and the constraints on the expansion of foreign trade in a command economy.

Levine, Herbert S. "The Effects of Foreign Trade on Soviet Planning Practices." In INTERNATIONAL TRADE AND CENTRAL PLANNING--AN ANALYSIS OF ECONOMIC INTERACTIONS, edited by Alan A. Brown and Egon Neuberger, pp. 255-76. Berkeley and Los Angeles: University of California Press, 1968.

> An assessment of the effects of foreign trade on Soviet planning methodology.

McMillan, Carl H. "Some Recent Developments in Soviet Foreign Trade Theory." CANADIAN SLAVONIC PAPERS 12 (Fall 1970): 243-72.

> A survey of the evolution of Soviet foreign trade theory from the traditional view of foreign trade (as a short-run instrument of plan balance) to the virtual acceptance of at least the essence of the theory of comparative advantage.

_____. "Soviet Specialization and Trade in Manufactures." SOVIET STUDIES 24 (April 1973): 522-32. Tables.

> An analysis of the pattern of specialization in Soviet trade; comparisons with the foreign trade of several industrial market economies.

Marer, Paul. SOVIET AND EAST EUROPEAN FOREIGN TRADE, 1946-1969. Bloomington: Indiana University Press, 1972. xviii, 408 p. Tables and figures.

> Statistical compendium of comprehensive data on the value of foreign trade of Eastern European countries during 1946-69.

Marer, Paul, and Neuberger, Egon. "Commercial Relations between the United States and Eastern Europe: Options and Prospects." In REORIENTATION

AND COMMERCIAL RELATIONS OF THE ECONOMIES OF EASTERN EUROPE, Joint Economic Committee, 93d Cong., 2d sess., pp. 556-98. Washington, D.C.: Government Printing Office, 1974. Tables and appendixes.

Factual background and forecasts of U.S.-East European trade and a discussion of the options open to the Eastern European countries for financing their imports from the United States.

Mendershausen, Horst. "The Terms of Soviet-Satellite Trade: A Broadened Analysis." REVIEW OF ECONOMICS AND STATISTICS 42 (May 1960): 152-63. Tables and figures.

An examination of price discrimination within the Soviet bloc.

_____. "Terms of Trade between the Soviet Union and Smaller Communist Countries, 1955-1957." REVIEW OF ECONOMICS AND STATISTICS 41 (May 1959): 106-18. Tables and figures.

An examination of intra-bloc foreign trade prices and possible price discrimination by the Soviet Union.

Michal, Jan M. "Czechoslovakia's Foreign Trade." SLAVIC REVIEW 27 (June 1968): 212-29. Tables.

An investigation of the quantum, value, and functions of Czechoslovakia's foreign trade.

Mitrofanova, N. "Concerning the Interrelationship between Internal and Foreign Trade Prices in European Socialist Countries." PROBLEMS OF ECONOMICS 17 (May 1974): 85-97.

A description of the determination of foreign trade prices, and their effect on internal prices.

_____. "Prospects for the Further Improvement of the Foreign Trade Prices of Socialist Countries." PROBLEMS OF ECONOMICS 17 (December 1974): 65-79. Tables.

Price index comparisons for contract, world, and wholesale prices.

Montias, John M[ichael]. "Rumania's Foreign Trade in the Postwar Period." SLAVIC REVIEW 25 (September 1966): 421-42. Tables.

A discussion of the volume, direction, and commodity composition of postwar Rumanian foreign trade.

_____. "Socialist Industrialization and Trade in Machinery Products: An Analysis Based on the Experience of Bulgaria, Poland, and Rumania." In INTERNATIONAL TRADE AND CENTRAL PLANNING--AN ANALYSIS OF ECONOMIC INTERACTIONS, edited by Alan A. Brown and Egon Neuberger, pp. 130-59. Berkeley and Los Angeles: University of California Press, 1968. Tables.

A discussion of both theoretical and empirical aspects of the volume and commodity composition of trade and balance of payments position of Bulgaria, Poland, and Rumania. A twenty-six-variable, six-sector simulation model is also presented in the paper.

Neuberger, Egon. "Is the USSR Superior to the West as a Market for Primary Products?" REVIEW OF ECONOMICS AND STATISTICS 46 (August 1964): 287-93. Tables.

An assessment of the validity of Soviet claims regarding the alleged superiority of the USSR over the Western industrialized countries as a market for primary products for the period 1955-61.

Nosko, P., and Poliakov, M. "The Currency Monopoly and the USSR's International Accounts." PROBLEMS OF ECONOMICS 11 (August 1968): 35-42.

A description of the financial aspects of Soviet foreign trade: definition of exchange rates, financing of international transactions, the role of the transferable ruble, and the functions of the International Bank for Economic Cooperation and of other banks involved in foreign trade.

Petrov, Milan. "Foreign Exchange Planning under the Conditions of the New System of Planning and Management of the National Economy." EASTERN EUROPEAN ECONOMICS 6 (Summer 1968): 44-54.

Comments on the Bulgarian economic reforms of the mid-1960s, including a discussion of the methods and scope of foreign exchange planning under the reform.

Plowiec, Urszula. "Poland's Foreign Trade Control System in 1971." SOVIET AND EASTERN EUROPEAN FOREIGN TRADE 9 (Winter 1973-74): 42-71.

An examination of the organization of foreign trade planning, methods of plan implementation, as well as the likely further changes in Polish foreign trade planning.

Prokhorov, G. "Optimization of the Foreign Economic Relations of Socialist Countries." PROBLEMS OF ECONOMICS 13 (August 1970): 63-80.

Consideration of questions of planned optimization, including optimality criteria, in intra-Comecon trade.

Pryor, Frederic L. THE COMMUNIST FOREIGN TRADE SYSTEM. Cambridge, Mass.: MIT Press, 1963. 296 p. Tables, appendixes, and index.

An analysis of the role of foreign trade in Communist countries, the planning of foreign trade, criteria for trade, pricing problems and exchange rates, mechanisms of intra-bloc foreign trade, and foreign trade reforms.

. "Foreign Trade Theory in the Communist Bloc." SOVIET STUDIES 14 (July 1962): 41-61.

A discussion of Communist views on pure trade theory and issues concerning intra-bloc pricing.

Rabinovich, I. "Soviet-American Trade Relations from 1923 to 1933." PROBLEMS OF ECONOMICS 3 (February 1961): 52-62. Tables.

A Soviet view of the nature and significance of American-Soviet trade relations.

Rubinshtein, G., and Baksht, M. "The Development of Soviet Foreign Trade." PROBLEMS OF ECONOMICS 5 (February 1963): 30-37. Tables and figures.

Comments on the growth of foreign trade volume and on the changes in the commodity structure of Soviet exports and imports.

Rux, Wiktor. "Polish Foreign Trade During the Five-Year Period 1971-1975." SOVIET AND EASTERN EUROPEAN FOREIGN TRADE 9 (Summer 1973): 83-107. Tables.

A description of Polish exports and imports, as well as the direction and commodity composition of foreign trade during 1971-75.

Sawyer, Carole A. COMMUNIST TRADE WITH DEVELOPING COUNTRIES: 1955-1965. New York: Frederick A. Praeger, 1966. x, 126 p. Tables and appendixes.

A concise, authoritative analysis of the volume and direction, commodity pattern, and balance of trade between the Communist countries and the developing nations from 1955 to 1965.

Scott, N.B. "Soviet Economic Relations with the Under-Developed Countries." SOVIET STUDIES 10 (July 1958): 36-53.

A discussion of Soviet aid to and trade patterns with the less developed countries.

Shagalov, G. "The Economic Efficiency of the Socialist Countries' Foreign Trade." PROBLEMS OF ECONOMICS 8 (December 1965): 49-60. Tables.

An explanation of indexes designed to measure the efficiency of Communist foreign trade.

Sirc, Ljubo. ECONOMIC DEVOLUTION IN EASTERN EUROPE. London: Longmans, Green and Co., 1969. xii, 165 p. Tables and appendix.

An analysis of Eastern European economic problems as they pertain to pricing, foreign trade, economic growth, planning methods, and economic reforms.

Smith, Glen Alden. SOVIET FOREIGN TRADE: ORGANIZATION OPERA-
TIONS, AND POLICY, 1918-1971. New York: Praeger, 1973. xvii, 360 p.
Tables and figures.

A discussion of Soviet foreign trade policy, organization, and
financing, Western trade restrictions, as well as Soviet trade with
the developing and Communist countries.

Snell, Edwin M. "Eastern Europe's Trade and Payments with the Industrial
West." In REORIENTATION AND COMMERCIAL RELATIONS OF THE ECON-
OMIES OF EASTERN EUROPE. Joint Economic Committee, 93d Cong., 2d
sess., pp. 682-724. Washington, D.C.: Government Printing Office, 1974.
Tables.

Illustrations of Eastern Europe's growing trade with the West, and
estimates of the growing payments deficits of Bulgaria, Czechoslovakia, German Democratic Republic, Hungary, Poland, and Rumania.

Spulber, Nicolas. "Problems of East-West Trade and Economic Trends in the
European Satellites of Soviet Russia." ECONOMIA INTERNAZIONALE 8
(1955): 597-617. Tables.

An analysis of the patterns and structural changes of intra and
extra-bloc trade and the respective roles of the New Course and
the strategic embargo.

Stackelberg, Georg A. von. "The Problem of Soviet Colonialism." STUDIES
ON THE SOVIET UNION 5 (1960): 15-30.

A discussion concerning ethnic minorities within the USSR and the
relations between the USSR and its satellites.

Staller, George J. "Patterns of Stability in Foreign Trade: OECD and
COMECON, 1950-1963." AMERICAN ECONOMIC REVIEW 57 (September
1967): 879-88. Tables.

Data and discussions of the results of empirical investigations of
import and export stabilities for CMEA and OECD blocs.

Thunberg, Penelope Hartland. "The Soviet Union in the World Economy."
In DIMENSIONS OF SOVIET ECONOMIC POWER, Joint Economic Commit-
tee, 87th Cong., 2d sess., pp. 409-38. Washington, D.C.: Government
Printing Office, 1962. Tables.

A careful examination of Soviet bloc foreign trade institutions,
foreign trade prices, exchange rates, and economic assistance, as
well as of the commodity composition and financial problems of
Soviet trade with the West.

United Nations. Economic Commission for Europe. "Foreign Trade and Economic
Development in Eastern Europe and the Soviet Union." ECONOMIC BULLETIN

FOR EUROPE 11 (June 1959): 39-76, appendix A: 1-31; appendix B: 1-2. Tables and appendixes.

A survey of the increase in the volume of trade, changes in its commodity composition and direction, problems of foreign trade organization and policy, and plans through 1965.

_____. "Note on Institutional Developments in the Foreign Trade of the Soviet Union and Eastern European Countries." ECONOMIC BULLETIN FOR EUROPE 20 (November 1968): 43-54. Appendix.

A discussion of the changes in foreign trade organization and pricing.

Vajda, Imre. THE ROLE OF FOREIGN TRADE IN A SOCIALIST ECONOMY-- NEW ESSAYS IN PERSUASION. Budapest: Corvina Press, 1965. 336 p. Tables and figures.

A collection of essays primarily examining the role of the Hungarian economy in the international division of labor, with special attention to CMEA trade.

Vajda, Imre, and Simai, Mihaly, eds. FOREIGN TRADE IN A PLANNED ECONOMY. London: Cambridge University Press, 1971. xii, 221 p. Tables, figures, and index.

A collection of eleven essays by Hungarian economists, dealing with the institutional mechanism of trade and payments within the Comecon, foreign trade aspects of Hungary's New Economic Mechanism, and various other trade related topics.

Valkenier, Elizabeth Kridl. "New Trends in Soviet Economic Relations with the Third World." WORLD POLITICS 22 (April 1970): 415-32.

A survey of new forms and methods in Soviet trade and aid and new Soviet thoughts on development.

Vasilev, Dimitur. "The International Socialist Division of Labor and Its Role in the Increased Profitability of Bulgaria's Foreign Trade." EASTERN EURO- PEAN ECONOMICS 8 (Fall 1969): 90-99.

A description of Bulgaria's foreign trade achievements, problems, and prospects within the Comecon.

Wilczynski, J. "Dumping and Central Planning." JOURNAL OF POLITICAL ECONOMY 74 (June 1966): 250-64. Tables.

An examination of the problem of dumping within the context of command-type central planning.

_____. SOCIALIST ECONOMIC DEVELOPMENT AND REFORMS. New York: Praeger, 1972. xvii, 350 p. Tables and index.

A discussion of growth strategy, orthodox planning practices, prices, financial and monetary policies, foreign trade criteria and practices, reforms, and growth performance in the Soviet-type economies.

_____. "The Theory of Comparative Costs and Centrally Planned Economies." ECONOMIC JOURNAL 75 (March 1965): 63-80.

Demonstration of the rejection of the theory of comparative costs in the Communist bloc (in 1965), followed by a discussion of accepted foreign trade criteria.

Wiles, P[eter]. J.D. COMMUNIST INTERNATIONAL ECONOMICS. New York: Frederick A. Praeger, 1969. xvi, 566 p. Tables and index.

Stimulating discussions of inflation in a Soviet-type economy, balance of payments and exchange rates, international integration, and problems of bilateralism, multilateralism, and international finance.

Zauberman, A[lfred]. "The Criterion of Efficiency of Foreign Trade in Soviet-type Economies." ECONOMICA 31 (February 1964): 5-12.

Description of the efficiency criteria proposed for Communist foreign trade.

Zlobin, I. "The World Socialist Market--Its Prices, Currency, and System of Settlements." PROBLEMS OF ECONOMICS 5 (November 1962): 12-21.

A discussion concerning Communist foreign trade principles, as well as price and exchange rate determination and system of settlements within the CMEA.

Zsoldos, Laszlo. THE ECONOMIC INTEGRATION OF HUNGARY INTO THE SOVIET BLOC: FOREIGN TRADE EXPERIENCE. Columbus: Ohio State University, College of Administrative Science, 1963. xvii, 149 p. Tables, figures, and appendixes.

Examination of the institutional aspects of Hungary's foreign trade, changes in the geographic and commodity patterns of Hungarian trade, and the impact of foreign trade on Hungary's economic development.

Zwass, Adam. "Currency in the Foreign Trade of the CMEA Countries." SOVIET AND EASTERN EUROPEAN FOREIGN TRADE 10 (Fall-Winter 1974-75): 46-96. Tables.

An instructive account of the general features of foreign trade in planned economies, the concepts of currency and exchange monopoly, functions of the exchange rate, and reforms in the foreign trade system of Soviet-type economies.

Zyzniewski, Stanley J. "The Soviet Economic Impact on Poland." AMERI-
CAN SLAVIC AND EAST EUROPEAN REVIEW 18 (April 1959): 205-25.
Tables.

> A description of the main features of postwar Polish-Soviet eco-
> nomic relations, with emphasis on the events of 1956.

CMEA

Adler-Karlsson, Gunnar. "The Council For Mutual Economic Assistance."
ECONOMICS OF PLANNING 3 (September 1963): 141-48.

> A survey of the background, goals, methods, and perspectives of
> the Comecon.

Aleksandrov, A. "In the Permanent Commissions of the Council of Mutual
Economic Assistance." PROBLEMS OF ECONOMICS 4 (March 1962): 55-61.

> An examination of the role performed by the various CMEA per-
> manent commissions.

Ames, Edward. "Economic Integration in the European Soviet Bloc?" AMER-
ICAN ECONOMIC REVIEW 49 (May 1959): 113-24.

> A theoretical analysis of the degree and extent of economic inte-
> gration within the Comecon.

Ausch, Sandor. THEORY AND PRACTICE OF CMEA COOPERATION. Translated by J. Racz and Gy. Hajdu. Budapest: Akademiai Kiado, 1972.
279 p. Tables, figures, and appendixes.

> A close look at problems of bilateralism and multilateralism in
> payments between CMEA countries, national plan coordination,
> CMEA foreign trade prices and practices, and certain aspects of
> specialization and cooperation within the CMEA.

Bilimovich, Aleksandr. "The Common Market and COMECON." STUDIES
ON THE SOVIET UNION 2, no. 2 (1962): 40-50.

> An examination of certain Comecon views concerning the EEC.

Bogomolov, O. "Economic Cooperation among the Comecon Countries."
PROBLEMS OF ECONOMICS 7 (January 1965): 39-46.

> An evaluation of the results, difficulties, and further tasks of
> intra-CMEA cooperation.

_____. "The International Socialist Division of Labor." PROBLEMS OF
ECONOMICS 3 (June 1960): 44-50.

> A discussion of the principles, policies, and achievements of eco-
> nomic integration within the CMEA.

Boltho, Andrea. FOREIGN TRADE CRITERIA IN SOCIALIST ECONOMIES. Cambridge: At the University Press, 1971. viii, 176 p. Tables, figures, appendix, and index.

A thorough examination of the theories and methods employed by the Soviet-type economies to implement their decisions concerning foreign trade. The Marxist approach to the foreign trade problem, the orthodox Soviet model of foreign trade planning, intra-CMEA specialization, and global and sectoral foreign trade models are discussed.

Bozyk, Pawel. "Domestic and Foreign Trade Prices in the Process of Integration in Comecon Countries." SOVIET AND EASTERN EUROPEAN FOREIGN TRADE 6 (Summer 1970): 125-39.

A discussion of domestic price formation, the relationships between domestic and foreign prices, the influence of domestic price structures on intra-Comecon specialization, and the role of foreign exchange rates in linking intra-Comecon domestic prices.

Braker, Hans. "Soviet Policy towards the Communist Countries with Special Reference to Its Economic Aspects." STUDIES ON THE SOVIET UNION 1, no. 2 (1961): 96-114.

A description of ideological principles and actual practices of economic cooperation within the Soviet bloc.

Brown, J.F. "Rumania Steps Out of Line." SURVEY 49 (October 1963): 19-34.

An analysis of the background and content of Rumania's dispute with the Comecon.

Council for Mutual Economic Assistance. A SURVEY OF TWENTY YEARS OF COUNCIL FOR MUTUAL ECONOMIC ASSISTANCE. Moscow: Council for Mutual Economic Assistance Secretariat, 1969. 107 p. Tables.

A brief survey of the activities of the CMEA during its first twenty years, including data on trade, the economic development of member countries, and intra-CMEA specialization and cooperation.

D'iachenko, V. "Main Trends in Improving Prices in Trade among Comecon Members." PROBLEMS OF ECONOMICS 11 (June 1968): 40-49.

An examination of the role and establishment of foreign trade prices within the Comecon, and a call for the establishment of Comecon's "own price basis."

Dudinskii, I. "Economic Consolidation of the Socialist Countries and European 'Integration.'" PROBLEMS OF ECONOMICS 5 (February 1963): 38-46. Tables and figures.

Proposals for the furtherance of the economic consolidation of the Soviet-bloc countries.

Fallenbuchl, Z[bigniew]. M. "Comecon Integration." PROBLEMS OF COMMUNISM 22 (March-April 1973): 25-39. Tables.

A review of the pattern and growth of Comecon foreign trade, and an assessment of the prospects for further integration in Eastern Europe.

_____. "East European Integration: Comecon." In REORIENTATION AND COMMERCIAL RELATIONS OF THE ECONOMIES OF EASTERN EUROPE, Joint Economic Committee, 93d Cong., 2d sess., pp. 79-134. Washington, D.C.: Government Printing Office, 1974. Tables.

A description of the evolution of CMEA principles and practices between 1949 and 1974.

Familton, R.J. "East-West Trade and Payments Relations." INTERNATIONAL MONETARY FUND STAFF PAPERS 17 (March 1970): 170-213. Tables and appendix.

A discussion of the CMEA countries' trade policies and arrangements and problems of East-West trade.

Foldi, T., and Kiss, T[ibor]., eds. SOCIALIST WORLD MARKET PRICES. Translated by Gy. Hajdu, P. Morvay, and J. Racz. Budapest: Akademiai Kiado, 1969. 205 p. Tables and figures.

A compendium of essays, selected from the papers presented at the international conference organized by the Permanent Economic Committee of the CMEA in April 1967 in Budapest. The selections vary in quality and deal with certain aspects of price formation within the CMEA.

Francuz, Henryk. "The International Bank for Economic Cooperation." INTERNATIONAL MONETARY FUND STAFF PAPERS 16 (November 1969): 489-503. Tables.

Thoughtful comments on IBEC's organization, structure, operations, and impact on the foreign trade of CMEA member countries.

Gamarnikow, Michael. "Industrial Cooperation: East Europe Looks West." PROBLEMS OF COMMUNISM 20 (May-June 1971): 41-48.

An exploration of the issues relevant to the emerging industrial cooperation between Eastern European enterprises and Western firms.

Heiss, Hertha W. "The Council for Mutual Economic Assistance--Developments since the Mid-1960's." In ECONOMIC DEVELOPMENTS IN COUNTRIES OF EASTERN EUROPE, Joint Economic Committee, 91st Cong., 2d sess., pp. 528-42. Washington, D.C.: Government Printing Office, 1970.

A discussion of important developments in CMEA during the late 1960s.

Henys, Otta. "The Council for Mutual Economic Assistance Established Twenty-Five Years Ago." SOVIET AND EASTERN EUROPEAN FOREIGN TRADE 10 (Summer 1974): 3-16.

An examination of the principles and experiences of CMEA integration with a perspective of twenty-five years of operation.

Hewett, Edward A. FOREIGN TRADE PRICES IN THE COUNCIL FOR MUTUAL ECONOMIC ASSISTANCE. New York: Cambridge University Press, 1974. 196 p. Tables, figures, and index.

Survey of literature on CMEA foreign trade price determination, analysis of CMEA foreign trade prices and their influence on intra-CMEA trade flows, and discussion of the proposals for reforming the CMEA pricing system.

Holzman, Franklyn D. "More on Soviet Bloc Trade Discrimination." SOVIET STUDIES 17 (July 1965): 44-65. Tables.

A concise, critical review of the argument concerning whether the USSR engaged in price discrimination toward its satellites during the 1950s.

Ivanov, Iu. A. "Improving the Foreign Exchange Relations of Comecon Member Nations." PROBLEMS OF ECONOMICS 17 (September 1974): 39-49.

A description of the role and functions of the International Bank for Economic Cooperation (IBEC), the International Investment Bank (IIB), and the transferable ruble.

Karpich, V. "The Development of Currency and Financial Relations among Comecon Countries." SOVIET AND EASTERN EUROPEAN FOREIGN TRADE 6 (Summer 1970): 103-24.

Familiarization with Comecon credits, payment relations, and multilateral clearinghouse operations.

Kaser, Michael [C.]. COMECON: INTEGRATION PROBLEMS OF THE PLANNED ECONOMIES. 2d ed. London: Oxford University Press, 1967. vii, 279 p. Tables, appendixes, and index.

An examination of the history of Comecon since the late 1940s, followed by an in-depth analysis of trade expansion and dependence, technical cooperation, pricing, and problems of integration within the Comecon.

_____. "Comecon's Commerce." PROBLEMS OF COMMUNISM 22 (July-

August 1973): 1-15. Tables.

A glance at the trade dependence of Comecon countries and the commodity structure of Comecon trade, accompanied by Comecon trade projections to 1980.

Kiss, Tibor. INTERNATIONAL DIVISION OF LABOR IN OPEN ECONOMIES, WITH SPECIAL REGARD TO THE CMEA. Translated by J. Racz. Budapest: Akademiai Kiado, 1971. 322 p. Tables and figures.

A basic introduction to the principles which govern foreign trade and economic growth. The author concentrates on the economic and financial aspects of CMEA integration and on certain problems of Socialist world market prices.

Montias, John M[ichael]. "Background and Origins of the Rumanian Dispute with Comecon." SOVIET STUDIES 16 (October 1964): 125-51. Tables.

An elucidation of the postwar history of Rumania's dispute with the Comecon.

_____. "Obstacles to the Economic Integration of Eastern Europe." STUDIES IN COMPARATIVE COMMUNISM 2 (July/October 1969): 38-60.

Thoughts on the political and strategic restrictions on integration and on the intra-Comecon institutional obstacles to cooperation.

_____. "The Structure of Comecon Trade and the Prospects for East-West Exchanges." In REORIENTATION AND COMMERCIAL RELATIONS OF THE ECONOMIES OF EASTERN EUROPE, Joint Economic Committee, 93d Cong., 2d sess., pp. 662-81. Washington, D.C.: Government Printing Office, 1974. Tables and appendixes.

An analysis of the commodity composition of intra-CMEA trade and the shares of CMEA members and the rest of the world in exchanges within broad commodity groups.

Oleinik, I. "Forms of International Division of Labor in the Socialist Camp." PROBLEMS OF ECONOMICS 4 (October 1961): 56-63.

A discussion of the methods and forms of specialization and coordination of production among the Communist countries.

Pinder, John. "EEC and Comecon." SURVEY 58 (January 1966): 101-17.

A brief outline of problems of Comecon integration and the Comecon's relations with GATT, EFTA, and the EEC.

Plaksin, A. "Fruitful Cooperation within the Council for Mutual Economic Assistance." PROBLEMS OF ECONOMICS 3 (February 1961): 47-51. Tables.

A description of the volume of trade and trade relations within the CMEA.

Polienko, A. "New Stage in Trade Between Countries of the Council for Mutual Economic Assistance." PROBLEMS OF ECONOMICS 6 (January 1964): 48-55.

An elaboration upon the principle of "socialist division of labor."

Rotleider, A. "The Convertible Ruble: The International Socialist Currency of Comecon Countries." PROBLEMS OF ECONOMICS 15 (November 1972): 83-96.

An assessment of the concept, uses, and alleged shortcomings of the transferable ruble.

Scheel, B. "Effective Division of Labor within the Comecon Nations." SOVIET AND EASTERN EUROPEAN FOREIGN TRADE 10 (Summer 1974): 60-70.

An explanation of the benefits of division of labor for CMEA members.

Schulz, U. "The Development of International Economic Organizations as Part of Socialist Economic Integration." SOVIET AND EASTERN EUROPEAN FOREIGN TRADE 9 (Fall 1973): 26-41.

An examination of the role of international economic organizations in the promotion of greater economic integration within the Soviet bloc.

Sergeev, V. "Structure of the Socialist Countries' Foreign Trade." PROBLEMS OF ECONOMICS 5 (November 1962): 3-12.

An examination of the commodity composition of trade within the CMEA.

Shaffer, Harry G. "Comecon Integration: Achievements, Problems, Prospects." SOVIET AND EASTERN EUROPEAN FOREIGN TRADE 9 (Fall 1973): 3-25.

A historical survey of CMEA cooperation since its beginnings in 1949, with emphasis on its role in engendering greater integration within the Soviet bloc and on the extent of Soviet control over its activities.

Spulber, Nicolas. "East-West Trade and the Paradoxes of the Strategic Embargo." In INTERNATIONAL TRADE AND CENTRAL PLANNING--AN ANALYSIS OF ECONOMIC INTERACTIONS, edited by Alan A. Brown and Egon Neuberger, pp. 104-26. Berkeley and Los Angeles: University of California Press, 1968. Tables.

An appraisal of the Western strategic embargo and its consequences for East-West and intra-CMEA trade.

Staller, George J. "Patterns of Stability in Foreign Trade: OECD and COMECON, 1950-1963." AMERICAN ECONOMIC REVIEW 57 (September 1967): 879-88. Tables.

A study of results of empirical investigations of import and export stabilities for CMEA and OECD blocs.

Suliaeva, L. "Currency and Financial Cooperation among Comecon Members." PROBLEMS OF ECONOMICS 10 (October 1967): 45-50.

Information about the functions of the International Bank for Economic Cooperation (IBEC).

Szawlowski, Richard. "The International Economic Organizations of Communist Countries: I." CANADIAN SLAVONIC PAPERS 10 (Autumn 1968): 254-77.

A survey of the creation and evolution of Comecon and of the other organizations belonging to the "Comecon family" as of 1968.

_____. "The International Economic Organizations of the Communist Countries: II." CANADIAN SLAVONIC PAPERS 11 (Spring 1969): 82-107.

Reflections on CMEA membership and organization and on the relations between CMEA and the EEC and OECD.

Tarnovskii, O. "Price Formation on the World Socialist Market." PROBLEMS OF ECONOMICS 12 (October 1969): 42-57.

An explanation of the prices used in CMEA trade (i.e., world market prices, corrected for cyclical and monopoly factors).

Vais, T., and Degtiar, L. "Collaboration of Comecon Countries in the Utilization of Labor Resources." PROBLEMS OF ECONOMICS 17 (June 1974): 24-34.

A call for the creation of joint enterprises and for temporary labor migration as ways of improving labor utilization within the Comecon.

Vajda, Imre. "Brakes and Bottlenecks in Hungary's Economic Growth." ECONOMICS OF PLANNING 6 (1966): 228-40.

Comments on Hungary's postwar growth experience and the role of the Comecon in that experience.

_____. THE ROLE OF FOREIGN TRADE IN A SOCIALIST ECONOMY--NEW ESSAYS IN PERSUASION. Budapest: Corvina Press, 1965. 336 p. Tables and figures.

A collection of essays primarily examining the role of the Hungarian economy in the international division of labor, with special attention to CMEA trade.

Vajda, Imre, and Simai, Mihaly, eds. FOREIGN TRADE IN A PLANNED ECONOMY. London: Cambridge University Press, 1971. xii, 221 p. Tables, figures, and index.

> A collection of eleven essays by Hungarian economists, dealing with the institutional mechanism of trade and payments within the Comecon, foreign trade aspects of Hungary's New Economic Mechanism, and various other trade related topics.

Vasilev, Dimitur. "The International Socialist Division of Labor and Its Role in the Increased Profitability of Bulgaria's Foreign Trade." EASTERN EUROPEAN ECONOMICS 8 (Fall 1969): 90-99.

> A discussion of Bulgaria's foreign trade achievements, problems, and prospects within the Comecon.

Wiesel, I. "The International Socialist Market." SOVIET AND EASTERN EUROPEAN FOREIGN TRADE 7 (Summer 1971): 109-18.

> An examination of the currency system and character of the Comecon and discussion of certain pricing problems in Comecon trade.

Wyczalkowski, Marcin R. "Communist Economics and Currency Convertibility." INTERNATIONAL MONETARY FUND STAFF PAPERS 8 (July 1966): 155-97.

> A discussion of the pre-1956 financial system of the Soviet bloc countries, followed by an outline of the financial reform discussions, current issues of convertibility and multilateralism within the CMEA, and the economic conditions for meaningful multilateralism and convertibility.

Zahalka, Vaclav. "Banks and Foreign Trade." SOVIET AND EASTERN EUROPEAN FOREIGN TRADE 8 (Summer 1972): 155-73.

> An explanation of the role of financial and banking institutions, including those within the CMEA, in the promotion of foreign trade.

Zauberman, Alfred. "Economic Integration: Problems and Prospects." PROBLEMS OF COMMUNISM 8 (July-August 1959): 23-29.

> An examination of the economic problems and political stumbling blocks of CMEA integration.

Zeman, Karel. "Development in the Position of the COMECON Complex in the World Economy." SOVIET AND EASTERN EUROPEAN FOREIGN TRADE 10 (Summer 1974): 30-59. Tables.

> Comments on the volume and structure of output and foreign trade of Comecon countries.

Zwass, Adam. "CMEA Monetary Institutions and Steering Instruments."

SOVIET AND EASTERN EUROPEAN FOREIGN TRADE 10 (Fall-Winter 1974–75): 97-158. Tables.

> A discussion of the formal organization of the CMEA, credits, prices, and clearing arrangements in intra-CMEA trade. Also considered are the roles of the International Investment Bank and International Bank for Economic Cooperation.

_____. "Convertibility in the Comecon Region? Proposals and Reverses." SOVIET AND EASTERN EUROPEAN FOREIGN TRADE 8 (Summer 1972): 99-132.

> A survey of the issues, proposals, and organizational changes related to convertibility within the CMEA.

_____. "The International Investment Bank and the Council for Mutual Economic Assistance." SOVIET AND EASTERN EUROPEAN FOREIGN TRADE 9 (Spring 1973): 3-50. Tables.

> A description of the organization, functions, capital, and other monetary reserves of the International Investment Bank, as well as some discussion concerning the functioning of the International Bank for Economic Cooperation.

_____. "Monetary Steering Instruments of East-West Trade." SOVIET AND EASTERN EUROPEAN FOREIGN TRADE 10 (Fall-Winter 1974-75): 159-233. Tables.

> A careful examination of the following aspects of East-West trade: Communist foreign trade relations with nonconvertibe currencies; Comecon and the international monetary and credit institutions; settlement, payments procedures, and credit in East-West trade; and the role of Eastern European banks in the West and that of Western banks in Eastern Europe.

EAST-WEST TRADE

Adler-Karlsson, Gunnar. "Problems of East-West Trade--A General Survey." ECONOMICS OF PLANNING 7 (1967): 119-82.

> A comprehensive survey of the history, mechanisms, and problems of East-West trade.

Allen, Robert Loring. "An Interpretation of East-West Trade." In COMPARISONS OF THE UNITED STATES AND SOVIET ECONOMIES, Joint Economic Committee, 86th Cong., 1st sess., pp. 403-26. Washington, D.C.: Government Printing Office, 1959. Appendix.

> An examination of the value and volume, commodity composition, and direction of Soviet bloc trade.

Familton, R.J. "East-West Trade and Payments Relations." INTERNATIONAL MONETARY FUND STAFF PAPERS 17 (March 1970): 170-213. Tables and appendix.

A discussion of the CMEA countries' trade policies and arrangements and problems of East-West trade.

Farrell, John T. "Soviet Payments Problems in Trade with the West." In SOVIET ECONOMIC PROSPECTS FOR THE SEVENTIES, Joint Economic Committee, 93d Cong., 1st sess., pp. 690-711. Washington, D.C.: Government Printing Office, 1973. Tables and appendix.

A survey of trends in commodity trade, Soviet hard currency problems, and future prospects for hard currency trade.

Holzman, Franklyn D. "East-West Trade and Investment Policy Issues: Past And Future." In SOVIET ECONOMIC PROSPECTS FOR THE SEVENTIES, Joint Economic Committee, 93d Cong., 1st sess., pp. 660-89. Washington, D.C.: Government Printing Office, 1973. Tables.

A review of the Export Control Act of 1949 and the Mutual Defense Assistance Control Act of 1951 for their appropriateness in light of the economic realities of the 1970s. Additionally, problems of currency inconvertibility and payments deficits of Soviet bloc countries are considered.

Montias, J[ohn]. M[ichael]. "The Structure of Comecon Trade and the Prospects for East-West Exchanges." In REORIENTATION AND COMMERCIAL RELATIONS OF THE ECONOMIES OF EASTERN EUROPE, Joint Economic Committee, 93d Cong., 2d sess., pp. 662-81. Washington, D.C.: Government Printing Office, 1974. Tables and appendixes.

An analysis of the commodity composition of intra-CMEA trade and the shares of CMEA members and the rest of the world in exchanges within broad commodity groups.

Notel, Rudolf. "Future Development of East-West Trade." ECONOMIA INTERNAZIONALE 23 (1970): 212-38. Tables.

Comments on the volume and future prospects of East-West trade.

Schonfeld, Roland. "The USA in Economic Relations between East and West." SOVIET AND EASTERN EUROPEAN FOREIGN TRADE 10 (Spring 1974): 3-18.

A discussion of the strategic embargo and the subsequent shifts in public opinion, trade agreements with the Soviet Union, and the limits to business dealings with the East.

Spulber, Nicolas. "East-West Trade and the Paradoxes of the Strategic Embargo." In INTERNATIONAL TRADE AND CENTRAL PLANNING--AN ANALYSIS OF ECONOMIC INTERACTIONS, edited by Alan A. Brown and Egon

Neuberger, pp. 104-26. Berkeley and Los Angeles: University of California Press, 1968. Tables.

A review and appraisal of the Western strategic embargo and its consequences for East-West and intra-CMEA trade.

United Nations. Economic Commission for Europe. "Developments in Trade between Eastern and Western Europe from 1950 to Mid-1952." ECONOMIC BULLETIN FOR EUROPE 4 (November 1952): 34-78. Tables and appendix.

A description of the changes in East-West trade in Europe during 1951-52.

_____. "Recent Developments in Trade between Eastern and Western Europe." ECONOMIC BULLETIN FOR EUROPE 3 (Second Quarter 1951): 49-66. Tables and appendix.

Illustration of the general course and commodity composition of trade between Eastern and Western Europe.

Wilczynski, J. "Dumping in Trade between Market and Centrally Planned Economies." ECONOMICS OF PLANNING 6 (1966): 211-27. Tables.

A survey of Australia's experiences with trading with the Soviet bloc.

_____. THE ECONOMICS AND POLITICS OF EAST-WEST TRADE. New York: Frederick A. Praeger, 1969. 416 p. Tables, figures, and index.

An illuminating introduction into the principles, policies, practices, and major issues of East-West trade.

_____. "Multilateralization of East-West Trade." ECONOMIA INTERNAZIONALE 21 (1968): 301-20.

Notes on the role of the IBEC and the relevance of the Soviet bloc reforms to the multilateralization of trade and payments.

_____. "Strategic Embargo in Perspective." SOVIET STUDIES 19 (July 1967): 74-86. Tables.

An examination of the rationale for the embargo as well as the effects of the embargo on the Soviet bloc and on the West.

Yalowitz, Kenneth. "U.S.S.R.--Western Industrial Cooperation." In SOVIET ECONOMIC PROSPECTS FOR THE SEVENTIES, Joint Economic Committee, 93d Cong., 1st sess., pp. 712-18. Washington, D.C.: Government Printing Office, 1973.

An exploration of the different forms of industrial cooperation and the possible obstacles that may arise.

Zwass, Adam. "Monetary Steering Instruments of East-West Trade." SOVIET AND EASTERN EUROPEAN FOREIGN TRADE 10 (Fall-Winter 1974-75): 159-233. Tables.

> A careful examination of the following aspects of East-West trade: Communist foreign trade relations with nonconvertible currencies; Comecon and the international monetary and credit institutions; settlement, payments procedures, and credit in East-West trade; and the role of Eastern European banks in the West and that of Western banks in Eastern Europe.

_____. "The Outlook for East-West Monetary Relations." SOVIET AND EASTERN EUROPEAN FOREIGN TRADE 10 (Fall-Winter 1974-75): 234-65.

> A discussion of monetary reform within the Comecon (role of transferable ruble, convertibility, etc.) and Comecon interest in a unified currency system. An appraisal of the future of East-West trade follows.

FOREIGN AID

Allen, Robert Loring. "The Soviet and East European Foreign Credit Program." AMERICAN SLAVIC AND EAST EUROPEAN REVIEW 16 (December 1957): 433-49.

> A discussion of Soviet-bloc credit policy and arrangements toward Afghanistan, Egypt, India, Indonesia, and Yugoslavia through 1956.

Aubrey, Henry G. "Sino-Soviet Economic Activities in Less Developed Countries." In COMPARISONS OF THE UNITED STATES AND SOVIET ECONOMIES, Joint Economic Committee, 86th Cong., 1st sess., pp. 445-66. Washington, D.C.: Government Printing Office, 1959. Tables.

> A review of Sino-Soviet foreign trade and aid activities during the 1950s along with a comparison with U.S. aid programs.

Berliner, Joseph S. SOVIET ECONOMIC AID: THE NEW TRADE POLICY IN UNDERDEVELOPED COUNTRIES. New York: Frederick A. Praeger, 1958. xv, 232 p. Tables, figures, appendixes, and index.

> An examination of the character, size, and expansion of the Soviet aid program and an analysis of the Soviet capacity to extend aid and of Soviet economic gains from the aid programs.

Carnett, George S., and Crawford, Morris H. "The Scope and Distribution of Soviet Economic Aid." In DIMENSIONS OF SOVIET ECONOMIC POWER, Joint Economic Committee, 87th Cong., 2d sess., pp. 457-74. Washington, D.C.: Government Printing Office, 1962. Tables and appendix.

> A discussion of the motives, scope, and distribution of Soviet economic, technical, and military assistance programs during 1954-62.

Cooper, Orah. "Soviet Economic Assistance to the Less Developed Countries of the Free World." In ECONOMIC PERFORMANCE AND MILITARY BURDEN IN THE SOVIET UNION, Joint Economic Committee, 91st Cong., 2d sess., pp. 117-22. Washington, D.C.: Government Printing Office, 1970.

> Data concerning Soviet foreign aid to the developing countries during 1954-69.

Glovinsky, Evgeny. "Soviet Economic Expansion in the Developing Countries." STUDIES ON THE SOVIET UNION 1, no. 2 (1961): 173-92. Tables.

> A survey of the Soviet Union's economic relations with the less developed countries.

Goldman, Marshall I. "A Balance Sheet of Soviet Foreign Aid." FOREIGN AFFAIRS 43 (January 1965): 349-60.

> An explanation of Soviet concepts on foreign aid and a description of specific Soviet-sponsored aid projects.

_____. SOVIET FOREIGN AID. New York: Frederick A. Praeger, 1967. xiv, 265 p. Tables, appendixes, and index.

> A valuable contribution to the understanding of Soviet foreign economic relations. The author presents case studies on Soviet foreign aid to India, Afghanistan, the UAR, Indonesia, as well as to other countries, makes revealing comparisons among the various methods of providing aid, and makes recommendations to American policy makers.

Horvath, Janos. "Economic Aid Flow from the USSR: A Recount of the First Fifteen Years." SLAVIC REVIEW 29 (December 1970): 613-32. Tables and figures.

> An account of the Soviet record of economic aid to the less developed countries, including its extent and recipients.

Klages, W.J. "Soviet Economic Thought and Economic Development: The Case of Foreign Aid." CANADIAN SLAVONIC PAPERS 12 (Winter 1970): 417-30.

> A brief survey of the Soviet foreign aid program toward the third world.

Prybyla, Jan S. "Soviet and Chinese Economic Competition within the Communist World." SOVIET STUDIES 15 (April 1964): 464-73.

> Thoughts on the Soviet-Chinese competition in North Vietnam, North Korea, and Outer Mongolia.

Rymalov, V. "Economic Competition of the Two Systems and the Problem of

Aid to Underdeveloped Countries." PROBLEMS OF ECONOMICS 3 (December 1960): 43-52. Tables.

> Soviet reflections on foreign aid.

Scott, N.B. "Soviet Economic Relations with the Under-Developed Countries." SOVIET STUDIES 10 (July 1958): 36-53.

> A discussion of Soviet aid to and trade patterns with the less developed countries.

Tansky, Leo. "Soviet Foreign Aid: Scope, Direction, and Trends." In SOVIET ECONOMIC PROSPECTS FOR THE SEVENTIES, Joint Economic Committee, 93d Cong., 1st sess., pp. 766-76. Washington, D.C.: Government Printing Office, 1973. Tables and appendix.

> An investigation of the ideological foundations, magnitude and direction, sectoral distribution, and terms and repayments of Soviet foreign aid between 1954 and 1972.

_____. "Soviet Foreign Aid to the Less Developed Economies." In NEW DIRECTIONS IN THE SOVIET ECONOMY, Joint Economic Committee, 89th Cong., 2d sess., pp. 947-74. Washington, D.C.: Government Printing Office, 1966. Tables.

> A discussion of the Soviet economic and military aid program and of its successes and failures. The magnitude and geographic distribution of Soviet economic aid, its sectoral distribution, and Soviet technical assistance are covered.

_____. U.S. AND U.S.S.R. AID TO DEVELOPING COUNTRIES: A COMPARATIVE STUDY OF INDIA, TURKEY, AND THE U.A.R. New York: Frederick A. Praeger, 1967. xvii, 192 p. Tables.

> Case study of U.S. foreign aid to Turkey, Soviet aid to India, and Indian and Soviet aid to the UAR. This work relies primarily on secondary sources.

Valkenier, Elisabeth Kridl. "New Trends in Soviet Economic Relations with the Third World." WORLD POLITICS 22 (April 1970): 415-32.

> General remarks on new forms and methods in Soviet trade and aid and new Soviet thoughts on development.

Chapter 14

ECONOMIC REFORMS

Abouchar, Alan. "Inefficiency and Reform in the Soviet Economy." SOVIET STUDIES 25 (July 1973): 67-76.

A brief summary of the Kosygin reforms and an analysis of the reasons for their failure.

Bachurin, A. "The Economic Reform in Operation." PROBLEMS OF ECONOMICS 11 (April 1969): 11-25. Tables.

A description of Soviet reform and an appraisal of further tasks.

Balassa, Bela [A.]. "The Economic Reform in Hungary." ECONOMICA 37 (February 1970): 1-22.

An investigation of the initial phase of Hungary's New Economic Mechanism.

_____. "The Firm in the New Economic Mechanism in Hungary." In PLAN AND MARKET: ECONOMIC REFORM IN EASTERN EUROPE, edited by Morris Bornstein, pp. 347-72. New Haven, Conn.: Yale University Press, 1973.

Comments on enterprise experiences during the initial phase of the Hungarian reform (1968-70). Short-term decision making, investment decisions, and export incentives are discussed.

Balinky, Alexander [S.], et al. PLANNING AND THE MARKET IN THE U.S.S.R.: THE 1960'S. New Brunswick, N.J.: Rutgers University Press, 1967. vi, 132 p.

A compendium of essays, dealing with the nature and implications of the Soviet economic reforms of the 1960s.

Balint, Jozsef. "On the Unfolding of the Economic Reform." EASTERN EUROPEAN ECONOMICS 9 (Fall 1970): 3-41.

An assessment of the initial results of the Hungarian economic reform of 1968 and prognostications of future alterations within the reform framework.

Batyrev, V. "The Economic Reform and the Increasing Role of Credit." PROBLEMS OF ECONOMICS 9 (September 1966): 50-58.

> An illustration of the role of credit in the Soviet economy following the announcement of reforms in 1965.

Baylis, Thomas A. "The New Economic System: The Role of the Technocrats in the DDR." SURVEY 61 (October 1966): 139-52.

> A discussion of the East German economic reform.

Bergson, Abram, et al. "Soviet Economic Performance and Reform: Some Problems of Analysis and Prognosis." SLAVIC REVIEW 25 (June 1966): 222-46.

> A round-table discussion of the Soviet economy, including such topics as the extent of decentralization, price reforms, innovation, and reduction of tautness.

Betz, Horst. "The Pattern of Economic Reform in East Germany: The Return to Increased Centralization?" ECONOMIA INTERNAZIONALE 26 (1973): 318-28.

> An evaluation of the initial expectations and the subsequent emasculation of the East German economic reform.

Blackman, James H. "The Kosygin Reforms: New Wine in Old Bottles?" In THE DEVELOPMENT OF THE SOVIET ECONOMY: PLAN AND PERFORMANCE, edited by Vladimir G. Treml, pp. 249-89. New York: Frederick A. Praeger, 1968.

> An assessment of the nature and scope of the Kosygin reforms of 1965.

Bornstein, Morris. "The Soviet Price Reform Discussion." QUARTERLY JOURNAL OF ECONOMICS 78 (February 1964): 15-48.

> An analysis of the 1956-63 Soviet price debates.

_____. PLAN AND MARKET: ECONOMIC REFORM IN EASTERN EUROPE. New Haven, Conn.: Yale University Press, 1973. viii, 416 p. Tables, figures, and appendixes.

> A collection of articles dealing with reasons for changes in economic systems, as well as with the measurement and evaluation of those changes.

Bottcher, Manfred. "Where Do We Stand with Planning in the New Economic System?" EASTERN EUROPEAN ECONOMICS 6 (Spring 1968): 50-54.

> A brief examination and evaluation of the East German planning reforms of the mid-1960s.

Branik, Julius. "Internal and World Prices in the New System of Management." EASTERN EUROPEAN ECONOMICS 5 (Spring 1967): 39-48. Tables.

A discussion of the expected impact of world prices on Czechoslovak internal prices as a result of the economic reform.

Brown, Alan A., and Marer, Paul. "Foreign Trade in the East European Reforms." In PLAN AND MARKET: ECONOMIC REFORM IN EASTERN EUROPE, edited by Morris Bornstein, pp. 153-205. New Haven, Conn.: Yale University Press, 1973. Tables, figures, and appendixes.

Observations concerning the role of foreign trade in centrally planned economies, primarily on the basis of Hungary's experiences. Relationships between foreign trade and economic reform.

Brown, Alan A., and Neuberger, Egon, eds. INTERNATIONAL TRADE AND CENTRAL PLANNING--AN ANALYSIS OF ECONOMIC INTERACTIONS. Berkeley and Los Angeles: University of California Press, 1968. 455 p. Tables, appendix, and index.

A collection of twelve high quality essays dealing with theoretical and empirical aspects of the foreign trade of the Soviet Union, Eastern Europe, and China.

Brown, J.F. "Reforms in Bulgaria." PROBLEMS OF COMMUNISM 15 (May-June 1966): 17-21.

A discussion of the background and content of the Bulgarian economic reform.

Buky, Barnabas. "Hungary's NEM on a Treadmill." PROBLEMS OF COMMUNISM 21 (September-October 1972): 31-39.

An assessment of the initial problems facing the 1968 Hungarian reform.

Burks, R.V. "The Political Hazards of Economic Reform." In REORIENTATION AND COMMERCIAL RELATIONS OF THE ECONOMIES OF EASTERN EUROPE, Joint Economic Committee, 93d Cong., 2d sess., pp. 51-78. Washington, D.C.: Government Printing Office, 1974.

An illustration of the political constraints to economic reform in Soviet-type economies.

_____. "The Political Implications of Economic Reform." In PLAN AND MARKET: ECONOMIC REFORM IN EASTERN EUROPE, edited by Morris Bornstein, pp. 373-402. New Haven, Conn.: Yale University Press, 1973.

A discussion of alternative reform programs, the political costs of market reform, and the Soviet dilemma regarding economic reforms in general.

Bush, Keith. "Agricultural Reforms Since Khrushchev." In NEW DIRECTIONS IN THE SOVIET ECONOMY, Joint Economic Committee, 89th Cong., 2d sess., pp. 451-72. Washington, D.C.: Government Printing Office, 1966. Tables.

>A survey of the Soviet agricultural reforms which were announced following Khrushchev's removal.

Campbell, Robert [W.]. "Economic Reform in the U.S.S.R." AMERICAN ECONOMIC REVIEW 58 (May 1968): 547-58.

>An examination of the Soviet reform of 1965-67 by means of reference to its principal features and unresolved issues.

_____. THE SOVIET-TYPE ECONOMIES: PERFORMANCE AND EVOLUTION. 3d ed. Boston: Houghton Mifflin Co., 1974. xi, 259 p. Figures, tables, and index. Paperback.

>Updated and expanded version of the first edition, published in 1960 under the title SOVIET ECONOMIC POWER: ITS ORGANIZATION, GROWTH, AND CHALLENGE. The expanded version includes discussions concerning basic economic institutions and organization, the Soviet growth model and its application in Eastern Europe, planning principles and practices, the record of Soviet growth, and economic reforms in the Soviet Union and Eastern Europe.

Conklin, David W. AN EVALUATION OF THE SOVIET PROFIT REFORMS; WITH SPECIAL REFERENCE TO AGRICULTURE. New York: Frederick A. Praeger, 1970. xiii, 192 p. Tables and figures.

>An analysis of the shift from traditional, command-type planning to a system which combines centralized and decentralized decisions as they apply to the agricultural sector.

Csikos-Nagy, Bela. "Macrostructural and Microstructural Performance of the Economy." SOVIET STUDIES 23 (January 1972): 474-83.

>An explanation of the guided market concept and the role of prices, as envisioned initially by the architects of the Hungarian reform of 1968.

Davies, R.W. "Planning a Mature Economy in the USSR." ECONOMICS OF PLANNING 6 (1966): 138-53.

>A survey of Soviet planning experience and a brief consideration of the prospects for reform.

Dellin, L.A.D. "Bulgarian Economic Reform--Advance and Retreat." PROBLEMS OF COMMUNISM 19 (September-October 1970): 44-52.

An examination of the pre-1968 Bulgarian economic reform blue-print and the subsequent reversals.

Dellin, L.A.D., and Gross, Hermann, eds. REFORMS IN THE SOVIET AND EASTERN EUROPEAN ECONOMIES. Lexington, Mass.: D.C. Heath, 1972. viii, 175 p. Index.

A collection of essays concerning the origin, nature, and direction of economic reforms in the USSR, Bulgaria, Czechoslovakia, Hungary, Poland, Rumania, and Yugoslavia.

Ellman, Michael [J.]. SOVIET PLANNING TODAY--PROPOSALS FOR AN OPTIMALLY FUNCTIONING ECONOMIC SYSTEM. Cambridge: At the University Press, 1971. xv, 219 p. Tables, figures, and appendixes.

Familiarization with Soviet planning theory and practices in light of the reforms.

Fedorenko, N[ikolay P.]. "The Reforms in Industry: Initial Results, Problems of Raising Efficiency." PROBLEMS OF ECONOMICS 10 (October 1967): 12-23.

General remarks on the problems of increasing the effectiveness of industrial reforms and evaluating the work of enterprises.

Feiwel, G[eorge]. R. "The Dynamics of Perpetuation: Some Observations on the Efficacy of Soviet Economic Reforms." ECONOMIA INTERNAZIONALE 26 (1973): 233-61.

Notes on plan tautness, technical progress and foreign trade, and obstacles to reform.

_____. THE ECONOMICS OF A SOCIALIST ENTERPRISE: A CASE STUDY OF THE POLISH FIRM. New York: Frederick A. Praeger, 1965. xvi, 398 p.

A very detailed review of the Polish economy after World War II, of the different planning philosophies, and of the actual plans as they affected Polish industrial enterprises. The views of leading Polish planners and economists, as related to greater decentralization in planning, are presented with great thoroughness.

_____. NEW ECONOMIC PATTERNS IN CZECHOSLOVAKIA: IMPACT OF GROWTH, PLANNING AND THE MARKET. New York: Frederick A. Praeger, 1968. xxiv, 589 p. Tables and figures.

A thorough discussion of the major currents of Czechoslovak economic development, planning, and reforms.

_____. PROBLEMS IN POLISH ECONOMIC PLANNING: CONTINUITY, CHANGE AND PROSPECTS. VOL. II. New York: Frederick A. Praeger, 1971. xvii, 454 p. Tables and figures.

A discussion of the economic reforms, the financing of investments, the existing planning system, and the revamping of the system for the 1970s.

_____. THE SOVIET QUEST FOR ECONOMIC EFFICIENCY--ISSUES, CONTROVERSIES, AND REFORMS. New York: Frederick A. Praeger, 1972. xxiv, 790 p.

An expanded and updated version of the first edition (1967). An exhaustive treatment of the issues related to Soviet economic development, planning, efficiency, reform proposals, and implementation.

Felker, Jere L. SOVIET ECONOMIC CONTROVERSIES: THE EMERGING MARKETING CONCEPT AND CHANGES IN PLANNING, 1960-1965. Cambridge, Mass.: MIT Press, 1966. x, 172 p. Index.

A careful examination of Soviet controversies regarding value, price, profit, trade, and reform as advanced during the first half of the 1960s.

Flakierski, H. "The Polish Economic Reform of 1970." CANADIAN JOURNAL OF ECONOMICS 6 (February 1973): 1-15.

A discussion of the 1970 Polish reform, with special attention to the proposed incentive system.

Friedrich, Gerd. "Problems of Economic Direction in the VVB's and Factories as Posed by Differentiated Conditions of Reproduction." EASTERN EUROPEAN ECONOMICS 6 (Winter 1967-68): 39-54.

An evaluation of the role and effectiveness of VVB's (Associations of Nationally Owned Factories) in the East German economy.

Friss, Istvan. "Practical Experiences of the Economic Reform in Hungary." EASTERN EUROPEAN ECONOMICS 11 (Spring 1973): 3-26.

An assessment of the initial successes and problems of the Hungarian reform of 1968.

Gado, Otto, ed. REFORM OF THE ECONOMIC MECHANISM IN HUNGARY: 1968-1971. Translated by T. Bacskai, G. Dienes, Gy. Hajdu, and J. Racz. Budapest: Akademiai Kiado, 1972. 314 p. Tables and appendix.

A compendium of twelve essays, providing a survey of the functioning of the economic regulators through 1971 and describing the main objectives of the Fourth Five-Year Plan.

Gamarnikow, Michael. "Balance Sheet on Economic Reforms." In REORIENTATION AND COMMERCIAL RELATIONS OF THE ECONOMIES OF EASTERN EUROPE, Joint Economic Committee, 93d Cong., 2d sess., pp. 164-213.

Washington, D.C.: Government Printing Office, 1974.

A survey of economic reforms in Bulgaria, Czechoslovakia, East Germany, Hungary, Poland, and Rumania between the first attempts and 1974.

_____. ECONOMIC REFORMS IN EASTERN EUROPE. Detroit: Wayne State University Press, 1968. 204 p. Index.

Based largely on a series of articles by the author, a thorough discussion of the Eastern European experience in economic reforms through the late 1960s.

_____. "A New Economic Approach." PROBLEMS OF COMMUNISM 21 (September-October 1972): 20-30.

An outline of Gomulka's economic legacies and Gierek's initial policies designed to deal with the major immediate problems facing the Polish economy.

_____. "Political Patterns and Economic Reforms." PROBLEMS OF COMMUNISM 18 (March-April 1969): 11-23.

An examination of the connections between political imperatives and economic reforms in Czechoslovakia, Hungary, and Yugoslavia.

Garbuzov, V. [F.]. "Finances and Economic Stimuli." PROBLEMS OF ECONOMICS 8 (February 1966): 3-10. Figures.

A description of the role of credit, prices, and profit under the Soviet economic reform of 1965.

Garetovskii, N. "The Role of Profit and Profitability under the New System for Economic Stimulation of Production." PROBLEMS OF ECONOMICS 12 (August 1969): 3-30. Tables.

A report on the place of profit under socialism, the incentive role of profit, and questions of price formation.

Glinski, Bohdan, and Pajestka, Jozef. "The Market and the Plan in the Light of Economic Reform in Poland." In PLANNING AND MARKETS: MODERN TRENDS IN VARIOUS ECONOMIC SYSTEMS, edited by John T. Dunlap and Nikolay P. Fedorenko, pp. 64-76. New York: McGraw-Hill Book Co., 1969.

A summary of the problems encountered in adjusting to the market by enterprises and an examination of the ways of increasing price flexibility for manufactured goods.

Golan, Galia. "The Road to Reform." PROBLEMS OF COMMUNISM 20 (May-June 1971): 11-21.

A review of the salient features of the Czechoslovak reform and a comparison of the several phases of its overall development with reforms in other countries.

Gregory, Paul R., and Stuart, Robert C. SOVIET ECONOMIC STRUCTURE AND PERFORMANCE. New York: Harper & Row Publishers, 1974. x, 478 p. Tables, figures, and index. Paperback.

A comprehensive analysis of significant issues in the Soviet economy. Included are discussions concerning the economic experiences of the periods of war communism and New Economic Policy, pricing, planning methods and principles, agriculture, growth strategy and performance, foreign trade, monetary and financial controls and policy, and economic reforms.

Grossman, Gregory. "Economic Reforms: A Balance Sheet." PROBLEMS OF COMMUNISM 15 (November-December 1966): 43-55.

Illuminating analysis of the causes, substantive content, problems, viability, and political implications of the reforms which were introduced in Eastern Europe during the mid-1960s.

Holesovsky, Vaclav. "Financial Aspects of the Czechoslovak Economic Reform." In MONEY AND PLAN--FINANCIAL ASPECTS OF THE EAST EUROPEAN ECONOMIC REFORMS, edited by Gregory Grossman, pp. 80-105. Berkeley and Los Angeles: University of California Press, 1968.

Information about the role of money and finance in the 1967 economic model.

_____. "Planning and the Market in Czechoslovak Reform." In PLAN AND MARKET: ECONOMIC REFORM IN EASTERN EUROPE, edited by Morris Bornstein, pp. 313-45. New Haven, Conn.: Yale University Press, 1973.

A review of the main features of the Czechoslovak reform of 1967 and the consequent recentralization.

_____. "Planning Reforms in Czechoslovakia." SOVIET STUDIES 19 (April 1968): 544-56.

A discussion of the background and outline of the reform, including the role of the central plan.

Holzman, Franklyn D. "Some Notes on Over-Full Employment Planning, Short-Run Balance, and the Soviet Economic Reforms." SOVIET STUDIES 22 (October 1970): 255-61.

An elaboration on the implications of over-full employment planning for input-output and for reforms, and on the possible advantages to planners of over-full employment planning.

Kalinov, Stefan, and Yordanov, Ivan. "Some Problems of Price Formation under the New System of Management of the National Economy." EASTERN EUROPEAN ECONOMICS 5 (Spring 1967): 9-16.

A discussion concerning methods of price formation and the role of prices under the Bulgarian reform.

Karcz, Jerzy F. "Agricultural Reform in Eastern Europe." In PLAN AND MARKET: ECONOMIC REFORM IN EASTERN EUROPE, edited by Morris Bornstein, pp. 207-43. New Haven, Conn.: Yale University Press, 1973. Tables.

A description of agricultural reforms in Bulgaria, Czechoslovakia, East Germany, Hungary, Poland, Rumania, and Yugoslavia.

_____. "Certain Aspects of New Economic Systems in Bulgaria and Czechoslovakia." In AGRARIAN POLICIES AND PROBLEMS IN COMMUNIST AND NON-COMMUNIST COUNTRIES, edited by W.A. Douglas Jackson, pp. 178-204. Seattle: University of Washington Press, 1971.

A discussion of the Czechoslovak and Bulgarian reforms as they pertained to agriculture.

Katz, Abraham. THE POLITICS OF ECONOMIC REFORM IN THE SOVIET UNION. New York: Praeger, 1972. viii, 230 p.

A brief survey of Soviet political and economic history provides the background for a discussion of the issues, problems, and content of the Soviet reforms of the 1960s.

Keren, Michael. "Concentration Amid Devolution in East Germany's Reforms." In PLAN AND MARKET: ECONOMIC REFORM IN EASTERN EUROPE, edited by Morris Bornstein, pp. 123-51. New Haven, Conn.: Yale University Press, 1973. Tables.

Familiarization with the changes in East German industrial concentration as manifested in that country's reformed centralism. There are some comparisons with the Hungarian reform.

_____. "The New Economic System in the GDR: An Obituary." SOVIET STUDIES 24 (April 1973): 554-87. Tables.

An evaluation of the course of the East German economic reform of 1963.

Khachaturov, T. "The Economic Reform and Problems of the Effectiveness of Capital Investments." PROBLEMS OF ECONOMICS 10 (March 1968): 12-24.

An examination of the principles and techniques for calculating the effectiveness of capital investments prior to and under the 1965 reform.

Klatt, Werner. "The Politics of Economic Reforms." SURVEY 70/71 (Winter/
Spring 1969): 154-65.

> A discussion of the political element in the Eastern European re-
> forms.

Komin, A. "Economic Reform and Tasks in Further Improving Price Formation."
PROBLEMS OF ECONOMICS 11 (December 1968): 39-46.

> A consideration of the role of wholesale prices and new methodol-
> ogical approaches to price formation.

Korda, B., and Moravcik, I. "Reflections on the 1965-1968 Czechoslovak
Economic Reform." CANADIAN SLAVONIC PAPERS 8 (Spring 1971): 45-65.

> An appraisal of the Czechoslovak reform movement.

Krylov, P., et al. "On the Procedure and Conditions for Changing to the
New System." PROBLEMS OF ECONOMICS 9 (September 1966): 3-14.
Tables.

> A brief description of the content of the Soviet reform.

Kuligin, P. "Improvement of Price Formation under the Economic Reform."
PROBLEMS OF ECONOMICS 12 (October 1969): 27-41.

> A call for the "further consolidation of centralized planning" as
> a method for improving price formation under the economic reform.

Kyn, Oldrich. "The Rise and Fall of Economic Reform in Czechoslovakia."
AMERICAN ECONOMIC REVIEW 60 (May 1970): 300-306. Tables.

> A short review of the reform movement in Czechoslovakia and of
> its 1969 demise.

Liberman, E.G. "Are We Flirting with Capitalism? Profits and 'Profits.'"
PROBLEMS OF ECONOMICS 8 (August 1965): 36-41.

> Liberman's famous response to TIME magazine in which he discusses
> the "essential character of profits."

_____. "The Plan, Direct Ties and Profitability." PROBLEMS OF ECO-
NOMICS 8 (January 1966): 27-31.

> An essay on the role of profitability in economic management in
> the USSR.

_____. "Profitability of Socialist Enterprises." PROBLEMS OF ECONOMICS
8 (March 1966): 3-10.

> Comments on the meaning and role of profitability for Socialist
> enterprises.

_____ . "The Role of Profits in the Industrial Incentive System of the U.S.S.R." INTERNATIONAL LABOUR REVIEW 97 (January 1968): 1-14.

> A discussion of the principles underlying the new system of management.

Liberman, E.G., and Zhitnitskii, Z. "Economic and Administrative Methods of Managing the Economy." PROBLEMS OF ECONOMICS 11 (August 1968): 3-11.

> A study, contrasting economic and bureaucratic-administrative methods of economic management.

Lippman, Heinz. "The Limits of Reform Communism." PROBLEMS OF COMMUNISM 19 (May-June 1970): 15-23.

> An examination of the emergence of reformism in East Germany during the 1950s and the subsequent rigid limits which were set by the party, including the partial reforms of the 1960s.

Lovell, C.A. Knox. "Profits and Cybernetics as Sources of Increased Efficiency in Soviet Planning." SOUTHERN ECONOMIC JOURNAL 34 (January 1968): 392-405. Tables.

> A review of the cybernetic approach to planning and Liberman's proposals.

Marczewski, Jan. CRISIS IN SOCIALIST PLANNING: EASTERN EUROPE AND THE USSR. Translated by Noel Lindsay. New York: Praeger, 1974. xvii, 245 p. Tables and index.

> A discussion of the orthodox Soviet-type planning system and planning reforms, primarily in Soviet and Eastern European industry. Foreign trade and monetary and financial planning and policies are also discussed.

Marschak, Thomas A. "Decentralizing the Command Economy: The Study of a Pragmatic Strategy for Reformers." In PLAN AND MARKET: ECONOMIC REFORM IN EASTERN EUROPE, edited by Morris Bernstein, pp. 22-63. New Haven, Conn.: Yale University Press, 1973.

> A theoretical analysis of performance indicators, of choices confronted by reformers, and of the consequences of these choices.

Michal, Jan [M.]. "The New Economic Model." SURVEY 59 (April 1966): 61-71. Tables.

> A familiarization with the Czechoslovakian economic reform program.

Miller, Dorothy, and Trend, Harry G. "Economic Reforms in East Germany." PROBLEMS OF COMMUNISM 15 (March-April 1966): 29-36.

A discussion of the substance and impact of the East German reform.

Montias, John Michael. "A Framework for Theoretical Analysis of Economic Reforms in Soviet-Type Economies." In PLAN AND MARKET: ECONOMIC REFORM IN EASTERN EUROPE, edited by Morris Bornstein, pp. 65-122. New Haven, Conn.: Yale University Press, 1973. Figures and appendixes.

Mathematical analysis of plan implementation in a centralized and in a reformed economy.

Moravcik, Ivo. "The Czechoslovak Economic Reform." CANADIAN SLAVONIC PAPERS 10 (Winter 1968): 430-50. Tables and appendix.

A discussion of the background and content of the aborted Czechoslovak economic reform.

Naor, Jacob. "How Dead is the GDR New Economic System?" SOVIET STUDIES 25 (October 1973): 276-82.

An illustration of state balances and indicators and the post-1970 economic role of profits, prices, and contracts in the GDR's New Economic System.

Neuberger, Egon. "Libermanism, Computopia, and Visible Hand: The Question of Informational Efficiency." AMERICAN ECONOMIC REVIEW 56 (May 1966): 131-44.

An appraisal of the "informational efficiency" of various reform alternatives for the Soviet economy.

Nove, Alec. "The Liberman Proposals." SURVEY 47 (April 1963): 113-18.

Elucidation of the famous Liberman proposals of 1962.

Nuti, Domenico Mario. "Investment Reforms in Czechoslovakia." SOVIET STUDIES 21 (January 1970): 360-70.

A summary of the investment rules prevailing in Czechoslovakia before and after 1967, and an analysis of their implications for economic planning.

Pashev, Apostol. "The New System of Management--An Important Stage in the Development of the Bulgarian Economy." EASTERN EUROPEAN ECONOMICS 5 (Spring 1967): 3-8.

An examination of the scope of the Bulgarian economic reform and its possible impact on the economic development of Bulgaria.

Pesek, Boris P. "The New Economic Model in Czechoslovakia." In MONEY AND PLAN--FINANCIAL ASPECTS OF EAST EUROPEAN ECONOMIC

REFORMS, edited by Gregory Grossman, pp. 106-28. Berkeley and Los Angeles: University of California Press, 1968.

> An evaluation of the fundamental aspects of the Czechoslovak economic reform of 1967.

Petrov, Milan. "Foreign Exchange Planning under the Conditions of the New System of Planning and Management of the National Economy." EASTERN EUROPEAN ECONOMICS 6 (Summer 1968): 44-54.

> Comments on the Bulgarian economic reforms of the mid-1960s, including a discussion of the methods and scope of foreign exchange planning under the reform.

Petrov, Tsvetan, and Kalinov, Stefan. "The Economic Mechanism of the New System in 1969 and 1970." EASTERN EUROPEAN ECONOMICS 8 (Fall 1969): 72-89.

> Thoughts concerning the further development of the Bulgarian economic reform.

Portes, Richard D. "Economic Reforms in Hungary." AMERICAN ECONOMIC REVIEW 60 (May 1970): 307-13.

> A short description of the Hungarian economic reform of 1968 and of its functioning through 1969.

_____. "The Strategy and Tactics of Economic Decentralization." SOVIET STUDIES 23 (April 1972): 629-58.

> An analysis of certain concepts and problems of decentralization, with special reference to the Hungarian reform of 1968.

Pryor, Frederic L. "Barriers to Market Socialism in Eastern Europe in the Mid 1960s." STUDIES IN COMPARATIVE COMMUNISM 3 (April 1970): 31-64. Tables.

> A survey of East European economic reforms, with special attention to the post-reform distribution of decision-making power by enterprises as well as to their structure and incentive systems.

Reiher, Klaus, and Schierz, Erich. "The Relation between Prices and Production-Financial Planning in the New Economic System." EASTERN EUROPEAN ECONOMICS 5 (Summer 1967): 40-51. Tables.

> An examination of the influence of prices on planning methods and of planning on prices in the East German economic reforms of the 1960s.

Ryavec, Karl W. "Soviet Industrial Managers, Their Superiors and the Economic Reform: A Study of an Attempt at Planned Behavioral Change." SOVIET STUDIES 21 (October 1969): 208-29.

A study of the extent to which a change took place in the relationship of industrial managers and their superiors as a result of the economic reform of 1965.

Schroeder, Gertrude E. "The 1966-67 Soviet Industrial Price Reform: A Study in Complications." SOVIET STUDIES 20 (April 1969): 462-77. Tables.

A discussion of the functioning of the Soviet price fixing apparatus, the objectives of price reform, as well as the main features and effects of the price revision.

_____. "The 'Reform' of the Supply System in Soviet Industry." SOVIET STUDIES 24 (July 1972): 97-119. Tables.

An examination of industrial supply problems and remedies instituted subsequent to the 1965 economic reform.

_____. "Soviet Economic 'Reforms': A Study in Contradictions." SOVIET STUDIES 20 (July 1968): 1-21.

A survey of the background of the 1965 Soviet economic reform and an evaluation of its provisions and effects.

_____. "Soviet Economic Reform at an Impasse." PROBLEMS OF COMMUNISM 20 (July-August 1970): 36-46.

An examination of the 1965 Soviet reform program, followed by a well documented account of its withering away.

Selucky, Radoslav. ECONOMIC REFORMS IN EASTERN EUROPE: POLITICAL BACKGROUND AND ECONOMIC SIGNIFICANCE. Translated by Zdenek Elias. New York: Frederick A. Praeger, 1972. x, 179 p.

An outline of the prereform system of the Eastern European countries, followed by observations on the economic reforms which took place in Czechoslovakia, Bulgaria, East Germany, Hungary, Poland, Rumania, and the Soviet Union. The author participated in the Czechoslovak reform movement.

Shaffer, Harry G. "What Price Economic Reforms?" PROBLEMS OF COMMUNISM 12 (May-June 1963): 18-26. Tables.

A brief review of the material incentive system which existed for Soviet managerial personnel during the early 1960s precedes a discussion of some of the proposed remedial changes.

Sharpe, Myron E., ed. PLANNING, PROFIT, AND INCENTIVES IN THE USSR. Vol. 1, THE LIBERMAN DISCUSSION--A NEW PHASE IN SOVIET ECONOMIC THOUGHT. White Plains, N.Y.: International Arts and Sciences Press, 1966. xiii, 314 p. Tables.

Translations of thirty-one articles covering a broad spectrum which appeared in Soviet publications. The central themes are prices, profits, and approaches to decentralization.

_____. PLANNING, PROFIT AND INCENTIVES IN THE USSR. Vol. 2, REFORM OF SOVIET ECONOMIC MANAGEMENT. White Plains, N.Y.: International Arts and Sciences Press, 1966. viii, 337 p. Tables.

A compilation of twenty selections dealing with the launching of reform and with problems of planned price formation.

Sik, Ota. "The Economic Impact of Stalinism." PROBLEMS OF COMMU-NISM 20 (May-June 1971): 1-10.

An interesting description of the impact of Stalinism on the growth and efficiency of the Czechoslovak economy by one of the chief architects of Czechoslovakia's economic reform program of 1965-68.

_____. PLAN AND MARKET UNDER SOCIALISM. Translated by Eleanor Wheeler. White Plains, N.Y.: International Arts and Sciences Press, 1967. 382 p. Tables, figures, and index.

A condemnation of the Stalinist form of central planning for a developed Socialist country and a call for the replacement of central commands by a modified market system.

Sitnin, V. "The Economic Reform and the Revision of Wholesale Prices for Industrial Goods." PROBLEMS OF ECONOMICS 9 (December 1966): 15-23.

An explanation of the role of prices and profitability and the need for wholesale price revisions.

Smolinski, Leon. "Planning Reforms in Poland." KYKLOS 21 (1968): 498-513.

An appraisal of the 1964-65 Polish reforms in comparison to similar reforms elsewhere in Eastern Europe.

_____. "Reforms in Poland." PROBLEMS OF COMMUNISM 15 (July-August 1966): 8-13.

A discussion of the content and prospects of the Polish economic reform of 1965.

Sokolov, V., et al. "The Firm and the Customer." PROBLEMS OF ECO-NOMICS 8 (August 1965): 3-14. Tables.

Familiarization with the Bol'shevichka-Maiak experiment.

Spigler, Iancu. ECONOMIC REFORMS IN RUMANIAN INDUSTRY. Eco-nomic Reforms in East European Industry Series. London: Oxford University

Press, 1973. xx, 176 p. Tables, figures, and index.

> Survey of the origins, provisions, and results of the Rumanian industrial planning reforms of the 1960s.

Staller, George J. "Czechoslovakia: The New Model of Planning and Management." AMERICAN ECONOMIC REVIEW 58 (May 1968): 559-67.

> An examination of the main features of the Czechoslovak reform, including its background, limitations, and prospects.

Szeplaki, Leslie. "Socialist Economic Reforms Revisited: A Reflection on the Major Issues." EAST EUROPEAN QUARTERLY 7 (Summer 1973): 167-81. Tables.

> An explanation of the major issues involved in the Hungarian economic reform of 1968.

Sztyber, Wladyslaw. "Theoretical Basis for the Reform of Sale Prices in Socialist Countries." EASTERN EUROPEAN ECONOMICS 9 (Winter 1970-71): 91-131.

> A discussion of the nature, scope, and extent of price reforms which were carried out in the Soviet-type economies during the 1960s.

Tatu, Michel. "Soviet Reforms: The Debate Goes On." PROBLEMS OF COMMUNISM 15 (January-February 1966): 28-34.

> A description of the background and political framework of the 1965 Soviet reforms.

Volin, Lazar. "Reforms in Agriculture." PROBLEMS OF COMMUNISM 8 (January-February 1959): 35-43.

> A discussion of post-Stalin developments in Soviet agriculture.

Zaleski, Eugene. PLANNING REFORMS IN THE SOVIET UNION, 1962-1966. AN ANALYSIS OF RECENT TRENDS IN ECONOMIC ORGANIZATION AND MANAGEMENT. Translated by Marie-Christine MacAndrew and G. Warren Nutter. Chapel Hill: University of North Carolina Press, 1967. viii, 203 p. Figures and index.

> An analytical discussion of the unchanged aspects or "permanent features" of Soviet administrative planning and of the obstacles to basic reform in the USSR. The author also gives a description of the course of the October 1965 reform to October 1966.

Zauberman, Alfred. "Liberman's Rules of the Game for Soviet Industry." SLAVIC REVIEW 22 (December 1963): 734-44.

> Comments on the proposals of the profit-oriented school.

Zhelev, Grudi. "Improving the Economic Mechanism of the Management of the National Economy." EASTERN EUROPEAN ECONOMICS 11 (Winter 1972-73): 47-63.

> Postscript to the Bulgarian economic reforms, as written by the deputy chief of the planning department of the Bulgarian Central Committee.

Zielinski, Janusz [G.]. "Centralisation and Decentralisation in Decision-Making." ECONOMICS OF PLANNING 3 (December 1963): 196-208.

> An analysis of the problems of multilevel structures, the concept and economic implications of decentralization, and construction of optimal plans.

_____. ECONOMIC REFORMS IN POLISH INDUSTRY. Economic Reforms in East European Industry Series. London: Oxford University Press, 1973. xxxiv, 333 p. Figures, tables, and index.

> Survey of the origins, provisions, and results of the Polish industrial planning reforms of the 1960s.

_____. "Economics and Politics of Economic Reforms in Eastern Europe." ECONOMICS OF PLANNING 9 (1969): 279-95.

> A close look at the differences between the two major types of reforms and the two approaches to implementation.

_____. "On the Effectiveness of the Polish Economic Reforms." SOVIET STUDIES 22 (January 1971): 406-32. Tables.

> An evaluation of the effectiveness, from the standpoint of planners' preferences, of the series of Polish industrial reforms.

_____. "On the Theory of Economic Reforms and Their Optimal Sequence." ECONOMICS OF PLANNING 8 (1968): 195-215.

> An illumination of the difficulties encountered because of the partial, gradual introduction of reforms. The planning process, problems of equilibrium, and the consequences of the lack of an overall system are analyzed within the framework of the Polish experience with economic reforms between 1956 and 1967.

Zwass, Adam. "The Outlook for East-West Monetary Relations." SOVIET AND EASTERN EUROPEAN FOREIGN TRADE 10 (Fall-Winter 1974-75): 234-65.

> An examination of questions of monetary reform within the Comecon (role of transferable ruble, convertibility, etc.) and Comecon interest in a unified currency system. An appraisal of the future of East-West trade follows.

AUTHOR INDEX

This index consists of authors, editors, compilers, translators, and other contributors to works cited in the text. Alphabetization is letter by letter.

A

Abouchar, Alan 85, 181
Adams, Arthur E. 117
Adams, Jan S. 117
Adler-Karlsson, Gunnar 166, 174
Aleksandrov, A. 143, 166
Allen, Robert Loring 153, 174, 177
Alton, Thad Paul 19-20, 25
Ames, Edward 9, 143
Andreassen, Knut 143
Antosenkov, E.G. 101
Arnold, Arthur Z. 73
Artemev, Vyacheslav 93
Atlas, Z. 51
Aubrey, Henry G. 177
Augustinovics, M. 153
Ausch, Sandor 73, 166
Azrael, Jeremy R. 51

B

Babitchev, Eugene 143
Bachurin, A. 51, 52, 181
Bacskai, T. 186
Bajt, Alexander 85
Baksht, M. 162
Balassa, Bela A. 52, 109, 181
Balinky, Alexander S. 52, 101
Balint, Jozsef 181
Bandera, V.N. 9

Baran, Paul A. 20
Barone, E. 15
Bartha, Ferenc 73
Bashkin, P. 126
Batra, Raveendra N. 126
Batyrev, V. 144
Baykov, Alexander 1, 153
Baylis, Thomas A. 182
Bazlova, A. 73
Becker, Abraham S. 20
Beckhart, Benjamin Haggott 146
Belik, Iu 52
Belkin, V. 52
Benz, G. William 80
Berend, Ivan T. 26
Berent, Jerzy 93
Berghianu, Maxim 52
Bergson, Abram 1, 15, 20, 21, 73,
    101, 109, 182
Berliner, Joseph S. 53, 110, 144,
    177
Bernasek, Miloslav 26
Berri, L. 21, 53
Beskid, Lidia 101
Bettelheim, Charles 85
Betz, Horst 182
Bhalla, A.S. 26
Bilimovich, Aleksandr 166
Birman, A. 52, 53, 144
Blackman, James H. 182
Block, Alexander 101-2

199

Author Index

Author Index

Author Index

O

Ofer, Gur 141
Oi, Walter Y. 129
Oleinik, I. 33, 170
Osborne, R.H. 5
Osofsky, Stephen 124
Oxenfeldt, Alfred R. 80
Oyrzanowski, Bronislaw 80

P

Pajestka, Jozef 187
Pantilie, N. 66
Pashev, Apostol 192
Pearce, Brian 37
Pervukhin, A. 52
Pesek, Boris P. 192
Pessel', M. 149
Petrov, Milan 161
Petrov, Tsvetan 193
Pickersgill, Gary M. 5
Pickersgill, Joyce E. 5, 80
Pinder, John 170
Plaksin, A. 170
Plowiec, Urszula 161
Polach, J.G. 139
Poletaev, P. 90
Poliakov, M. 149
Polienko, A. 171
Portes, Richard D. 66, 193
Porwit, Krzysztof 66
Postyshev, A. 67
Powell, Raymond P. 37, 46, 89, 150
Pozdniakova, N. 105
Preobrazhensky, Evgeny 37
Prociuk, S.G. 98
Prokhorov, G. 161
Prosandeev, A. 141
Prybyla, Jan S. 105, 124, 178
Pryor, Frederic L. 11, 24, 150, 161-62, 193

R

Rabinovich, G. 143
Rabinovich, I. 162
Racz, J. 158, 166, 168, 186
Rakowski, Mieczyslaw 90

Ranki, G. 26
Rapawy, Stephen 96
Raskin, G. 90
Redding, A. David 98, 136
Reiher, Klaus 81
Richman, Barry M. 67
Rimlinger, Gaston V. 98
Roberts, Paul Craig 16, 37
Robertson, Wade E. 43
Robinson, E.A.G. 26
Romanchenko, G. 124
Romanowski, Jacek I. 138
Ronimmois, H.E. 134
Rotleider, A. 171
Rubinshtein, G. 162
Rubinshtein, M. 81
Rutgaizer, V. 37, 141
Rux, Wiktor 162
Ryavec, Karl W. 193
Rybakov, O. 67
Rychetnik, Ludek 81
Rychlewski, Eugeniusz 90
Rymalov, V. 178

S

Sadowski, Zdzislaw 33
Sawyer, Carole A. 162
Scheel, B. 171
Schierz, Erich 81
Schinke, Eberhard 124
Schlesinger, Rudolf 67-68, 124
Schnitzer, Martin 5
Schonfeld, Roland 175
Schroeder, Gertrude E. 68, 81, 98, 105, 194
Schulz, U. 171
Schwartz, Harry 5
Scott, N.B. 162
Searing, Marjory E. 37, 155
Seers, Dudley 24
Selucky, Radoslav 194
Semenov, I. 139
Senchagov, V. 90
Sergeev, V. 171
Seton, Francis 24, 38
Severin, Barbara S. 102
Shabad, Theodore 134
Shaffer, Harry G. 177, 194
Shagalov, G. 113
Sharpe, Myron E. 194-95

Author Index

TITLE INDEX

This index is alphabetized letter by letter. In some cases titles have been shortened.

Title Index

Title Index

SUBJECT INDEX

In this index of subjects, USSR will not be found as a main entry but as a subentry under various economic terms. Numbers refer to pages and underlined numbers are main areas of emphasis within that subject. Alphabetization is letter by letter.

A

Accounting practices in economics 54
Afghanistan, foreign aid to 177
Age distributions, Soviet 97
Agricultural policy and productivity 25, 73, 117-31
  comparisons with the U.S. 110
  efficiency in 112, 113, 123
  financial and investment policy in 86, 90, 119, 124, 125, 126, 149
  labor supply in 100, 125
  organization of 119, 121
  prices in 21, 73, 74, 77, 117, 118, 124, 128, 129
  private enterprise in 123, 125, 126, 127, 128, 129, 130
  procurement and costs in 80
  profit in 118, 184
  reforms in 117, 118, 121, 122, 184, 188, 189, 196
  relationship to industry 35
  statistics 124
  wages and income in 98, 124, 125, 129, 131
  by geographical area
    Bulgaria 121, 189
    Czechoslovakia 4, 11, 64, 117, 121, 189

Eastern Europe 113, 121, 122, 123, 189
Germany, East 5, 11, 24, 47, 126
Hungary 5, 27, 36, 65, 118
Poland 25, 51, 117, 123
Rumania 35, 39, 119
USSR 1, 5, 6, 9, 10, 11, 12, 21, 24, 26, 28, 31, 36, 39, 40, 42, 44, 48, 52, 59, 73, 74, 79, 80, 88, 96, 98, 100, 111, 113, 117, 118, 119, 120, 121, 122, 123, 124, 125, 126, 127, 128, 129, 130, 132, 136, 145, 184, 188, 196
  See also Collectivization; Migrant labor; State farms
Allocation of resources. See Resource allocation
Ames, Edward 58
Asia, economic growth in Soviet 27, 37
Associations of Nationally Owned Factories 10, 186
Australia, trade with the Soviet bloc 176
Automation. See Technology and technological policy

213

Subject Index

B

Balance of payments 133, 151, 155, 157, 161, 165. See also Payments, international
Balance of trade 162
Balances 10, 21, 82
  interbranch 10, 53, 55, 56, 59, 60, 62, 86, 119
  intersectoral 55
  material 58, 62, 65, 70
Balkan countries 6
  trade with Bulgaria 155
  See also names of specific Balkan countries
Banks and banking 151
  Eastern Europe 146, 149, 152, 173, 174, 177
  Germany, East 5
  USSR 73, 143, 144, 146, 147, 149, 152, 156, 161
  See also Gosbank; International Bank for Economic Cooperation; Savings and thrift; Soviet Bank for Foreign Trade
Barone, E. 15
Bilateralism 151, 165, 166
Birth rates, Soviet 94
Bol'shevicka-Maiak experiment 195
Bonuses 53, 59, 62, 63. See also Incentive systems
Brezhnev, Leonid 102, 119, 121, 124
Budget, national 148, 151
  Czechoslovakia 4, 11, 64
  USSR 76, 78, 144, 145, 148, 149, 150
Bulgaria 1, 2, 28, 55
  agriculture in 121, 127
  commerce of 155, 160-61, 164, 173
  economic growth and development of 34
  economic reforms in 183, 184-85, 189, 192, 193, 197
  economic organization in 12, 39
  industry in 133

C

Capital 59, 85-91
  charges 90, 135, 149
  effect of prices on 79
  fixed 86
  labor substitution for 86
  productivity 19, 90, 109, 114
  resources 11
  role of 114
  stock 21, 26, 88, 89
  by geographical area
    Eastern Europe 19, 88, 109, 114
    Hungary 46, 114
    USSR 11, 21, 26, 85, 86, 88, 89, 90, 91, 135
  See also Credit policies; Investment
Capitalism 15
  compared with socialism 3, 4, 37, 89, 107, 109
  profit factor in 51
Capital-output ratios 34, 88, 89, 90, 91, 114, 124
Ceausescu, N. 10
Centralization in economics 6, 13, 17, 26, 62-63, 64, 65, 66, 69, 70, 72, 76, 78, 79, 80, 89, 112, 118, 146, 154, 158, 164, 165, 176, 182, 184, 190, 192, 195, 197. See also Decentralization in economics
Chemical industries, East European 133
Child welfare programs 96, 105
China
  commerce of 183
  economic growth and development of 38, 40
  foreign aid of 177, 178
  transportation in 33, 136
Clearinghouse operations, East European 148, 151, 169
Climatic conditions 138
  agriculture and 122
CMEA. See Council for Mutual Economic Assistance
Coal industry, Soviet 43, 131, 138

Subject Index

Subject Index

Subject Index